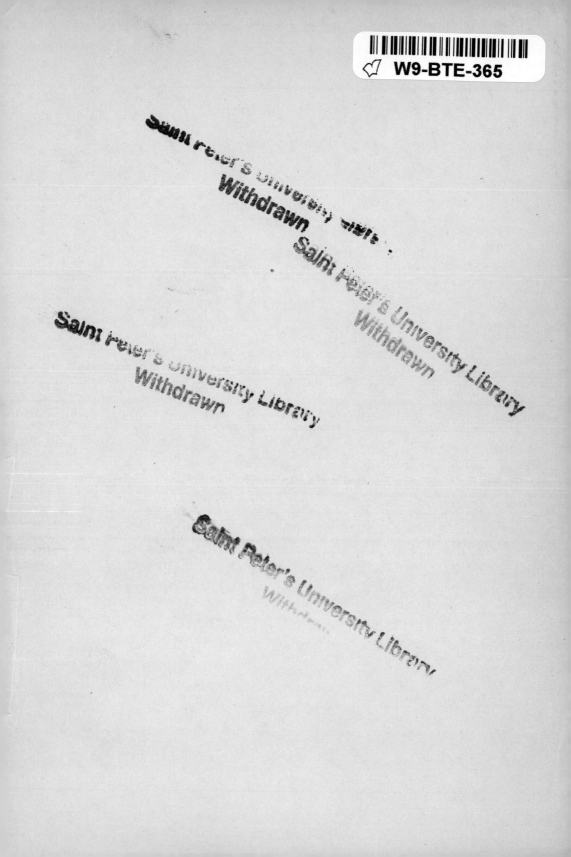

THE WORKS OF JOHN MILTON

THE WORKS OF
JOHN MILTON

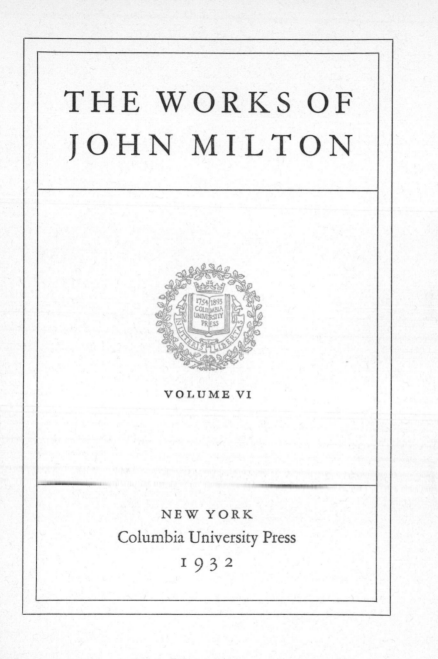

VOLUME VI

NEW YORK
Columbia University Press
1 9 3 2

PRINTED IN THE UNITED STATES OF AMERICA
BY THE PRINTING HOUSE OF WILLIAM EDWIN RUDGE, INC.
MOUNT VERNON, NEW YORK

EDITORIAL BOARD

CONTENTS

vii

viii

ILLUSTRATIONS

A TREATISE OF CIVIL POWER
IN ECCLESIASTICAL CAUSES

359

A TREATISE OF Civil power

IN
Ecclesiastical causes:

SHEWING
That it is not lawfull for any
power on earth to compell
in matters of

Religion.

The author J. M.

London, Printed by *Tho. Newcomb*, *Anno* 1659.

To the Parlament

of the Commonwealth of England with the
dominions therof.

I Have prepar'd, supream Councel, against the much
expected time of your sitting, this treatise; which,
though to all Christian magistrates equally belonging,
and therfore to have bin written in the common language
5 of Christendom, natural dutie and affection hath confin'd,
and dedicated first to my own nation: and in a season
wherin the timely reading therof, to the easier accomplishment of your great work, may save you much labor and
interruption: of two parts usually propos'd, civil and ec-
10 clesiastical, recommending civil only to your proper care,
ecclesiastical to them only from whom it takes both that
name and nature. Yet not for this cause only do I require
or trust to finde acceptance, but in a two-fold respect besides: first as bringing cleer evidence of scripture and
15 protestant maxims to the Parlament of England, who in
all thir late acts, upon occasion, have professd to assert
only the true protestant Christian religion, as it is con-
taind in the holy scriptures: next, in regard that your
power being but for a time, and having in your selves a
20 Christian libertie of your own, which at one time or other
may be oppressd, therof truly sensible, it will concern you
while you are in power, so to regard other mens consciences,

as you would your own should be regarded in the power of
others; and to consider that any law against conscience is
alike in force against any conscience, and so may one way
or other justly redound upon your selves. One advantage
5 *I make no doubt of, that I shall write to many eminent*
persons of your number, alreadie perfet and resolvd in
this important article of Christianitie. Some of whom I
remember to have heard often for several years, at a councel
next in autoritie to your own, so well joining religion with
10 *civil prudence, and yet so well distinguishing the different*
power of either, and this not only voting, but frequently
reasoning why it should be so, that if any there present had
bin before of an opinion contrary, he might doubtless have
departed thence a convert in that point, and have confessd,
15 *that then both commonwealth and religion will at length, if*
ever, flourish in Christendom, when either they who govern
discern between civil and religious, or they only who so dis-
cern shall be admitted to govern. Till then nothing but
troubles, persecutions, commotions can be expected; the in-
20 *ward decay of true religion among our selves, and the utter*
overthrow at last by a common enemy. Of civil libertie I
have written heretofore by the appointment, and not without
the approbation of civil power: of Christian liberty I write
now; which others long since having don with all freedom
25 *under heathen emperors, I should do wrong to suspect,*
that I now shall with less under Christian governors, and
such especially as profess openly thir defence of Christian
libertie; although I write this not otherwise appointed or

*induc'd then by an inward perswasion of the Christian
dutie which I may usefully discharge herin to the common
Lord and Master of us all, and the certain hope of his
approbation, first and chiefest to be sought: In the hand of*
5 *whose providence I remain, praying all success and good
event on your publick councels to the defence of true religion and our civil rights.*

JOHN MILTON.

A Treatise of Civil power in Ecclesiastical causes

TWO things there be which have bin ever found working much mischief to the church of God, and the advancement of truth; force on the one side restraining, and hire on the other side corrupting the teachers thereof.
5 Few ages have bin since the ascension of our Saviour, wherin the one of these two, or both together have not prevaild. It can be at no time therfore unseasonable to speak of these things; since by them the church is either in continual detriment and oppression, or in continual danger. The former
10 shall be at this time my argument; the latter as I shall finde God disposing me, and opportunity inviting. What I argue, shall be drawn from the scripture only; and therin from true fundamental principles of the gospel; to all knowing Christians undeniable. And if the governors of this common-
15 wealth since the rooting out of prelats have made least use of force in religion, and most have favord Christian liberty of any in this Iland before them since the first preaching of the gospel, for which we are not to forget our thanks to God, and their due praise, they may, I doubt not, in this treatise finde
20 that which not only will confirm them to defend still the Christian liberty which we enjoy, but will incite them also to enlarge it, if in aught they yet straiten it. To them who perhaps herafter, less experienc'd in religion, may come to gov-

ern or give us laws, this or other such, if they please, may be a timely instruction: however to the truth it will be at all times no unneedfull testimonie; at least some discharge of that general dutie which no Christian but according to what he hath
5 receivd, knows is requir'd of him if he have aught more conducing to the advancement of religion then what is usually endeavourd, freely to impart it.

It will require no great labor of exposition to unfold what is here meant by matters of religion; being as soon appre-
10 hended as defin'd, such things as belong chiefly to the knowledge and service of God: and are either above the reach and light of nature without revelation from above, and therfore liable to be variously understood by humane reason, or such things as are enjoind or forbidden by divine precept, which
15 els by the light of reason would seem indifferent to be don or not don; and so likewise must needs appeer to everie man as the precept is understood. Whence I here mean by conscience or religion, that full perswasion whereby we are assur'd that our beleef and practise, as far as we are able to apprehend and
20 probably make appeer, is according to the will of God & his Holy Spirit within us, which we ought to follow much rather then any law of man, as not only his word every where bids us, but the very dictate of reason tells us. *Act.*
4. 19. *whether it be right in the sight of God, to hearken to*
25 *you more then to God, judge ye.* That for beleef or practise in religion according to this conscientious perswasion no man ought be punished or molested by any outward force on earth whatsoever, I distrust not, through Gods implor'd

assistance, to make plane by these following arguments.

First it cannot be deni'd, being the main foundation of our protestant religion, that we of these ages, having no other divine rule or autoritie from without us warrantable to one

5 another as a common ground but the holy scripture, and no other within us but the illumination of the Holy Spirit so interpreting that scripture as warrantable only to our selves and to such whose consciences we can so perswade, can have no other ground in matters of religion but only from the scrip-

10 tures. And these being not possible to be understood without this divine illumination, which no man can know at all times to be in himself, much less to be at any time for certain in any other, it follows cleerly, that no man or body of men in these times can be the infallible judges or determiners in matters of

15 religion to any other mens consciences but thir own. And therfore those Beroeans are commended, *Act.* 17. 11, who after the preaching even of S. *Paul, searchd the scriptures daily, whether those things were so.* Nor did they more then what God himself in many places commands us by the same

20 apostle, to search, to try, to judge of these things our selves: And gives us reason also, *Gal.* 6. 4, 5. *let every man prove his own work, and then shall he have rejoicing in himself alone, and not in another: for every man shall bear his own burden.* If then we count it so ignorant and irreligious in the papist

25 to think himself dischargd in Gods account, beleeving only as the church beleevs, how much greater condemnation will it be to the protestant his condemner, to think himself justified, beleeving only as the state beleevs? With good cause therfore

it is the general consent of all sound protestant writers, that
neither traditions, councels nor canons of any visible church,
much less edicts of any magistrate or civil session, but the
scripture only can be the final judge or rule in matters of re-
5 ligion, and that only in the conscience of every Christian to
himself. Which protestation made by the first publick reformers of our religion against the imperial edicts of *Charls*
the fifth, imposing church-traditions without scripture, gave
first beginning to the name of *Protestant;* and with that name
10 hath ever bin receivd this doctrine, which preferrs the scripture before the church, and acknowledges none but the Scripture sole interpreter of it self to the conscience. For if the
church be not sufficient to be implicitly beleevd, as we hold
it is not, what can there els be nam'd of more autoritie then
15 the church but the conscience; then which God only is greater,
1 *Joh.* 3.20? But if any man shall pretend, that the scripture
judges to his conscience for other men, he makes himself
greater not only then the church, but also then the scripture,
then the consciences of other men; a presumption too high
20 for any mortal; since every true Christian able to give a reason
of his faith, hath the word of God before him, the promisd
Holy Spirit, and the minde of Christ within him, 1 *Cor.* 2.
16; a much better and safer guide of conscience, which as far
as concerns himself he may far more certainly know then any
25 outward rule impos'd upon him by others whom he inwardly
neither knows nor can know; at least knows nothing of them
more sure then this one thing, that they cannot be his judges
in religion. 1 *Cor.* 2. 15. *the spiritual man judgeth all things,*

but he himself is judgd of no man. Chiefly for this cause do all true protestants account the pope antichrist, for that he assumes to himself this infallibilitie over both the conscience and the scripture; *siting in the temple of God,* as it were op-
5 posite to God, *and exalting himself above all that is called god, or is worshipd,* 2 Thess. 2. 4. That is to say not only above all judges and magistrates, who though they be calld gods, are far beneath infallible, but also above God himself, by giving law both to the scripture, to the conscience, and to
10 the spirit it self of God within us. Whenas we finde, *James* 4. 12, *there is one lawgiver, who is able to save and to destroy: who art thou that judgest another?* That Christ is the only lawgiver of his church and that it is here meant in religious matters, no well grounded Christian will deny. Thus
15 also *S. Paul,* Rom. 14. 4. *who art thou that judgest the servant of another? to his own Lord he standeth or falleth: but he shall stand; for God is able to make him stand.* As therfore of one beyond expression bold and presumptuous, both these apostles demand, *who art thou* that presum'st to impose other
20 law or judgment in religion then the only lawgiver and judge Christ, who only can save and can destroy, gives to the conscience? And the forecited place to the *Thessalonians* by compar'd effects resolvs us, that be he or they who or wherever they be or can be, they are of far less autoritie then the
25 church, whom in these things as protestants they receive not, and yet no less antichrist in this main point of antichristianism, no less a pope or popedom then he at *Rome,* if not much more; by setting up supream interpreters of scripture either

those doctors whom they follow, or, which is far worse, themselves as a civil papacie assuming unaccountable supremacie to themselves not in civil only but ecclesiastical causes. Seeing then that in matters of religion, as hath been prov'd, none can judge or determin here on earth, no not church-governors themselves against the consciences of other beleevers, my inference is, or rather not mine but our Saviours own, that in those matters they neither can command nor use constraint; lest they run rashly on a pernicious consequence, forewarnd in that parable *Mat.* 13. from the 26 to the 31 verse: *least while ye gather up the tares, ye root up also the wheat with them. Let both grow together until the harvest: and in the time of harvest I will say to the reapers, Gather ye together first the tares &c.* whereby he declares that this work neither his own ministers nor any els can discerningly anough or judgingly perform without his own immediat direction, in his own fit season; and that they ought till then not to attempt it. Which is further confirmd 2 *Cor.* 1. 24. *not that we have dominion over your faith, but are helpers of your joy.* If apostles had no dominion or constraining powr over faith or conscience, much less have ordinary ministers. 1 *Pet.* 5. 2, 3. *Feed the flock of God not by constraint &c. neither as being lords over Gods heritage.* But some will object, that this overthrows all church-discipline, all censure of errors, if no man can determin. My answer is, that what they hear is plane scripture; which forbids not church-sentence or determining, but as it ends in violence upon the conscience unconvinc'd. Let who so will interpret or determin,

so it be according to true church-discipline; which is exercis'd
on them only who have willingly joind themselves in that
covnant of union, and proceeds only to a separation from the
rest, proceeds never to any corporal inforcement or forfeture
5 of monie; which in spiritual things are the two arms of Antichrist, not of the true church; the one being an inquisition,
the other no better then a temporal indulgence of sin for
monie, whether by the church exacted or by the magistrate;
both the one and the other a temporal satisfaction for what
10 Christ hath satisfied eternally; a popish commuting of penaltie, corporal for spiritual; a satisfaction to man especially
to the magistrate, for what and to whom we owe none: these
and more are the injustices of force and fining in religion,
besides what I most insist on, the violation of Gods express
15 commandment in the gospel, as hath bin shewn. Thus then
if church-governors cannot use force in religion, though but
for this reason, because they cannot infallibly determin to
the conscience without convincement, much less have civil
magistrates autoritie to use force where they can much less
20 judge; unless they mean only to be the civil executioners of
them who have no civil power to give them such commission,
no nor yet ecclesiastical to any force or violence in religion.
To summe up all in brief, if we must beleeve as the magistrate appoints, why not rather as the church? if not as either
25 without convincement, how can force be lawfull? But some
are ready to cry out, what shall then be don to blasphemie?
Them I would first exhort not thus to terrifie and pose the
people with a Greek word: but to teach them better what it

is; being a most usual and common word in that language to
signifie any slander, any malitious or evil speaking, whether
against God or man or any thing to good belonging: blasphemie or evil speaking against God malitiously, is far from
5 conscience in religion; according to that of *Marc 9. 39. there
is none who doth a powerfull work in my name, and can
likely speak evil of me.* If this suffice not, I referre them to
that prudent and well deliberated act *August 9.* 1650; where
the Parlament defines blasphemie against God, as far as it is
10 a crime belonging to civil judicature, *pleniùs ac meliùs Chry-
sippo & Crantore;* in plane English more warily, more
judiciously, more orthodoxally then twice thir number of
divines have don in many a prolix volume: although in
all likelihood they whose whole studie and profession these
15 things are should be most intelligent and authentic therin, as
they are for the most part, yet neither they nor these unnerr-
ing always or infallible. But we shall not carrie it thus; another Greek apparition stands in our way, *heresie* and *heretic;* in like manner also rail'd at to the people as in a tongue
20 unknown. They should first interpret to them, that heresie,
by what it signifies in that language, is no word of evil note;
meaning only the choise or following of any opinion good or
bad in religion or any other learning: and thus not only in
heathen authors, but in the New testament it self without
25 censure or blame. *Acts* 15. 5. *certain of the heresie of the
Pharises which beleevd,* and 26. 5. *after the exactest heresie
of our religion I livd a Pharise.* In which sense Presbyterian
or Independent may without reproach be calld a heresie.

Where it is mentioned with blame, it seems to differ little from schism 1 *Cor.* 11. 18, 19. *I hear that there be schisms among you* &c. *for there must also heresies be among you* &c; though some who write of heresie after their own heads, would make it far worse then schism; whenas on the contrarie, schism signifies division, and in the worst sense; heresie, choise only of one opinion before another, which may bee without discord. In apostolic times therfore ere the scripture was written, heresie was a doctrin maintaind against the doctrin by them deliverd: which in these times can be no otherwise defin'd then a doctrin maintaind against the light, which we now only have, of the scripture. Seeing therfore that no man, no synod, no session of men, though calld the church, can judge definitively the sense of scripture to another mans conscience, which is well known to be a general maxim of the Protestant religion, it follows planely, that he who holds in religion that beleef or those opinions which to his conscience and utmost understanding appeer with most evidence or probabilitie in the scripture, though to others he seem erroneous, can no more be justly censur'd for a heretic then his censurers; who do but the same thing themselves while they censure him for so doing. For ask them, or any Protestant, which hath most autoritie, the church or the scripture? they will answer, doubtless, that the scripture: and what hath most autoritie, that no doubt but they will confess is to be followd. He then who to his best apprehension follows the scripture, though against any point of doctrine by the whole church receivd, is not the heretic; but he who

follows the church against his conscience and perswasion
grounded on the scripture. To make this yet more undeniable, I shall only borrow a plane similie, the same which
our own writers, when they would demonstrate planest that
5 we rightly preferre the scripture before the church, use frequently against the Papist in this manner. As the Samaritans
beleevd Christ, first for the womans word, but next and much
rather for his own, so we the scripture; first on the churches
word, but afterwards and much more for its own, as the word
10 of God; yea the church it self we beleeve then for the scripture. The inference of it self follows: if by the Protestant doctrine we beleeve the scripture not for the churches saying, but
for its own as the word of God, then ought we to beleeve
what in our conscience we apprehend the scripture to say,
15 though the visible church with all her doctors gainsay; and
being taught to beleeve them only for the scripture, they who
so do are not heretics, but the best protestants: and by their
opinions, whatever they be, can hurt no protestant, whose
rule is not to receive them but from the scripture: which to
20 interpret convincingly to his own conscience none is able but
himself guided by the Holy Spirit; and not so guided, none
then he to himself can be a worse deceiver. To protestants
therfore whose common rule and touchstone is the scripture,
nothing can with more conscience, more equitie, nothing
25 more protestantly can be permitted then a free and lawful
debate at all times by writing, conference or disputation of
what opinion soever, disputable by scripture: concluding, that
no man in religion is properly a heretic at this day, but he

who maintains traditions or opinions not probable by scripture; who, for aught I know, is the papist only; he the only
heretic, who counts all heretics but himself. Such as these, indeed, were capitally punishd by the law of *Moses,* as the only
5 true heretics, idolaters, plane and open deserters of God and
his known law: but in the gospel such are punishd by excommunion only. *Tit. 3. 10. an heretic, after the first and second
admonition, reject.* But they who think not this heavie anough
and understand not that dreadfull aw and spiritual efficacie
10 which the apostle hath expressd so highly to be in church-
discipline, 2 *Cor.* 10. of which anon, and think weakly that
the church of God cannot long subsist but in a bodilie fear, for
want of other prooff will needs wrest that place of S. *Paul Rom.*
13. to set up civil inquisition, and give power to the magis-
15 trate both of civil judgment and punishment in causes ecclesiastical. But let us see with what strength of argument. *Let
every soul be subject to the higher powers.* First, how prove
they that the apostle means other powers then such as they to
whom he writes were then under; who medld not at all in
20 ecclesiastical causes, unless as tyrants and persecuters; and
from them, I hope, they will not derive either the right of
magistrates to judge in spiritual things, or the dutie of such
our obedience. How prove they next, that he intitles them
here to spiritual causes, from whom he witheld, as much as
25 in him lay, the judging of civil; 1 *Cor.* 6. 1, &c. If he himself
appeald to *Cesar,* it was to judge his innocence, not his religion. *For rulers are not a terror to good works, but to the
evil.* then are they not a terror to conscience, which is the

rule or judge of good works grounded on the scripture. But
heresie, they say, is reck'nd among evil works *Gal.* 5. 20: as
if all evil works were to be punishd by the magistrate; wherof
this place, thir own citation, reck'ns up besides heresie a suf-
5 ficient number to confute them; *uncleanness, wantonness,*
enmitie, strife, emulations, animosities, contentions, envy-
ings; all which are far more *manifest* to be judgd by him then
heresie, as they define it; and yet I suppose they will not subject these evil works nor many more such like to his cogni-
10 sance and punishment. *Wilt thou then not be affraid of the*
power? do that which is good and thou shalt have praise of
the same. This shews that religious matters are not here
meant; wherin from the power here spoken of they could
have no praise. *For he is the minister of God to thee for good.*
15 true; but in that office and to that end and by those means
which in this place must be cleerly found, if from this place
they intend to argue. And how for thy good by forcing, op-
pressing and insnaring thy conscience? Many are the ministers of God, and thir offices no less different then many;
20 none more different then state and church-government. Who
seeks to govern both must needs be worse then any lord
prelat or church-pluralist: for he in his own facultie and profession, the other not in his own and for the most part not
throughly understood makes himself supream lord or pope
25 of the church as far as his civil jurisdiction stretches, and all
the ministers of God therin, his ministers, or his curates rather
in the function onely, not in the government: while he himself assumes to rule by civil power things to be rul'd only by

spiritual: when as this very chapter v. 6 appointing him his peculiar office, which requires utmost attendance, forbids him this worse then church-plurality from that full and waightie charge, wherin alone he is *the minister of God, at-*
5 *tending continually on this very thing.* To little purpose will they here instance *Moses,* who did all by immediate divine direction, no nor yet *Asa, Jehosaphat,* or *Josia,* who both might when they pleasd receive answer from God, and had a commonwealth by him deliverd them, incorporated with a
10 national church exercis'd more in bodily then in spiritual worship, so as that the church might be calld a commonwealth and the whole commonwealth a church: nothing of which can be said of Christianitie, deliverd without the help of magistrates, yea in the midst of thir opposition; how little
15 then with any reference to them or mention of them, save onely of our obedience to thir civil laws, as they countnance good and deterr evil: which is the proper work of the magistrate, following in the same verse, and shews distinctly wherin he is the minister of God, *a revenger to execute wrath*
20 *on him that doth evil.* But we must first know who it is that doth evil: the heretic they say among the first. Let it be known then certainly who is a heretic: and that he who holds opinions in religion professdly from tradition or his own inventions and not from Scripture but rather against it, is the
25 only heretic; and yet though such, not alwaies punishable by the magistrate, unless he do evil against a civil Law, properly so calld, hath been already prov'd without need of repetition. *But if thou do that which is evil, be affraid.* To do by scrip-

ture and the gospel according to conscience is not to do evil;
if we therof ought not to be affraid, he ought not by his judging to give cause; causes therfore of Religion are not here
meant. *For he beareth not the sword in vain.* Yes altogether
5 in vain, if it smite he knows not what; if that for heresie
which not the church it self, much less he, can determine absolutely to be so; if truth for error, being himself so often
fallible, he bears the sword not in vain only, but unjustly and
to evil. *Be subject not only for wrath, but for conscience sake:*
10 how for conscience sake against conscience? By all these
reasons it appeers planely that the apostle in this place gives
no judgment or coercive power to magistrates, neither to
those then nor these now in matters of religion; and exhorts
us no otherwise then he exhorted those *Romans.* It hath now
15 twice befaln me to assert, through Gods assistance, this most
wrested and vexd place of scripture; heretofore against *Sal-
masius* and regal tyranie over the state; now against *Erastus*
and state-tyranie over the church. If from such uncertain or
rather such improbable grounds as these they endue magis-
20 tracie with spiritual judgment, they may as well invest him
in the same spiritual kinde with power of utmost punishment, excommunication; and then turn spiritual into corporal, as no worse authors did then *Chrysostom, Jerom* and
Austin, whom *Erasmus* and others in thir notes on the New
25 Testament have cited to interpret that *cutting off* which S.
Paul wishd to them who had brought back the Galatians to
circumcision, no less then the amercement of thir whole vi-
rilitie; and *Grotius* addes that this concising punishment of

circumcisers became a penal law therupon among the *Visi-*
gothes: a dangerous example of beginning in the spirit to end
so in the flesh: wheras that cutting off much likelier seems
meant a cutting off from the church, not unusually so termd
5 in scripture, and a zealous imprecation, not a command. But
I have mentiond this passage to shew how absurd they often
prove who have not learnd to distinguish rightly between
civil power and ecclesiastical. How many persecutions then,
imprisonments, banishments, penalties and stripes; how
10 much bloodshed have the forcers of conscience to answer for,
and protestants rather then papists! For the papist, judging
by his principles, punishes them who beleeve not as the church
beleevs though against the scripture: but the protestant,
teaching every one to beleeve the scripture though against the
15 church, counts heretical and persecutes, against his own principles, them who in any particular so beleeve as he in general
teaches them; them who most honor and beleeve divine scripture, but not against it any humane interpretation though
universal; them who interpret scripture only to themselves,
20 which by his own position none but they to themselves can
interpret; them who use the scripture no otherwise by his
own doctrine to thir edification, then he himself uses it to thir
punishing: and so whom his doctrine acknowledges a true
beleever, his discipline persecutes as a heretic. The papist ex-
25 acts our beleef as to the church due above scripture; and by
the church, which is the whole people of God, understands
the pope, the general councels prelatical only and the sur-
nam'd fathers: but the forcing protestant though he deny

such beleef to any church whatsoever, yet takes it to himself
and his teachers, of far less autorite then to be calld the
church and above scripture beleevd: which renders his practice both contrarie to his beleef, and far worse then that be-
5 leef which he condemns in the papist. By all which well considerd, the more he professes to be a true protestant, the more
he hath to answer for his persecuting then a papist. No protestant therfore of what sect soever following scripture only,
which is the common sect wherin they all agree, and the
10 granted rule of everie mans conscience to himself, ought, by
the common doctrine of protestants, to be forc'd or molested
for religion. But as for poperie and idolatrie, why they also
may not hence plead to be tolerated, I have much less to say.
Their religion the more considerd, the less can be acknowl-
15 edgd a religion; but a Roman principalitie rather, endevour-
ing to keep up her old universal dominion under a new name
and meer shaddow of a catholic religion; being indeed more
rightly nam'd a catholic heresie against the scripture; supported mainly by a civil, and, except in *Rome,* by a forein
20 power: justly therfore to be suspected, not tolerated by the
magistrate of another countrey. Besides, of an implicit faith,
which they profess, the conscience also becoms implicit; and
so by voluntarie servitude to mans law, forfets her Christian
libertie. Who then can plead for such a conscience, as being
25 implicitly enthrald to man instead of God, almost becoms no
conscience, as the will not free, becoms no will. Nevertheless
if they ought not to be tolerated, it is for just reason of state
more then of religion; which they who force, though pro-

fessing to be protestants, deserve as little to be tolerated themselves, being no less guiltie of poperie in the most popish
point. Lastly, for idolatrie, who knows it not to be evidently
against all scripture both of the Old and New Testament, and
5 therfore a true heresie, or rather an impietie; wherin a right
conscience can have naught to do; and the works therof so
manifest, that a magistrate can hardly err in prohibiting and
quite removing at least the publick and scandalous use therof.

From the riddance of these objections I proceed yet to an-
10 other reason why it is unlawfull for the civil magistrate to use
force in matters of religion; which is, because to judge in
those things, though we should grant him able, which is
prov'd he is not, yet as a civil magistrate he hath no right.
Christ hath a government of his own, sufficient of it self to
15 all his ends and purposes in governing his church; but much
different from that of the civil magistrate; and the difference
in this verie thing principally consists, that it governs not by
outward force, and that for two reasons. First because it deals
only with the inward man and his actions, which are all spir-
20 itual and to outward force not lyable: secondly to shew us the
divine excellence of his spiritual kingdom, able without
worldly force to subdue all the powers and kingdoms of
this world, which are upheld by outward force only. That
the inward man is nothing els but the inward part of man,
25 his understanding and his will, and that his actions thence
proceeding, yet not simply thence but from the work of
divine grace upon them, are the whole matter of religion
under the gospel, will appeer planely by considering what

that religion is; whence we shall perceive yet more planely
that it cannot be forc'd. What evangelic religion is, is told
in two words, faith and charitie; or beleef and practise.
That both these flow either the one from the understanding,
5 the other from the will, or both jointly from both, once indeed naturally free, but now only as they are regenerat and
wrought on by divine grace, is in part evident to common
sense and principles unquestiond, the rest by scripture: concerning our beleef, *Mat.* 16. 17. *flesh and blood hath not re-*
10 *veald it unto thee, but my father which is in heaven:* concerning our practise, as it is religious and not meerly civil, *Gal.*
5. 22, 23 and other places declare it to be the fruit of the
spirit only. Nay our whole practical dutie in religion is contained in charitie, or the love of God and our neighbour, no
15 way to be forc'd, yet the fulfilling of the whole law; that is to
say, our whole practise in religion. If then both our beleef
and practise, which comprehend our whole religion, flow
from faculties of the inward man, free and unconstrainable
of themselves by nature, and our practise not only from fac-
20 ulties endu'd with freedom, but from love and charitie besides, incapable of force, and all these things by transgression
lost, but renewd and regenerated in us by the power and gift
of God alone, how can such religion as this admit of force
from man, or force be any way appli'd to such religion, espe-
25 cially under the free offer of grace in the gospel, but it must
forthwith frustrate and make of no effect both the religion
and the gospel? And that to compell outward profession,
which they will say perhaps ought to be compelld though

inward religion cannot, is to compell hypocrisie not to advance religion, shall yet, though of it self cleer anough, be
ere the conclusion further manifest. The other reason why
Christ rejects outward force in the goverment of his church,
5 is, as I said before, to shew us the divine excellence of his spiritual kingdom, able without worldly force to subdue all the
powers and kingdoms of this world, which are upheld by
outward force only: by which to uphold religion otherwise
then to defend the religious from outward violence, is no
10 service to Christ or his kingdom, but rather a disparagement,
and degrades it from a divine and spiritual kingdom to a
kingdom of this world: which he denies it to be,—because it
needs not force to confirm it: *Joh.* 18. 36. *if my kingdom
were of this world, then would my servants fight, that I
15 should not be deliverd to the Jewes.* This proves the kingdom of Christ not governd by outward force; as being none
of this world, whose kingdoms are maintaind all by force
onely: and yet disproves not that a Christian commonwealth
may defend it self against outward force in the cause of re-
20 ligion as well as in any other; though Christ himself, coming
purposely to dye for us, would not be so defended. 1 *Cor.*
1. 27. *God hath chosen the weak things of the world to con-
found the things which are mighty.* Then surely he hath not
chosen the force of this world to subdue conscience and con-
25 scientious men, who in this world are counted weakest; but
rather conscience, as being weakest, to subdue and regulate
force, his adversarie, not his aide or instrument in governing
the church. 2 *Cor.* 10. 3, 4, 5, 6. *for though we walk in the*

flesh, we do not warre after the flesh: for the weapons of our
warfare are not carnal; but mightie through God to the pulling
down of strong holds; casting down imaginations and everie
high thing that exalts it self against the knowledge of God;
and bringing into captivitie everie thought to the obedience
of Christ: and having in a readiness to aveng all disobedience.
It is evident by the first and second verses of this chapter, that
the apostle here speaks of that spiritual power by which Christ
governs his church, how allsufficient it is, how powerful to
reach the conscience and the inward man with whom it
chiefly deals and whom no power els can deal with. In comparison of which as it is here thus magnificently describ'd,
how uneffectual and weak is outward force with all her bois-
trous tooles, to the shame of those Christians and especially
those churchmen, who to the exercising of church discipline
never cease calling on the civil magistrate to interpose his
fleshlie force; an argument that all true ministerial and spiritual power is dead within them: who think the gospel,
which both began and spread over the whole world for above
three hundred years under heathen and persecuting emperors, cannot stand or continue, supported by the same divine
presence and protection to the worlds end, much easier under the defensive favor onely of a Christian magistrate, unless
it be enacted and settled, as they call it, by the state, a statute
or a state-religion: and understand not that the church it self
cannot, much less the state, settle or impose one tittle of religion upon our obedience implicit, but can only recommend
or propound it to our free and conscientious examination:

unless they mean to set the state higher then the church in religion, and with a grosse contradiction give to the state in thir settling petition that command of our implicit beleef, which they deny in thir setled confession both to the state

5 and to the church. Let them cease then to importune and interrupt the magistrate from attending to his own charge in civil and moral things, the settling of things just, things honest, the defence of things religious settled by the churches within themselves; and the repressing of thir contraries de-

10 terminable by the common light of nature; which is not to constrain or to repress religion, probable by scripture, but the violaters and persecuters therof: of all which things he hath anough and more then anough to do, left yet undon; for which the land groans and justice goes to wrack the while:

15 let him also forbear force where he hath no right to judge; for the conscience is not his province: least a worse *woe* arrive him, for worse offending, then was denounc'd by our Saviour *Matt.* 23. 23. against the Pharises: ye have forc'd the conscience, which was not to be forc'd; but judgment and mercy

20 ye have not executed: this ye should have don, and the other let alone. And since it is the councel and set purpose of God in the gospel by spiritual means which are counted weak, to overcom all power which resists him; let them not go about to do that by worldly strength which he hath decreed to do

25 by those means which the world counts weakness, least they be again obnoxious to that saying which in another place is also written of the Pharises, *Luke* 7. 30. *that they frustrated the councel of God.* The main plea is, and urgd with much

vehemence to thir imitation, that the kings of *Juda,* as I
touchd before, and especially *Josia* both judgd and us'd
force in religion. 2 *Chr.* 34. 33. *he made all that were pres-*
ent in Israel to serve the Lord thir God: an argument, if it be
5 well weighed, worse then that us'd by the false prophet
Shemaia to the high priest, that in imitation of *Jehoiada* he
ought to put *Jeremie* in the stocks, *Jer.* 29. 24, 26, &c. for
which he receivd his due denouncement from God. But to
this besides I return a threefold answer: first, that the state of
10 religion under the gospel is far differing from what it was
under the law: then was the state of rigor, childhood, bondage and works, to all which force was not unbefitting; now
is the state of grace, manhood, freedom and faith; to all
which belongs willingness and reason, not force: the law was
15 then written on tables of stone, and to be performd according to the letter, willingly or unwillingly; the gospel, our
new covnant, upon the heart of every beleever, to be inter-
preted only by the sense of charitie and inward perswasion:
the law had no distinct government or governors of church
20 and commonwealth, but the Priests and Levites judg'd in all
causes not ecclesiastical only but civil, *Deut.* 17. 8, &c. which
under the gospel is forbidden to all church-ministers, as a
thing which Christ thir master in his ministerie disclam'd
Luke 12, 14; as a thing beneathe them 1 *Cor.* 6. 4; and by
25 many of our statutes, as to them who have a peculiar and far
differing government of thir own. If not, why different the
governors? why not church-ministers in state-affairs, as well
as state-ministers in church-affairs? If church and state shall

be made one flesh again as under the law, let it be withall considerd, that God who then joind them hath now severd them; that which, he so ordaining, was then a lawfull conjunction, to such on either side as join again what he hath
5 severd, would be nothing now but thir own presumptuous fornication. Secondly, the kings of *Juda* and those magistrates under the law might have recours, as I said before, to divine inspiration; which our magistrates under the gospel have not, more then to the same spirit, which those whom
10 they force have oft times in greater measure then themselves: and so, instead of forcing the Christian, they force the Holy Ghost; and, against that wise forewarning of *Gamaliel,* fight against God. Thirdly, those kings and magistrates us'd force in such things only as were undoubtedly known and forbid-
15 den in the law of *Moses,* idolatrie and direct apostacie from that national and strict enjoind worship of God; wherof the corporal punishment was by himself expressly set down: but magistrates under the gospel, our free, elective and rational worship, are most commonly busiest to force those things
20 which in the gospel are either left free, nay somtimes abolishd when by them compelld, or els controverted equally by writers on both sides, and somtimes with odds on that side which is against them. By which means they either punish that which they ought to favor and protect, or that with cor-
25 poral punishment and of thir own inventing, which not they but the church hath receivd command to chastise with a spiritual rod only. Yet some are so eager in thir zeal of forcing, that they refuse not to descend at length to the utmost shift

of that parabolical prooff *Luke* 14. 16, &c. *compell them to come in.* therfore magistrates may compell in religion. As if a parable were to be straind through every word or phrase, and not expounded by the general scope therof: which is no
5 other here then the earnest expression of Gods displeasure on those recusant Jewes, and his purpose to preferre the gentiles on any terms before them; expressd here by the word *compell.* But how compells he? doubtless no otherwise then he draws, without which no man can come to him, *Joh.* 6. 44:
10 and that is by the inward perswasive motions of his spirit and by his ministers; not by the outward compulsions of a magistrate or his officers. The true people of Christ, as is foretold *Psal.* 110. 3, *are a willing people in the day of his power.* then much more now when he rules all things by outward
15 weakness, that both his inward power and their sinceritie may the more appeer. *God loveth a chearfull giver:* then certainly is not pleasd with an unchearfull worshiper; as the verie words declare of his evangelical invitations. *Esa.* 55. 1. *ho, everie one that thirsteth, come. Joh.* 7. 37. *if any man*
20 *thirst. Rev.* 3. 18. *I counsel thee.* and 22, 17. *whosoever will, let him take the water of life freely.* And in that grand commission of preaching to invite all nations *Marc* 16. 16, as the reward of them who come, so the penaltie of them who come not is only spiritual. But they bring now some reason with
25 thir force, which must not pass unanswerd; that the church of *Thyatira* was blam'd *Rev.* 2. 20 for suffering the false *prophetess to teach and to seduce.* I answer, that seducement is to be hinderd by fit and proper means ordaind in church-

discipline; by instant and powerfull demonstration to the contrarie; by opposing truth to error, no unequal match; truth the strong to error the weak though slie and shifting. Force is no honest confutation; but uneffectual, and for the 5 most part unsuccessfull, oft times fatal to them who use it: sound doctrine diligently and duely taught, is of herself both sufficient, and of herself (if some secret judgment of God hinder not) alwaies prevalent against seducers. This the *Thya-tirians* had neglected, suffering, against Church-discipline, 10 that woman to teach and seduce among them: civil force they had not then in thir power; being the Christian part only of that citie, and then especially under one of those ten great persecutions, wherof this the second was raisd by *Domitian:* force therfore in these matters could not be re-15 quir'd of them, who were then under force themselves.

I have shewn that the civil power hath neither right nor can do right by forcing religious things: I will now shew the wrong it doth; by violating the fundamental privilege of the gospel, the new-birthright of everie true beleever, Christian 20 libertie. 2 *Cor.* 3. 17. *where the spirit of the Lord is, there is libertie. Gal.* 4. 26. *Jerusalem which is above, is free; which is the mother of us all.* and 31. *we are not children of the bondwoman but of the free.* It will be sufficient in this place to say no more of Christian libertie, then that it sets us free 25 not only from the bondage of those ceremonies, but also from the forcible imposition of those circumstances, place and time in the worship of God: which though by him commanded in the old law, yet in respect of that veritie and freedom which

is evangelical, S. *Paul* comprehends both kindes alike, that is
to say, both ceremonie and circumstance, under one and the
same contemtuous name of *weak and beggarly rudiments,*
Gal. 4. 3. 9, 10. *Col.* 2. 8. with 16: conformable to what our
5 Saviour himself taught *John* 4. 21, 23. *neither in this moun-*
tain nor yet at Jerusalem. In spirit and in truth: for the fa-
ther seeketh such to worship him. that is to say, not only sincere of heart, for such he sought ever, but also, as the words
here chiefly import, not compelld to place, and by the same
10 reason, not to any set time; as his apostle by the same spirit
hath taught us *Rom.* 14. 6, &c. *one man esteemeth one day*
above another, another &c. Gal. 4. 10. *Ye observe dayes, and*
moonths &c. Coloss. 2. 16. These and other such places of
scripture the best and learnedest reformed writers have
15 thought evident anough to instruct us in our freedom not
only from ceremonies but from those circumstances also,
though impos'd with a confident perswasion of moralitie
in them, which they hold impossible to be in place or time.
By what warrant then our opinions and practises herin are of
20 late turnd quite against all other Protestants, and that which
is to them orthodoxal, to us become scandalous and punishable by statute, I wish were once again better considerd; if we
mean not to proclame a schism in this point from the best
and most reformed churches abroad. They who would seem
25 more knowing, confess that these things are indifferent, but
for that very cause by the magistrate may be commanded. As
if God of his special grace in the gospel had to this end freed
us from his own commandments in these things, that our

freedom should subject us to a more greevous yoke, the commandments of men. As well may the magistrate call that
common or unclean which God hath cleansd, forbidden to
S. *Peter Acts* 10. 15; as well may he loos'n that which God
5 hath strait'nd, or strait'n that which God hath loos'nd, as he
may injoin those things in religion which God hath left free,
and lay on that yoke which God hath taken off. For he hath
not only given us this gift as a special privilege and excellence of the free gospel above the servile law, but strictly also
10 hath commanded us to keep it and enjoy it. *Gal.* 5. 13. *you
are calld to libertie.* 1 *Cor.* 7. 23. *be not made the servants of
men. Gal.* 5. 14. *stand fast therfore in the libertie wherwith
Christ hath made us free; and be not intangl'd again with the
yoke of bondage.* Neither is this a meer command, but for
15 the most part in these forecited places accompanied with the
verie waightiest and inmost reasons of Christian religion:
Rom. 14. 9, 10. *for to this end Christ both dy'd and rose and
reviv'd, that he might be Lord both of the dead and living.
But why dost thou judge thy brother? &c.* how presum'st
20 thou to be his lord, to be whose only Lord, at least in these
things, Christ both dy'd and rose and livd again? *We shall
all stand before the judgment seat of Christ.* why then dost
thou not only judge, but persecute in these things for which
we are to be accountable to the tribunal of Christ only, our
25 Lord and lawgiver? 1 *Cor.* 7. 23. *ye are bought with a price;
be not made the servants of men.* some trivial price belike,
and for some frivolous pretences paid in their opinion, if
bought and by him redeemd who is God from what was once

the service of God, we shall be enthrald again and forc'd by
men to what now is but the service of men. *Gal.* 4. 31, with
5. 1. *we are not children of the bondwoman* &c. *stand fast
therfore* &c. *Col.* 2. 8. *beware least any man spoil you,* &c.
5 *after the rudiments of the world, and not after Christ.* Solid
reasons wherof are continu'd through the whole chapter. *v.*
10. *ye are complete in him, which is the head of all principalitie and power.* not completed therfore or made the more
religious by those ordinances of civil power, from which
10 Christ thir head hath dischargd us; *blotting out the hand-
writing of ordinances, that was against us, which was contrarie to us; and took it out of the way, nailing it to his cross,
v.* 14: blotting out ordinances written by God himself, much
more those so boldly written over again by men, ordinances
15 which were against us, that is, against our frailtie, much more
those which are against our conscience. *Let no man therfore
judge you in respect of* &c. *v.* 16. *Gal.* 4. 3, &c. *even so we,
when we were children, were in bondage under the rudiments of the world: but when the fullness of time was come,
20 God sent forth his son* &c. *to redeem them that were under
the law, that we might receive the adoption of sons* &c.
Wherfore thou art no more a servant, but a son &c. *But now*
&c. *how turn ye again to the weak and beggarly rudiments,
wherunto ye desire again to be in bondage? ye observe dayes*
25 &c. Hence it planely appeers, that if we be not free we are not
sons, but still servants unadopted; and if we turn again to
those weak and beggarly rudiments, we are not free; yea
though willingly and with a misguided conscience we desire

to be in bondage to them; how much more then if unwillingly and against our conscience? Ill was our condition
chang'd from legal to evangelical, and small advantage got-
ten by the gospel, if for the spirit of adoption to freedom,
5 promisd us, we receive again the spirit of bondage to fear; if
our fear which was then servile towards God only, must be
now servile in religion towards men: strange also and prepos-
terous fear, if when and wherin it hath attaind by the redemption of our Saviour to be filial only towards God, it must be
10 now servile towards the magistrate. Who by subjecting us to
his punishment in these things, brings back into religion that
law of terror and satisfaction, belonging now only to civil
crimes; and thereby in effect abolishes the gospel by establishing again the law to a far worse yoke of servitude upon us
15 then before. It will therfore not misbecome the meanest
Christian to put in minde Christian magistrates, and so much
the more freely by how much the more they desire to be
thought Christian (for they will be thereby, as they ought to
be in these things, the more our brethren and the less our
20 lords) that they meddle not rashly with Christian libertie,
the birthright and outward testimonie of our adoption: least
while they little think it, nay think they do God service, they
themselves like the sons of that bondwoman be found persecuting them who are freeborne of the spirit; and by a sacri-
25 lege of not the least aggravation bereaving them of that sacred libertie which our Saviour with his own blood purchas'd
for them.

A fourth reason why the magistrate ought not to use force

in religion, I bring from the consideration of all those ends
which he can likely pretend to the interposing of his force
therin: and those hardly can be other then first the glorie of
God; next either the spiritual good of them whom he forces,
5 or the temporal punishment of their scandal to others. As
for the promoting of Gods glory, none, I think, will say that
his glorie ought to be promoted in religious things by unwarrantable means, much less by means contrarie to what he
hath commanded. That outward force is such, and that Gods
10 glory in the whole administration of the gospel according to
his own will and councel ought to be fulfilld by weakness, at
least so refuted, not by force; or if by force, inward and spiritual, not outward and corporeal, is already prov'd at large.
That outward force cannot tend to the good of him who is
15 forc'd in religion, is unquestionable. For in religion whatever we do under the gospel, we ought to be therof perswaded without scruple; and are justified by the faith we
have, not by the work we do. *Rom.* 14. 5. *Let every man be
fully perswaded in his own mind.* The other reason which
20 follows necessarily, is obvious *Gal.* 2. 16, and in many other
places of St. *Paul,* as the groundwork and foundation of the
whole gospel, that we are *justified by the faith of Christ, and
not by the works of the law.* if not by the works of Gods law,
how then by the injunctions of mans law? Surely force can-
25 not work perswasion, which is faith; cannot therfore justifie
nor pacifie the conscience; and that which justifies not in the
gospel, condemns; is not only not good, but sinfull to do.
Rom. 14. 23. *Whatsoever is not of faith, is sin.* It concerns

the magistrate then to take heed how he forces in religion
conscientious men: least by compelling them to do that wherof they cannot be perswaded, that wherin they cannot finde
themselves justified, but by thir own consciences condemnd,
5 instead of aiming at thir spiritual good, he force them to do
evil; and while he thinks himself *Asa, Josia, Nehemia,* he be
found *Jeroboam,* who causd Israel to sin; and thereby draw
upon his own head all those sins and shipwracks of implicit
faith and conformitie, which he hath forc'd, and all the
10 wounds given to those *little ones,* whom to offend he will
finde worse one day then that violent drowning mentioned
Matt. 18. 6. Lastly as a preface to force, it is the usual pretence, that although tender consciences shall be tolerated, yet
scandals thereby given shall not be unpunishd, prophane and
15 licentious men shall not be encourag'd to neglect the performance of religious and holy duties by color of any law
giving libertie to tender consciences. By which contrivance
the way lies ready open to them heerafter who may be so
minded, to take away by little and little, that liberty which
20 Christ and his gospel, not any magistrate, hath right to give:
though this kinde of his giving be but to give with one hand
and take away with the other, which is a deluding not a giving. As for scandals, if any man be offended at the conscientious liberty of another, it is a taken scandal not a given. To
25 heal one conscience we must not wound another: and men
must be exhorted to beware of scandals in Christian libertie,
not forc'd by the magistrate; least while he goes about to
take away the scandal, which is uncertain whether given or

taken, he take away our liberty, which is the certain and the sacred gift of God, neither to be touchd by him, nor to be parted with by us. None more cautious of giving scandal then St. *Paul*. Yet while he made himself *servant to all,* that
5 he *might gain the more,* he made himself so of his own accord, was not made so by outward force, testifying at the same time that he *was free from all men,* 1 *Cor.* 9. 19: and therafter exhorts us also *Gal.* 5. 13. *ye were calld to libertie* &c. *but by love serve one another:* then not by force. As for
10 that fear least prophane and licentious men should be encourag'd to omit the performance of religious and holy duties, how can that care belong to the civil magistrate, especially to his force? For if prophane and licentious persons must not neglect the performance of religious and holy duties,
15 it implies, that such duties they can perform; which no Protestant will affirm. They who mean the outward performance, may so explane it; and it will then appeer yet more plancly, that such performance of religious and holy duties especialy by prophane and licentious persons, is a dis-
20 honoring rather then a worshiping of God; and not only by him not requir'd but detested: *Prov.* 21. 27. *the sacrifice of the wicked is an abomination: how much more when he bringeth it with a wicked minde?* To compell therfore the prophane to things holy in his prophaneness, is all one under
25 the gospel, as to have compelld the unclean to sacrifise in his uncleanness under the law. And I adde withall, that to compell the licentious in his licentiousness, and the conscientious against his conscience, coms all to one; tends not to the honor

of God, but to the multiplying and the aggravating of sin to them both. We read not that Christ ever exercis'd force but once; and that was to drive prophane ones out of his temple, not to force them in: and if thir beeing there was an offence,

5 we finde by many other scriptures that thir praying there was an abomination: and yet to the Jewish law that nation, as a servant, was oblig'd; but to the gospel each person is left voluntarie, calld only, as a son, by the preaching of the word; not to be driven in by edicts and force of arms. For if by the

10 apostle, *Rom.* 12. 1, we are *beseechd* as *brethren by the mercies of God* to *present* our *bodies a living sacrifice, holy, acceptable to God, which is* our *reasonable service* or worship, then is no man to be forc'd by the compulsive laws of men to present his body a dead sacrifice, and so under the gospel

15 most unholy and unacceptable, because it is his unreasonable service, that is to say, not only unwilling but unconscionable. But if prophane and licentious persons may not omit the performance of holy duties, why may they not partake of holy things? why are they prohibited the Lords supper; since

20 both the one and the other action may be outward; and outward performance of dutie may attain at least an outward participation of benefit? The church denying them that communion of grace and thanksgiving, as it justly doth, why doth the magistrate compell them to the union of perform-

25 ing that which they neither truly can, being themselves unholy, and to do seemingly is both hatefull to God, and perhaps no less dangerous to perform holie duties irreligiously then to receive holy signes or sacraments unworthily. All

prophane and licentious men, so known, can be considerd
but either so without the church as never yet within it, or departed thence of thir own accord, or excommunicate: if never
yet within the church, whom the apostle, and so consequently
5 the church have naught to do to judge, as he professes 1 *Cor.*
5. 12, then by what autoritie doth the magistrate judge, or,
which is worse, compell in relation to the church? if departed
of his own accord, like that lost sheep *Luke* 15. 4, &c. the
true church either with her own or any borrowd force wor-
10 ries him not in again, but rather in all charitable manner
sends after him; and if she finde him, layes him gently on her
shoulders; bears him, yea bears his burdens; his errors, his in-
firmities any way tolerable, *so fulfilling the law of Christ,*
Gal. 6. 2: if excommunicate, whom the church hath bid go
15 out, in whose name doth the magistrate compell to go in?
The church indeed hinders none from hearing in her publick
congregation, for the doors are open to all: nor excommu-
nicates to destruction, but, as much as in her lies, to a final
saving. Her meaning therfore must needs bee, that as her driv-
20 ing out brings on no outward penaltie, so no outward force
or penaltie of an improper and only a destructive power
should drive in again her infectious sheep; therfore sent out
because infectious, and not driven in but with the danger not
only of the whole and sound, but also of his own utter per-
25 ishing. Since force neither instructs in religion nor begets
repentance or amendment of life, but, on the contrarie, hardness of heart, formalitie, hypocrisie, and, as I said before,
everie way increase of sin; more and more alienates the minde

from a violent religion expelling out and compelling in, and
reduces it to a condition like that which the *Britains* com-
plain of in our storie, driven to and fro between the *Picts* and
the sea. If after excommunion he be found intractable, in-
5 curable, and will not hear the church, he becoms as one
never yet within her pale, *a heathen or a publican, Mat.* 18.
17; not further to be judgd, no not by the magistrate, unless
for civil causes; but left to the final sentence of that judge,
whose coming shall be in flames of fire; that *Maran athà,* 1
10 *Cor.* 16. 22; then which to him so left nothing can be more
dreadful and ofttimes to him particularly nothing more
speedie, that is to say, the Lord cometh: In the mean while
deliverd up to Satan, 1 *Cor.* 5. 5. 1 *Tim.* 1. 20. that is, from
the fould of Christ and kingdom of grace to the world again
15 which is the kingdom of Satan; and as he was receivd *from
darkness to light, and from the power of Satan to God, Acts*
26, 18, so now deliverd up again from light to darkness, and
from God to the power of Satan; yet so as is in both places
manifested, to the intent of saving him, brought sooner to
20 contrition by spiritual then by any corporal severitie. But
grant it belonging any way to the magistrate, that prophane
and licentious persons omit not the performance of holy
duties, which in them were odious to God even under the
law, much more now under the gospel, yet ought his care
25 both as a magistrate and a Christian, to be much more that
conscience be not inwardly violated, then that licence in these
things be made outwardly conformable: since his part is undoubtedly as a Christian, which puts him upon this office

much more then as a magistrate, in all respects to have more
care of the conscientious then of the prophane; and not for
their sakes to take away (while they pretend to give) or to
diminish the rightfull libertie of religious consciences.

5   On these four scriptural reasons as on a firm square this
truth, the right of Christian and evangelic liberty, will stand
immoveable against all those pretended consequences of license and confusion which for the most part men most licentious and confus'd themselves, or such as whose severitie
10 would be wiser then divine wisdom, are ever aptest to object
against the waies of God: as if God without them when he
gave us this libertie, knew not of the worst which these men
in thir arrogance pretend will follow: yet knowing all their
worst, he gave us this liberty as by him judgd best. As to those
15 magistrates who think it their work to settle religion, and
those ministers or others, who so oft call upon them to do so,
I trust, that having well considerd what hath bin here argu'd,
neither they will continue in that intention, nor these in that
expectation from them: when they shall finde that the settle-
20 ment of religion belongs only to each particular church by
perswasive and spiritual means within it self, and that the
defence only of the church belongs to the magistrate. Had
he once learnt not further to concern himself with church affairs, half his labor might be spar'd, and the commonwealth
25 better tended. To which end, that which I premis'd in the
beginning, and in due place treated of more at large, I desire
now concluding, that they would consider seriously what religion is: and they will find it to be in summe, both our be-

leef and our practise depending upon God only. That there
can be no place then left for the magistrate or his force in the
settlement of religion, by appointing either what we shall
beleeve in divine things or practise in religious (neither of
5 which things are in the power of man either to perform himself or to enable others) I perswade me in the Christian inge-
nuitie of all religious men, the more they examin seriously,
the more they will finde cleerly to be true: and finde how
false and deceivable that common saying is, which is so much
10 reli'd upon, that the Christian Magistrate is *custos utriusque
tabulæ,* keeper of both tables; unless is meant by keeper the
defender only: neither can that maxim be maintaind by any
prooff or argument which hath not in this discours first or
last bin refuted. For the two tables, or ten commandements,
15 teach our dutie to God and our neighbour from the love of
both; give magistrates no autoritie to force either: they seek
that from the judicial law; though on false grounds, especially in the first table, as I have shewn; and both in first and
second execute that autoritie for the most part not according
20 to Gods judicial laws but thir own. As for civil crimes and of
the outward man, which all are not, no not of those against
the second table, as that of coveting; in them what power they
have, they had from the beginning, long before *Moses* or the
two tables were in being. And whether they be not now as
25 little in being to be kept by any Christian as they are two
legal tables, remanes yet as undecided, as it is sure they never
were yet deliverd to the keeping of any Christian magistrate.
But of these things perhaps more some other time; what may

serve the present hath bin above discourst sufficiently out of
the scriptures: and to those produc'd might be added testimonies, examples, experiences of all succeeding ages to
these times asserting this doctrine: but having herin the scrip-
5 ture so copious and so plane, we have all that can be properly calld true strength and nerve; the rest would be but
pomp and incumbrance. Pomp and ostentation of reading is
admir'd among the vulgar: but doubtless in matters of religion he is learnedest who is planest. The brevitie I use, not
10 exceeding a small manual, will not therfore, I suppose, be
thought the less considerable, unless with them perhaps who
think that great books only can determin great matters. I
rather chose the common rule, not to make much ado where
less may serve. Which in controversies and those especially
15 of religion, would make them less tedious, and by consequence read ofter, by many more, and with more benefit.

The End.

CONSIDERATIONS
TOUCHING THE LIKELIEST MEANS
TO REMOVE HIRELINGS
OUT OF THE CHURCH

Confiderations

TOUCHING
The likelieft means to remove

HIRELINGS

out of the church.

Wherein is alfo difcourc'd

Of { *Tithes,*
Church-fees,
Church-revenues;

And whether any maintenance
of minifters can be fettl'd
by law.

The author *J. M.*

LONDON:
Printed by *T. N.* for *L. Chap-*
man at the Crown in Popes-
head Alley. 1659.

To the Parlament

of the Commonwealth of England with the
dominions therof.

Owing to your protection, supream Senat, this
libertie of writing which I have us'd these *18
years* on all occasions to assert the just rights
and freedoms both of church and state, and so far approv'd,
5 as to have bin trusted with the representment and defence
of your actions to all Christendom against an adversarie
of no mean repute, to whom should I address what I still
publish on the same argument, but to you whose magnanimous councels first opend and unbound the age from a
10 double bondage under prelatical and regal tyrannie; above
our own hopes heartning us to look up at last like men and
Christians from the slavish dejection, wherin from father
to son we were bred up and taught; and thereby deserving
of these nations, if they be not barbarously ingrateful, to be
15 acknowledgd, next under God, the authors and best patrons
of religious and civil libertie, that ever these Ilands brought
forth. The care and tuition of whose peace and safety,
after a short but scandalous night of interruption, is now
again by a new dawning of Gods miraculous providence
20 among us, revolvd upon your shoulders. And to whom
more appertain these considerations which I propound,
then to your selves and the debate before you, though I

trust of no difficultie, yet at present of great expectation,
not whether ye will gratifie, were it no more then so, but
whether ye will hearken to the just petition of many thou-
sands best affected both to religion and to this your returne,
5 *or whether ye will satisfie, which you never can, the covet-*
ous pretences and demands of insatiable hirelings, whose
disaffection ye well know both to your selves and your reso-
lutions. That I, though among many others in this com-
mon concernment, interpose to your deliberations what my
10 *thoughts also are, your own judgment and the success therof*
hath given me the confidence: which requests but this, that
if I have prosperously, God so favoring me, defended the
publick cause of this commonwealth to foreiners, ye would
not think the reason and abilitie, wheron ye trusted once,
15 *and repent not, your whole reputation to the world, either*
grown less by more maturitie and longer studie, or less
available in English *then in another tongue: but that if it*
suffic'd som years past to convince and satisfie the unin-
gag'd of other nations in the justice of your doings, though
20 *then held paradoxal, it may as well suffice now against*
weaker opposition in matters, except here in England *with*
a spiritualtie of men devoted to thir temporal gain, of no
controversie els among Protestants. *Neither do I doubt,*
seeing daily the acceptance which they finde who in thir
25 *petitions venture to bring advice also and new modells of a*
commonwealth, but that you will interpret it much more
the dutie of a Christian to offer what his conscience per-
swades him may be of moment to the freedom and better

constituting of the church: since it is a deed of highest charitie to help undeceive the people, and a work worthiest your autoritie, in all things els authors, assertors and now recoverers of our libertie, to deliver us, the only people of all
5 *Protestants left still undeliverd, from the oppressions of a Simonious decimating clergie; who shame not against the judgment and practice of all other churches reformd, to maintain, though very weakly, thir Popish and oft refuted positions, not in a point of conscience, wherin they might*
10 *be blameles, but in a point of covetousnes and unjust claim to other mens goods; a contention foul and odious in any man, but most of all in ministers of the gospel, in whom contention, though for thir own right, scarce is allowable. Till which greevances be remov'd and religion set free from*
15 *the monopolie of hirelings, I dare affirme, that no modell whatsoever of a commonwealth will prove succesful or undisturbd; and so perswaded, implore divine assistance on your pious councels and proceedings to unanimitie in this and all other truth.*

JOHN MILTON.

Considerations touching the likeliest means to remove hirelings out of the Church.

THE former treatise, which leads in this, begann with two things ever found working much mischief to the church of God, and the advancement of truth; force on the one side restraining, and hire on the other side corrupting the teachers therof. The latter of these is by much the more dangerous: for under force, though no thank to the forcers, true religion oft-times best thrives and flourishes: but the corruption of teachers, most commonly the effect of hire, is the very bane of truth in them who are so corrupted. Of force not to be us'd in matters of religion, I have already spoken; and so stated matters of conscience and religion in faith and divine worship, and so severd them from blasphemie and heresie, the one being such properly as is despiteful, the other such as stands not to the rule of Scripture, and so both of them not matters of religion, but rather against it, that to them who will yet use force, this only choise can be left, whether they will force them to beleeve, to whom it is not given from above, being not forc'd thereto by any principle of the gospel, which is now the only dispensation of God to all men, or whether being Protestants, they will punish in those things wherin the Protestant religion denies them

to be judges, either in themselves infallible or to the consciences of other men, or whether, lastly, they think fit to
punish error, supposing they can be infallible that it is so,
being not wilful, but conscientious, and, according to the
5 best light of him who errs, grounded on scripture: which
kinde of error all men religious, or but only reasonable, have
thought worthier of pardon; and the growth therof to be
prevented by spiritual means and church-discipline, not by
civil laws and outward force; since it is God only who gives
10 as well to beleeve aright, as to beleeve at all; and by those
means which he ordaind sufficiently in his church to the full
execution of his divine purpose in the gospel. It remanes now
to speak of hire; the other evil so mischeevous in religion:
wherof I promisd then to speak further, when I should finde
15 God disposing me, and opportunity inviting. Opportunity I
finde now inviting; and apprehend therin the concurrence of
God disposing; since the maintenance of church-ministers, a
thing not properly belonging to the magistrate, and yet with
such importunity call'd for, and expected from him, is at
20 present under publick debate. Wherin least any thing may
happen to be determind and establishd prejudicial to the
right and freedom of church, or advantageous to such as may
be found hirelings therin, it will be now most seasonable, and
in these matters wherin every Christian hath his free suffrage,
25 no way misbecoming Christian meeknes to offer freely, without disparagement to the wisest, such advice as God shall incline him and inable him to propound. Since heretofore in
commonwealths of most fame for government, civil laws

were not establishd till they had been first for certain dayes publishd to the view of all men, that who so pleasd might speak freely his opinion therof, and give in his exceptions, ere the law could pass to a full establishment. And where
5 ought this equity to have more place, then in the libertie which is unseparable from Christian religion? This, I am not ignorant, will be a work unpleasing to some: but what truth is not hateful to some or other, as this, in likelihood, will be to none but hirelings. And if there be among them
10 who hold it thir duty to speak impartial truth, as the work of thir ministry, though not performd without monie, let them not envie others who think the same no less their duty by the general office of Christianity, to speak truth, as in all reason may be thought, more impartially and unsuspectedly without
15 monie.

Hire of it self is neither a thing unlawful, nor a word of any evil note, signifying no more then a due recompence or reward; as when our Saviour saith, *the laborer is worthy of his hire.* That which makes it so dangerous in the church,
20 and properly makes the *hireling,* a word always of evil signi-fication, is either the excess thereof, or the undue manner of giving and taking it. What harme the excess therof brought to the church, perhaps was not found by experience till the days of *Constantine:* who out of his zeal thinking he could be
25 never too liberally a nursing father of the church, might be not unfitly said to have either overlaid it or choakd it in the nursing. Which was foretold, as is recorded in ecclesiastical traditions, by a voice heard from heaven on the very day that

those great donations and church-revenues were given, cry-
ing aloud, *This day is poison pourd into the church.* Which
the event soon after verifi'd; as appeers by another no less
ancient observation, *That religion brought forth wealth, and*
5 *the daughter devourd the mother.* But long ere wealth came
into the church, so soone as any gain appeerd in religion,
hirelings were apparent; drawn in long before by the very
sent thereof. *Judas* therefor, the first hireling, for want of
present hire answerable to his coveting, from the small num-
10 ber or the meanness of such as then were the religious, sold
the religion it self with the founder therof, his master. *Simon*
Magus the next, in hope only that preaching and the gifts of
the holy ghost would prove gainful, offerd beforehand a sum
of monie to obtain them. Not long after, as the apostle fore-
15 told, hirelings like wolves came in by herds, *Acts* 20. 29. *For,*
I know this, that after my departing shall greevous wolves
enter in among you, not sparing the flock. Tit. 1. 11. *Teach-*
ing things which they ought not, for filthy lucres sake. 2 Pet.
2. 3. *And through covetousnes shall they with feigned words*
20 *make merchandise of you.* Yet they taught not fals doctrin
only, but seeming piety: 1 *Tim. 6. 5. supposing that gain is*
Godlines. Neither came they in of themselves only, but in-
vited oft-times by a corrupt audience: 2 *Tim.* 4. 3. *For the*
time will come, when they will not endure sound doctrin, but
25 *after thir own lusts they will heap to themselves teachers,*
having itching ears: and they on the other side, as fast heap-
ing to themselves disciples, *Acts* 20. 30, doubtles had as
itching palmes. 2 *Pet.* 2. 15. *Following the way of* Balaam,

the son of Bosor, *who lovd the wages of unrighteousnes.*
Jude 11. *They ran greedily after the error of* Balaam *for re-*
ward. Thus we see that not only the excess of hire in wealth-
iest times, but also the undue and vitious taking or giving
5 it, though but small or mean, as in the primitive times, gave
to hirelings occasion, though not intended, yet sufficient, to
creep at first into the church. Which argues also the difficulty,
or rather the impossibility, to remove them quite; unless every
minister were, as St. *Paul,* contented to teach *gratis:* but few
10 such are to be found. As therefor we cannot justly take away
all hire in the church, because we cannot otherwise quite
remove all hirelings, so are we not for the impossibility of
removing them all, to use therefor no endevor that fewest
may come in: but rather, in regard the evil, do what we can,
15 will always be incumbent and unavoidable, to use our utmost diligence, how it may be least dangerous. Which will
be likeliest effected, if we consider, first, what recompence
God hath ordain should be given to ministers of the church;
(for that a recompence ought to be given them, and may by
20 them justly be received, our Saviour himself from the very
light of reason and of equity hath declar'd: *Luke* 10. 7. *The*
laborer is worthy of his hire) next by whom; and lastly, in
what manner.

What recompence ought be given to church-ministers, God
25 hath answerably ordain according to that difference which
he hath manifestly put between those his two great dispen-
sations, the law and the gospel. Under the law he gave them
tithes; under the gospel, having left all things in his church

to charity and Christian freedom, he hath given them only
what is justly given them. That, as well under the gospel as
under the law, say our English divines, and they only of all
Protestants, is tithes; and they say true, if any man be so
5 minded to give them of his own the tenth or twentith: but
that the law therefor of tithes is in force under the gospel, all
other Protestant divines, though equally concernd, yet constantly deny. For although hire to the laborer be of moral
and perpetual right, yet that special kinde of hire, the tenth,
10 can be of no right or necessity, but to that special labor for
which God ordain it. That special labor was the Levitical
and ceremonial service of the tabernacle, *Numb.* 18. 21, 31.
which is now abolishd: the right therefor of that special hire
must needs be withall abolishd, as being also ceremonial.
15 That tithes were ceremonial, is plane; not being given to the
Levites till they had bin first offerd a heave-offering to the
Lord, *Vers.* 24, 28. He then who by that law brings tithes
into the gospel, of necessity brings in withall a sacrifice, and
an altar; without which tithes by that law were unsanctifi'd
20 and polluted, *Vers.* 32. and therefor never thought on in the
first Christian times, till ceremonies, altars, and oblations, by
an ancienter corruption were brought back long before. And
yet the *Jewes* ever since thir temple was destroid, though they
have Rabbies and teachers of thir law, yet pay no tithes, as
25 having no Levites to whom, no temple where to pay them,
no altar wheron to hallow them; which argues that the *Jewes*
themselves never thought tithes moral, but ceremonial only.
That Christians therefor should take them up, when *Jewes*

have laid them down, must needs be very absurd and pre-
posterous. Next, it is as cleer in the same chapter, that the
priests and Levites had not tithes for their labor only in the
tabernacle, but in regard they were to have no other part nor
5 inheritance in the land, *Vers.* 20, 24. and by that means for
a tenth lost a twelfth. But our levites undergoing no such
law of deprivement, can have no right to any such compen-
sation: nay, if by this law they will have tithes, can have no
inheritance of land, but forfeit what they have. Besides this,
10 tithes were of two sorts, those of every year, and those of every
third year: of the former, every one that brought his tithes,
was to eat his share. *Deut.* 14. 23. *Thou shalt eat before the
Lord thy God, in the place which he shall chuse to place his
name there, the tithe of thy corn, of thy wine, and of thine
15 oyle, &c.* Nay, though he could not bring his tithe in kinde,
by reason of his distant dwelling from the tabernacle or temple, but was thereby forc'd to turn it into monie, he was to
bestow that monie on whatsoever pleasd him; oxen, sheep,
wine, or strong drink; and to eat and drink therof there be-
20 fore the Lord both he and his houshold, *Ver.* 24, 25, 26. As
for the tithes of every third year, they were not given only to
the Levite, but to the stranger, the fatherles, and the widdow,
Vers. 28, 29. & *Chap.* 26. 12, 13. So that ours, if they will
have tithes, must admitt of these sharers with them. Nay,
25 these tithes were not paid in at all to the Levite, but the Levite
himself was to come with those his fellow guests and eat his
share of them only at his house who provided them; and this
not in regard of his ministerial office, but because he had no

part nor inheritance in the land. Lastly, the priests and Levites, a tribe, were of a far different constitution from this of
our ministers under the gospel: in them were orders and degrees both by family, dignity and office, mainly distinguishd;
5 the high priest, his brethren and his sons, to whom the Levites themselves paid tithes, and of the best, were eminently
superior, *Num.* 18. 28, 29. No Protestant, I suppose, will
liken one of our ministers to a high priest, but rather to a
common Levite. Unless then, to keep their tithes, they mean
10 to bring back again bishops, archbishops and the whole gang
of prelatry, to whom will they themselves pay tythes, as by
that law it was a sin to them, if they did not, *v.* 32. Certainly
this must needs put them to a deep demurr, while the desire
of holding fast thir tithes without sin, may tempt them to
15 bring back again bishops as the likenes of that hierarchy that
should receive tithes from them, and the desire to pay none,
may advise them to keep out of the church all orders above
them. But if we have to do at present, as I suppose we have,
with true reformed Protestants, not with Papists or prelates,
20 it will not be deni'd that in the gospel there be but two ministerial degrees, presbyters and deacons: which if they contend
to have any succession, reference or conformity with those
two degrees under the law, priests & Levites, it must needs be
such whereby our presbyters or ministers may be answerable
25 to priests, and our deacons to Levites: by which rule of proportion it will follow, that we must pay our tithes to the deacons only, and they only to the ministers. But if it be truer
yet that the priesthood of *Aaron* typifi'd a better reality, 1

Pet. 2. 5. signifying the Christian true and *holy priesthood, to offer up spiritual sacrifice;* it follows hence, that we are now justly exempt from paying tithes, to any who claim from *Aaron,* since that priesthood is in us now real, which in him

5   was but a shaddow. Seeing then by all this which hath bin shewn that the law of tithes is partly ceremonial, as the work was for which they were given, partly judicial, not of common, but of particular right to the tribe of *Levi,* nor to them alone, but to the owner also and his houshold, at the time of

10 thir offering, and every three year to the stranger, the fatherles, and the widdow, thir appointed sharers, and that they were a tribe of priests and deacons improperly compar'd to the constitution of our ministery, and the tithes given by that people to those deacons only, it follows that our ministers at

15 this day, being neither priests nor Levites, nor fitly answering to either of them, can have no just title or pretence to tithes, by any consequence drawn from the law of *Moses.* But they think they have yet a better plea in the example of *Melchisedec,* who took tithes of *Abram* ere the law was given:

20 whence they would inferr tithes to be of moral right. But they ought to know, or to remember, that not examples, but express commands oblige our obedience to God or man: next, that whatsoever was don in religion before the law written, is not presently to be counted moral, when as so many things

25 were then don both ceremonial and Judaically judicial, that we need not doubt to conclude all times before Christ, more or less under the ceremonial law. To what end servd els those altars and sacrifices, that distinction of clean and unclean

entring into the ark, circumcision and the raising up of seed
to the elder brother, *Gen*. 38. 8 ? If these things be not moral,
though before the law, how are tithes, though in the example
of *Abram* and *Melchisedec?* But this instance is so far from
5 being the just ground of a law, that after all circumstances
duly waighd both from *Gen*. 14. and *Heb*. 7, it will not be
allowd them so much as an example. *Melchisedec,* besides his
priestly benediction, brought with him bread and wine sufficient to refresh *Abram* and his whole armie; incited to do so,
10 first, by the secret providence of God, intending him for a
type of Christ and his priesthood; next by his due thankful-
nes and honor to *Abram,* who had freed his borders of *Salem*
from a potent enemie: *Abram* on the other side honors him
with the tenth of all, that is to say, (for he took not sure his
15 whole estate with him to that warr) of the spoiles, *Heb*. 7. 4.
Incited he also by the same secret providence, to signifie as
grandfather of *Levi,* that the Levitical priesthood was excelld
by the priesthood of Christ. For the giving of a tenth declar'd, it seems in those countreys and times, him the greater
20 who receivd it. That which next incited him, was partly his
gratitude to requite the present, partly his reverence to the
person and his benediction: to his person, as a king and
priest; greater therefor then *Abram;* who was a priest also,
but not a king. And who unhir'd will be so hardy as to say,
25 that *Abram* at any other time ever paid him tithes, either before or after; or had then, but for this accidental meeting and
obligement; or that els *Melchisedec* had demanded or exacted them, or took them otherwise, then as the voluntarie

gift of *Abram?* But our ministers, though neither priests nor
kings more then any other Christian, greater in thir own esteem then *Abraham* and all his seed, for the verbal labor of a
seventh dayes preachment, not bringing, like *Melchisedec,*
5 bread or wine at thir own cost, would not take only at the
willing hand of liberality or gratitude, but require and exact
as due the tenth, not of spoiles, but of our whole estates and
labors; nor once, but yearly. We then it seems by the example
of *Abram* must pay tithes to these *melchisedecs:* but what if
10 the person of *Abram* can either no way represent us, or will
oblige the ministers to pay tithes no less then other men?
Abram had not only a priest in his loines, but was himself a
priest; and gave tithes to *Melchisedec* either as grandfather
of *Levi,* or as father of the faithful. If as grandfather (though
15 he understood it not) of *Levi,* he oblig'd not us but *Levi* only,
the inferior priest, by that homage (as the apostle to the
Hebrewes cleerly anough explanes) to acknowledge the
greater. And they who by *Melchisedec* claim from *Abram*
as *Levi's* grandfather, have none to seek thir tithes of but the
20 Levites, where they can finde them. If *Abram* as father of
the faithful paid tithes to *Melchisedec,* then certainly the
ministers also, if they be of that number, paid in him equally
with the rest. Which may induce us to beleeve, that as both
Abram and *Melchisedec,* so tithes also in that action typical
25 and ceremonial, signifi'd nothing els but that subjection,
which all the faithful, both ministers and people owe to
Christ, our high priest and king. In any literal sense from
this example they never will be able to extort that the people

in those dayes paid tithes to priests; but this only, that one
priest once in his life, of spoiles only, and in requital partly of
a liberal present, partly of a benediction, gave voluntary
tithes, not to a greater priest then himself as far as *Abram*
5 could then understand, but rather to a priest and king joind
in one person. They will reply, perhaps, that if one priest
paid tithes to another, it must needs be understood that the
people did no less to the priest. But I shall easily remove that
necessitie by remembring them that in those dayes was no
10 priest, but the father, or the first born of each familie; and
by consequence no people to pay him tithes, but his own
children and servants, who had not wherewithall to pay him,
but of his own. Yet grant that the people then paid tithes,
there will not yet be the like reason to enjoin us: they being
15 then under ceremonies, a meer laitie, we now under Christ, a
royal priesthood, 1 *Pet.* 2. 9, as we are coheirs, kings and
priests with him, a priest for ever after the order or manner
of *Melchisedec.* As therefor *Abram* paid tithes to *Melchise-*
dec because *Levi* was in him, so we ought to pay none be-
20 cause the true *Melchisedec* is in us, and we in him who can
pay to none greater, and hath freed us by our union with
himself, from all compulsive tributes and taxes in his church.
Neither doth the collateral place, *Heb.* 7, make other use of
this story, then to prove Christ, personated by *Melchisedec,*
25 a greater priest then *Aaron: Vers.* 4. *Now consider how great*
this man was, &c. and proves not in the least manner that
tithes be of any right to ministers, but the contrary: first the
Levites had *a commandment to take tithes of the people ac-*

cording to the law, that is of thir brethren, though they com
out of the loines of Abraham, Vers. 5. The commandment
then was, it seems, to take tithes of the *Jewes* only, and according to the law. That law changing of necessity with the
5 priesthood, no other sort of ministers, as they must needs be
another sort, under another priesthood, can receive that trib-
ute of tithes which fell with that law, unless renu'd by another express command and according to another law: no
such law is extant. Next, *Melchisedec* not as a minister, but
10 as Christ himself in person blessd *Abraham, who had the*
promises, Vers. 6; and in him blessd all both ministers and
people, both of the law and gospel: that blessing declar'd him
greater and better then whom he blessd, *Vers.* 7; receiving
tithes from them all not as a maintenance, which *Melchisedec*
15 needed not, but as a signe of homage and subjection to thir
king and priest: wheras ministers bear not the person of
Christ in his priesthood or kingship, bless not as he blesses,
are not by their blessing greater then *Abraham,* and all the
faithful with themselves included in him, cannot both give
20 and take tithes in *Abram,* cannot claim to themselves that
signe of our allegiance due only to our eternal king and priest,
cannot therefor derive tithes from *Melchisedec.* Lastly, the
eighth verse hath thus: *Here men that die receive tithes:*
There he received them, of whom it is witnesd that he liveth.
25 Which words intimate that as he offerd himself once for us,
so he received once of us in *Abraham,* and in that place the
typical acknowledgment of our redemption: which had it
bin a perpetual annuitie to Christ, by him claimd as his due,

Levi must have paid it yearly, as well as then, *Vers*. 9. and our ministers ought still to som *Melchisedec* or other, as well now as they did in *Abraham*. But that Christ never claimd any such tenth as his annual due, much less resign'd it to the
5 ministers, his so officious receivers without express commission or assignement, will be yet cleerer as we proceed. Thus much may at length assure us, that this example of *Abram* & *Melchisedec,* though I see of late they build most upon it, can so little be the ground of any law to us, that it will not so
10 much avail them as to the autoritie of an example. Of like impertinence is that example of *Jacob, Gen*. 28. 22, who of his free choise, not enjoind by any law, vowd the tenth of all that God should give him : which, for aught appeers to the contrarie, he vowd as a thing no less indifferent before his
15 vow, then the foregoing part thereof; That the stone which he had set there for a pillar, should be God's house. And to whom vowd he this tenth, but to God; not to any priest; for we read of none to him greater then himself? and to God, no doubt, but he paid what he vowd; both in the building of
20 that *Bethel* with other altars els where, and the expence of his continual sacrifices, which none but he had right to offer. However therefor he paid his tenth, it could in no likelihood, unless by such an occasion as befell his grandfather, be to any priest. But, say they, *All the tithe of the land, whether*
25 *of the seed of the land, or of the fruit of the tree, is the Lords, holy unto the Lord, Levit*. 27. 30. And this before it was given to the Levites; therefor since they ceasd. No question; *For the whole earth is the Lords, and the fulnes therof, Psal*.

24. 1; and the light of nature shews us no less: but that the tenth is his more then the rest, how know I, but as he so declares it? He declares it so here of the land of *Canaan* only, as by all circumstance appeers; and passes by deed of gift this
5 tenth to the Levite; yet so as offerd to him first a heave-offring, and consecrated on his altar, *Numb.* 18. all which I had as little known, but by that evidence. The Levites are ceasd, the gift returns to the giver. How then can we know that he hath given it to any other, or how can these men presume to
10 take it unofferd first to God, unconsecrated, without an other cleer and express donation, wherof they shew no evidence or writing? Besides, he hath now alienated that holy land: who can warrantably affirme, that he hath since hallowd the tenth of this land; which none but God hath power to do or can
15 warrant? Thir last prooff they cite out of the gospel, which makes as little for them; *Matth.* 23. 23; where our Saviour denouncing woe to the Scribes and Pharises, who paid tithe so exactly, and omitted waightier matters, tels them, that these they ought to have don, that is, to have paid tithes. For
20 our Saviour spake then to those who observd the law of *Moses,* which was yet not fully abrogated, till the destruction of the temple. And by the way here we may observe out of thir own prooff, that the Scribes and Pharises, though then chief teachers of the people, such at least as were not Levites,
25 did not take tithes, but paid them: So much less covetous were the Scribes and Pharises in those worst times then ours at this day. This is so apparent to the reformed divines of other countreys, that when any one of ours hath attempted

in Latine to maintain this argument of tithes, though a man
would think they might suffer him without opposition in a
point equally tending to the advantage of all ministers, yet
they forbear not to oppose him, as in a doctrin not fit to pass
5 unoppos'd under the gospel. Which shews the modestie, the
contentednes of those forein pastors with the maintenance
given them, thir sinceritie also in the truth, though less gainful, and the avarice of ours: who through the love of their
old Papistical tithes, consider not the weak arguments, or
10 rather conjectures and surmises which they bring to defend
them. On the other side, although it be sufficient to have
prov'd in general the abolishing of tithes, as part of the Judaical or ceremonial law, which is abolishd all, as well that
before as that after *Moses,* yet I shall further prove them ab-
15 rogated by an express ordinance of the gospel, founded not
on any type, or that municipal law of *Moses,* but on moral,
and general equitie, given us instead: 1 *Cor.* 9. 13, 14. *Know
ye not, that they who minister about holy things, live of the
things of the temple; and they which wait at the altar, are
20 partakers with the altar? so also the Lord hath ordaind, that
they who preach the gospel, should live of the gospel.* He
saith not, Should live on things which were of the temple or
of the altar, of which were tithes, for that had given them a
cleer title: but abrogating that former law of *Moses,* which
25 determind what and how much, by a later ordinance of
Christ, which leaves the what and how much indefinit and
free, so it be sufficient to live on, he saith, *The Lord hath so
ordaind, that they who preach the gospel, should live of the*

gospel; which hath neither temple, altar nor sacrifice: *Heb.*
7. 13. For he of whom these things are spoken, pertaineth to
another tribe, of which no man gave attendance at the altar:
his ministers therefor cannot thence have tithes. And where
5 the Lord hath so ordaind, we may finde easily in more then
one evangelist: *Luke* 10. 7, 8. *In the same house remaine,*
eating and drinking such things as they give: For the laborer
is worthy of his hire, &c. And into whatsoever citie you
enter, and they receive you, eat such things as are set before
10 *you.* To which ordinance of Christ it may seem likeliest, that
the apostle referrs us both here and 1 *Tim.* 5. 18, where he
cites this as the saying of our Saviour, *That the laborer is*
worthy of his hire: and both by this place of *Luke,* and that
of *Matth.* 10. 9, 10, 11, it evidently appeers that our Saviour
15 ordaind no certain maintenance for his apostles or ministers
publickly or privatly in house or citie receivd, but that, what
ever it were, which might suffice to live on: and this not commanded or proportiond by *Abram* or by *Moses,* whom he
might easily have here cited, as his manner was, but declar'd
20 only by a rule of common equitie which proportions the hire
as well to the abilitie of him who gives as to the labor of him
who receives, and recommends him only as worthy, not in-
vests him with a legal right. And mark wheron he grounds
this his ordinance; not on a perpetual right of tithes from
25 *Melchisedec,* as hirelings pretend, which he never claimd
either for himself, or for his ministers, but on the plane and
common equitie of rewarding the laborer; worthy somtimes
of single, somtimes of double honor, not proportionable by

tithes. And the apostle in this forecited chapter to the *Corinthians, Vers.* 11, affirms it to be no great recompence, if carnal things be reapd for spiritual sown; but to mention tithes, neglects here the fittest occasion that could be offerd
5 him, and leaves the rest free and undetermind. Certainly if Christ or his apostles had approv'd of tithes, they would have either by writing or tradition recommended them to the church: and that soone would have appeerd in the practise of those primitive and the next ages. But for the first three
10 hundred years and more, in all the ecclesiastical storie, I finde no such doctrin or example: though error by that time had brought back again priests, altars and oblations; and in many other points of religion had miserably Judaiz'd the church. So that the defenders of tithes, after a long pomp and tedious
15 preparation out of Heathen authors, telling us that tithes were paid to *Hercules* and *Apollo,* which perhaps was imitated from the *Jewes,* and as it were bespeaking our expectation, that they will abound much more with autorities out of Christian storie, have nothing of general approbation to be-
20 ginn with from the first three or four ages, but that which abundantly serves to the confutation of thir tithes; while they confess that churchmen in those ages livd meerly upon free-will offerings. Neither can they say, that tithes were not then paid for want of a civil magistrate to ordain them, for Chris-
25 tians had then also lands, and might give out of them what they pleasd; and yet of tithes then given we finde no mention. And the first Christian emperors, who did all things as bishops advis'd them, suppli'd what was wanting to the clergy

not out of tithes, which were never motiond, but out of thir
own imperial revenues; as is manifest in *Eusebius, Theodorit*
and *Sozomen,* from *Constantine* to *Arcadius.* Hence those
ancientest reformed churches of the *Waldenses,* if they rather
5 continu'd not pure since the apostles, deni'd that tithes were
to be given, or that they were ever given in the primitive
church; as appeers by an ancient tractate inserted in the
Bohemian historie. Thus far hath the church bin alwaies,
whether in her prime, or in her ancientest reformation, from
10 the approving of tithes: nor without reason; for they might
easily perceive that tithes were fitted to the *Jewes* only, a
national church of many incomplete synagogues, uniting
the accomplishment of divine worship in one temple; and
the Levites there had thir tithes paid where they did thir
15 bodilie work; to which a particular tribe was set apart by
divine appointment, not by the peoples election: but the
Christian church is universal; not ti'd to nation, dioces or
parish, but consisting of many particular churches complete
in themselves; gatherd, not by compulsion or the accident of
20 dwelling nigh together, but by free consent chusing both thir
particular church and thir church-officers. Wheras if tithes be
set up, all these Christian privileges will be disturbd and
soone lost, and with them Christian libertie. The first autoritie which our adversaries bring, after those fabulous apos-
25 tolic canons, which they dare not insist upon, is a provincial
councel held at *Cullen,* where they voted tithes to be *Gods
rent,* in the year three hundred fifty six; at the same time perhaps when the three kings reignd there, and of like autoritie.

For to what purpose do they bring these trivial testimonies,
by which they might as well prove altars, candles at noone,
and the greatest part of those superstitions, fetchd from Paganism or Jewism, which the Papist, inveigl'd by this fond
5 argument of antiquitie, retains to this day? to what purpose
those decrees of I know not what bishops, to a Parlament and
people who have thrown out both bishops and altars, and
promisd all reformation by the word of God? And that altars
brought tithes hither, as one corruption begott another, is
10 evident by one of those questions which the monk *Austin*
propounded to the Pope, *Concerning those things, which by
offerings of the faithful came to the altar;* as *Beda* writes, *l.* 1.
c. 27. If then by these testimonies we must have tithes continu'd, we must again have altars. Of fathers, by custom so
15 calld, they quote *Ambrose, Augustin,* and som other ceremonial doctors of the same leaven: whose assertion without
pertinent scripture, no reformed church can admitt; and
what they vouch, is founded on the law of *Moses,* with which,
every where pitifully mistaken, they again incorporate the
20 gospel; as did the rest also of those titular fathers, perhaps an
age or two before them, by many rights and ceremonies, both
Jewish and Heathenish introduc'd; whereby thinking to gain
all, they lost all: and instead of winning Jewes and Pagans to
be Christians, by too much condescending they turnd Chris-
25 tians into Jewes and Pagans. To heap such unconvincing citations as these in religion, wherof the scripture only is our rule,
argues not much learning nor judgment, but the lost labor of
much unprofitable reading. And yet a late hot Quærist for

tithes, whom ye may know by his wits lying ever beside him
in the margent, to be ever beside his wits in the text, a fierce
reformer once, now ranckl'd with a contrary heat, would
send us back, very reformedly indeed, to learn reformation
5 from *Tyndarus* and *Rebuffus,* two canonical Promooters.
They produce next the ancient constitutions of this land,
Saxon laws, edicts of kings, and thir counsels, from *Athel-
stan,* in the year nine hundred twenty eight, that tithes by
statute were paid: and might produce from *Ina,* above two
10 hundred years before, that *Romescot,* or *Peters* penny, was by
as good statute law paid to the Pope, from seven hundred
twenty five, and almost as long continu'd. And who knows
not that this law of tithes was enacted by those kings and
barons upon the opinion they had of thir divine right, as the
15 very words import of *Edward* the Confessor, in the close of
that law: *For so blessed* Austin *preachd and taught;* meaning the monk, who first brought the *Romish* religion into
England from *Gregory* the Pope. And by the way I add, that
by these laws, imitating the law of *Moses,* the third part of
20 tithes only was the priests due; the other two were appointed
for the poor, and to adorne or repare churches; as the canons
of *Ecbert* and *Elfric* witnes: *Concil. Brit.* If then these laws
were founded upon the opinion of divine autoritie, and that
autoritie be found mistaken and erroneous, as hath bin fully
25 manifested, it follows, that these laws fall of themselves with
thir fals foundation. But with what face or conscience can
they alleage *Moses,* or these laws for tithes, as they now enjoy
or exact them; wherof *Moses* ordains the owner, as we heard

before, the stranger, the fatherles and the widdow partakers
with the Levite; and these fathers which they cite, and these
though Romish rather then English laws, allotted both to
priest and bishop the third part only. But these our Protes-
5 tant, these our new reformed English presbyterian divines,
against thir own cited authors, and to the shame of thir pretended reformation, would engross to themselves all tithes by
statute; and supported more by thir wilful obstinacie and
desire of filthie lucre then by these both insufficient and im-
10 pertinent autorities, would perswade a Christian magistracie
and parlament, whom we trust God hath restor'd for a happier reformation, to impose upon us a Judaical ceremonial
law, and yet from that law to be more irregular and unwarrantable, more complying with a covetous clergie, then any
15 of those Popish kings and parlaments alleagd. Another shift
they have to plead, that tithes may be moral as well as the
sabbath, a tenth of fruits as well as a seaventh of dayes. I
answer, that the prelats who urge this argument, have least
reason to use it; denying morality in the sabbath, and therin
20 better agreeing with reformed churches abroad then the rest
of our divines: As therefor the seaventh day is not moral, but
a convenient recourse of worship in fit season, whether seaventh or other number, so neither is the tenth of our goods, but
only a convenient subsistence morally due to ministers. The
25 last and lowest sort of thir arguments, that men purchas'd
not thir tithe with thir land and such like pettifoggerie, I
omitt; as refuted sufficiently by others: I omitt also thir violent and irreligious exactions, related no less credibly: thir

seising of pots and pans from the poor, who have as good right to tithes as they; from som, the very beds; thir sueing and imprisoning; worse then when the canon law was in force; worse then when those wicked sons of *Eli* were priests,

5 whose manner was thus to seise thir pretended priestly due by force, 1 *Sam.* 2. 12, *&c. Whereby men abhorrd the offering of the Lord;* and it may be feard that many will as much abhorr the gospel, if such violence as this be sufferd in her ministers, and in that which they also pretend to be the offer-

10 ing of the Lord. For those sons of *belial* within som limits made seisure of what they knew was thir own by an undoubted law; but these, from whom there is no sanctuarie, seise out of mens grounds, out of mens houses thir other goods of double, somtimes of treble value, for that, which

15 did not covetousnes and rapine blinde them, they know to be not thir own by the gospel which they preach. Of som more tolerable then these, thus severely God hath spoken: *Esa.* 46. 10, *&c. They are greedy dogs; they all look to thir own way, every one for his gain, from his quarter.* With what anger

20 then will he judge them who stand not looking, but under colour of a divine right, fetch by force that which is not thir own, taking his name not in vain, but in violence? Nor content as *Gehazi* was to make a cunning, but a constraind advantage of what thir master bids them give freely, how can

25 they but returne smitten, worse then that sharking minister, with a spiritual leprosie? And yet they cry out sacrilege, that men will not be gulld and baffl'd the tenth of thir estates by giving credit to frivolous pretences of divine right. Where

did God ever cleerly declare to all nations, or in all lands (and none but fooles part with thir estates, without cleerest evidence, on bare supposals and presumptions of them who are the gainers thereby) that he requir'd the tenth as due to him
5 or his son perpetually and in all places? Where did he demand it, that we might certainly know, as in all claimes of temporal right is just and reasonable? or if demanded, where did he assigne it, or by what evident conveyance to ministers? unless they can demonstrate this by more then conjectures,
10 thir title can be no better to tithes then the title of *Gehazi* was to those things which by abusing his masters name he rookd from *Naaman*. Much less where did he command that tithes should be fetchd by force, where left not under the gospel whatever his right was, to the freewill-offrings of men?
15 Which is the greater sacrilege, to bely divine autoritic, to make the name of Christ accessory to violence, and, robbing him of the very honor which he aimd at in bestowing freely the gospel, to committ Simonie and rapin, both secular and ecclesiastical, or on the other side, not to give up the tenth of
20 civil right and proprietie to the tricks and impostures of clergie men, contriv'd with all the art and argument that thir bellies can invent or suggest; yet so ridiculous and presuming on the peoples dulnes or superstition, as to think they prove the divine right of thir maintenance by *Abram* paying
25 tithes to *Melchisedec,* when as *Milchisedec* in that passage rather gave maintenance to *Abram;* in whom all both priests and ministers, as well as lay-men paid tithes, not receivd them. And because I affirmd above, beginning this first part

of my discourse, that God hath given to ministers of the gospel that maintenance only which is justly given them, let us
see a little what hath bin thought of that other maintenance
besides tithes, which of all Protestants, our English divines
5 either only or most apparently both require and take. Those
are, fees for christnings, marriages, and burials: which,
though whoso will may give freely, yet being not of right,
but of free gift, if they be exacted or establishd, they become
unjust to them who are otherwise maintaind; and of such
10 evil note, that even the councel of *Trent, l. 2. p.* 240, makes
them lyable to the laws against Simonie, who take or demand fees for the administring of any sacrament: *Che la
sinodo volendo levare gli abusi introdotti, &c.* And in the
next page, with like severity condemns the giving or taking
15 for a benefice, and the celebrating of marriages, christnings,
and burials, for fees exacted or demanded: nor counts it less
Simonie to sell the ground or place of burial. And in a state
assembly at *Orleans,* 1561, it was decreed, *Che non si potesse
essiger cosa alcuna, &c, p.* 429. *That nothing should be ex-*
20 *acted for the administring of sacraments, burials, or any other
spiritual function.* Thus much that councel, of all others the
most Popish, and this assembly of Papists, though, by thir
own principles, in bondage to the clergie, were induc'd, either
by thir own reason and shame, or by the light of reformation
25 then shining in upon them, or rather by the known canons
of many councels and synods long before, to condemne of
Simonie spiritual fees demanded. For if the minister be
maintaind for his whole ministry, why should he be twice

paid for any part therof? why should he, like a servant, seek
vailes over and above his wages? As for christnings, either
they themselves call men to baptism, or men of themselves
com: if ministers invite, how ill had it becomd *John* the Bap-
5 tist to demand fees for his baptising, or Christ for his christnings? Far less becoms it these now, with a greediness lower
then that of tradesmen calling passengers to thir shop, and
yet paid beforehand, to ask again, for doing that which those
thir founders did freely. If men of themselves com to be bap-
10 tiz'd, they are either brought by such as already pay the minister, or com to be one of his disciples and maintainers: of
whom to ask a fee as it were for entrance, is a piece of paultry
craft or caution, befitting none but beggarly artists. Burials
and marriages are so little to be any part of thir gain, that
15 they who consider well, may finde them to be no part of thir
function. At burials thir attendance they alleage on the corps;
all the guests do as much unhir'd: But thir praiers at the
grave; superstitiously requir'd: yet if requir'd, thir last performance to the deceasd of thir own flock. But the funeral
20 sermon: at thir choise: or if not, an occasion offerd them to
preach out of season, which is one part of thir office. But
somthing must be spoken in praise: if due, thir duty; if undue, thir corruption: a peculiar Simonie of our divines in
England only. But the ground is broken, and especially thir
25 unrighteous possession, the chancel. To sell that will not
only raise up in judgment the Councel of *Trent* against them,
but will lose them the best champion of tithes, thir zealous
antiquary, Sir *Hen: Spelman;* who in a book written to that

purpose, by many cited canons, and som even of times cor-
ruptest in the church, proves that fees exacted or demanded
for sacraments, marriages, burials, and especially for inter-
ring, are wicked, accursed, Simoniacal and abominable. Yet
5 thus is the church, for all this noise of reformation, left still
unreformd, by the censure of thir own synods, thir own
favorers, a den of theeves and robbers. As for marriages that
ministers should meddle with them, as not sanctifi'd or legit-
imat without their celebration, I finde no ground in scripture
10 either of precept or example. Likeliest it is (which our *Selden*
hath well observd, *l. 2, c. 28, ux. Eb.*) that in imitation of
heathen priests who were wont at nuptials to use many rites
and ceremonies, and especially, judging it would be profitable, and the increase of thir autoritie, not to be spectators
15 only in busines of such concernment to the life of man, they
insinuated that marriage was not holy without their benediction, and for the better colour, made it a sacrament; being
of it self a civil ordinance, a houshold contract, a thing indifferent and free to the whole race of mankinde, not as re-
20 ligious, but as men: best, indeed, undertaken to religious
ends, and, as the apostle saith, 1 *Cor. 7, in the Lord.* Yet not
therefor invalid or unholy without a minister and his pretended necessary hallowing, more then any other act, enter-
prise or contract of civil life, which ought all to be don also
25 in the Lord and to his glorie. All which, no less then marriage, were by the cunning of priests heretofore, as material
to thir profit, transacted at the altar. Our divines denie it to
be a sacrament; yet retain the celebration, till prudently a

late parlament recoverd the civil liberty of marriage from thir incroachment; and transferrd the ratifying and registring therof from the canonical shop to the proper cognisance of civil magistrates. Seeing then, that God hath given to minis-
5 ters under the gospel, that only which is justly given them, that is to say, a due and moderat livelihood, the hire of thir labor, and that the heave-offering of tithes is abolishd with the altar, yea though not abolishd, yet lawles, as they enjoy them, thir Melchisedecian right also trivial and groundles,
10 and both tithes and fees, if exacted or establishd, unjust and scandalous, we may hope, with them remov'd, to remove hirelings in som good measure, whom these tempting baits, by law especially to be recoverd, allure into the church.

The next thing to be considerd in the maintenance of min-
15 isters, is by whom it should be given. Wherin though the light of reason might sufficiently informe us, it will be best to consult the scripture: *Gal.* 6. 6. *let him that is taught in the word, communicate, to him that teacheth, in all good things:* that is to say, in all manner of gratitude, to his abilitie. 1 *Cor.*
20 9. 11. *if we have sown unto you spiritual things, is it a great matter if we reap your carnal things?* to whom therefor hath not bin sown, from him wherefor should be reapd? 1 *Tim.* 5. 17. *let the elders that rule well, be counted worthie of double honor; especially they who labor in the word and*
25 *doctrin.* By these places we see, that recompence was given either by every one in particular who had bin instructed, or by them all in common, brought into the church-treasurie, and distributed to the ministers according to thir several la-

bors: and that was judgd either by som extraordinarie person, as *Timothie,* who by the apostle was then left evangelist at *Ephesus, 2 Tim.* 4. 5, or by som to whom the church deputed that care. This is so agreeable to reason and so cleer, that any
5 one may perceive what iniquitie and violence hath prevaild since in the church, whereby it hath bin so orderd, that they also shall be compelld to recompence the parochial minister, who neither chose him for thir teacher, nor have receivd instruction from him, as being either insufficient, or not resi-
10 dent, or inferior to whom they follow; wherin to barr them thir choise, is to violate Christian liberty. Our law-books testifie, that before the councel of *Lateran,* in the year 1179, and the fifth of our *Henry* 2, or rather before a decretal epistle of Pope *Innocent* the third, about 1200, and the first of king
15 *John, any man might have given his tithes to what spiritual person he would:* and, as the L. *Coke* notes on that place, *instit. part* 2, that *this decretal bound not the subjects of this realm; but, as it seemd just and reasonable.* The Pope took his reason rightly from the above cited place, 1 *Cor.* 9. 11:
20 but falsly suppos'd every one to be instructed by his parish-priest. Whether this were then first so decreed or rather long before, as may seem by the laws of *Edgar* and *Canute,* that tithes were to be paid, not to whom he would that paid them, but to the cathedral church or the parish-priest, it imports
25 not; since the reason which they themselves bring, built on fals supposition, becomes alike infirme and absurd, that he should reap from me, who sows not to me; bee the cause either his defect, or my free choise. But here it will be readily

objected, What if they who are to be instructed be not able to maintain a minister, as in many villages? I answer, that the scripture shews in many places what ought to be don herin. First I offer it to the reason of any man, whether he think the
5 knowledge of Christian religion harder then any other art or science to attain. I suppose he will grant that it is far easier; both of it self, and in regard of Gods assisting spirit, not particularly promisd us to the attainment of any other knowledge, but of this only: since it was preachd as well to the
10 shepherds of *Bethleem* by angels, as to the eastern Wisemen by that starr: and our Saviour declares himself anointed to preach the gospel to the poore, *Luke* 4. 18. then surely to thir capacitie. They who after him first taught it, were otherwise unlearned men: they who before *Hus* and *Luther* first re-
15 formd it, were for the meanenes of thir condition calld, *the poore men of Lions:* and in *Flanders* at this day, *les gueus,* which is to say, beggars. Therefor are the scriptures translated into every vulgar tongue, as being held in main matters of belief and salvation, plane and easie to the poorest: and
20 such no less then thir teachers have the spirit to guide them in all truth, *Joh.* 14. 26, *&* 16. 13. Hence we may conclude, if men be not all thir life time under a teacher to learn Logic, natural Philosophie, Ethics or Mathematics, which are more difficult, that certainly it is not necessarie to the attainment of
25 Christian knowledge that men should sit all thir life long at the feet of a pulpited divine; while he, a lollard indeed over his elbow-cushion, in almost the seaventh part of 40. or 50. years teaches them scarce half the principles of religion; and

Christ. Learning easy.

his sheep oft-times sit the while to as little purpose of beni-
fiting as the sheep in thir pues at *Smithfield;* and for the most
part by som Simonie or other, bought and sold like them: or,
if this comparison be too low, like those woemen, 1 *Tim.*
5 3. 7. *ever learning and never attaining;* yet not so much
through thir own fault, as through the unskilful and im-
methodical teaching of thir pastor, teaching here and there
at random out of this or that text as his ease or fansie, and
oft-times as his stealth guides him. Seeing then that Chris-
10 tian religion may be so easily attaind, and by meanest capacities, it cannot be much difficult to finde waies, both
how the poore, yea all men may be soone taught what is
to be known of Christianitie, and they who teach them,
recompenc'd. First, if ministers of thir own accord, who
15 pretend that they are calld and sent to preach the gospel,
those especially who have no particular flock, would imitate
our Saviour and his disciples who went preaching through
the villages, not only through the cities, *Matth.* 9. 35, *Mark*
6. 6, *Luke* 13. 22, *Acts* 8. 25. and there preachd to the poore
20 as well as to the rich, looking for no recompence but in
heaven: *John* 4. 35, 36. *Looke on the fields; for they are
white alreadie to harvest: and he that reapeth, receiveth
wages, and gathereth fruit unto life eternal.* This was their
wages. But they will soone reply, we our selves have not
25 wherewithall; who shall bear the charges of our journey? To
whom it may as soone be answerd, that in likelihood they are
not poorer then they who did thus; and if they have not the
same faith which those disciples had to trust in God and the

promise of Christ for thir maintenance as they did, and yet
intrude into the ministerie without any livelihood of thir
own, they cast themselves into a miserable hazzard or temp-
tation, and oft-times into a more miserable necessitie, either
5 to starve, or to please thir paymasters rather then God: and
give men just cause to suspect, that they came neither calld
nor sent from above to preach the word, but from below, by
the instinct of thir own hunger, to feed upon the church. Yet
grant it needful to allow them both the charges of thir jor-
10 ney and the hire of thir labor, it will belong next to the charitie of richer congregations, where most commonly they
abound with teachers, to send som of thir number to the villages round, as the apostles from *Jerusalem* sent *Peter* and
John to the citie and villages of *Samaria, Acts* 8, 14, 25; or
15 as the church at *Jerusalem* sent *Barnabas* to *Antioch, chap.*
11. 22; and other churches joining sent *Luke* to travail with
Paul, 2 Cor. 8. 19: though whether they had thir charges
born by the church or no, it be not recorded. If it be objected
that this itinerarie preaching will not serve to plant the gos-
20 pel in those places, unless they who are sent, abide there som
competent time, I answer, that if they stay there a year or
two, which was the longest time usually staid by the apostles
in one place, it may suffice to teach them, who will attend
and learn, all the points of religion necessary to salvation;
25 then sorting them into several congregations of a moderat
number, out of the ablest and zealousest among them to create elders, who, exercising and requiring from themselves
what they have learnd (for no learning is retaind without

constant exercise and methodical repetition) may teach and
govern the rest: and so exhorted to continue faithful and
stedfast, they may securely be committed to the providence
of God and the guidance of his holy spirit, till God may offer
5 som opportunitie to visit them again and to confirme them:
which when they have don, they have don as much as the
apostles were wont to do in propagating the gospel, *Acts* 14.
23. *And when they had ordaind them elders in every church,
and had praied with fasting, they commended them to the
10 Lord, on whom they beleevd.* And in the same chapter, *Vers.*
21, 22, *When they had preachd the gospel to that citie, and
had taught many, they returned again to* Lystra *and to* Icon-
ium *and* Antioch, *confirming the soules of the disciples, and
exhorting them to continue in the faith.* And *Chap.* 15. 36.
15 *Let us go again and visit our brethren.* And *Vers.* 41. *He
went thorow* Syria *and* Cilicia, *confirming the churches.* To
these I might add other helps, which we enjoy now, to make
more easie the attainment of Christian religion by the meanest: the entire scripture translated into English with plenty of
20 notes; and som where or other, I trust, may be found som
wholsom bodie of divinitie, as they call it, without schoole
terms and metaphysical notions, which have obscur'd rather
then explan'd our religion, and made it seem difficult without cause. Thus taught once for all, and thus now and then
25 visited and confirmd, in the most destitute and poorest places
of the land, under the government of thir own elders performing all ministerial offices among them, they may be
trusted to meet and edifie one another whether in church or

chappel, or, to save them the trudging of many miles thether, neerer home, though in a house or barn. For notwithstanding the gaudy superstition of som devoted still ignorantly to temples, we may be well assur'd that he who disdaind not to
5 be laid in a manger, disdains not to be preachd in a barn; and that by such meetings as these, being, indeed, most apostolical and primitive, they will in a short time advance more in Christian knowledge and reformation of life, then by the many years preaching of such an incumbent, I may say, such
10 an incubus oft times, as will be meanly hir'd to abide long in those places. They have this left perhaps to object further, that to send thus and to maintaine, though but for a year or two, ministers and teachers in several places, would prove chargeable to the churches, though in towns and cities round
15 about. To whom again I answer, that it was not thought so by them who first thus propagated the gospel, though but few in number to us, and much less able to sustain the expence. Yet this expence would be much less, then to hire incumbents or rather incumbrances, for life-time; and a great
20 means (which is the subject of this discourse) to diminish hirelings. But be the expence less or more, if it be found burdensom to the churches, they have in this land an easie remedie in thir recourse to the civil magistrate; who hath in his hands the disposal of no small revenues; left, perhaps, an-
25 ciently to superstitious, but meant undoubtedly to good and best uses; and therefor, once made publick, appliable by the present magistrate to such uses as the church or solid reason from whomsoever shall convince him to think best. And

Hirelings to preach.

those uses may be, no doubt, much rather then as glebes and augmentations are now bestowd, to grant such requests as these of the churches; or to erect in greater number all over the land schooles and competent libraries to those schooles, where languages and arts may be taught free together, without the needles, unprofitable and inconvenient removing to another place. So all the land would be soone better civiliz'd, and they who are taught freely at the publick cost, might have thir education given them on this condition, that therewith content, they should not gadd for preferment out of thir own countrey, but continue there thankful for what they receivd freely, bestowing it as freely on thir countrey, without soaring above the meannes wherin they were born. But how they shall live when they are thus bred and dismissd, will be still the sluggish objection. To which is answerd, that those publick foundations may be so instituted, as the youth therin may be at once brought up to a competence of learning and to an honest trade; and the hours of teaching so orderd, as thir studie may be no hindrance to thir labor or other calling. This was the breeding of S. *Paul,* though born of no mean parents, a free citizen of the Roman empire: so little did his trade debase him, that it rather enabld him to use that magnanimitie of preaching the gospel through *Asia* and *Europe* at his own charges: thus those preachers among the poor *Waldenses,* the ancient stock of our reformation, without these helps which I speak of, bred up themselves in trades, and especially in physic and surgery as well as in the studie of scripture (which is the only true theologie) that they might

be no burden to the church; and by the example of Christ,
might cure both soul and bodie; through industry joining
that to their ministerie, which he joind to his by gift of the
spirit. Thus relates *Peter Gilles* in his historie of the *Wal-*
5 *denses* in *Piemont*. But our ministers think scorn to use a
trade, and count it the reproach of this age, that tradesmen
preach the gospel. It were to be wishd they were all tradesmen; they would not then so many of them, for want of another trade, make a trade of thir preaching: and yet they
10 clamor that tradesmen preach; and yet they preach, while
they themselves are the worst tradesmen of all. As for church-
endowments and possessions, I meet with none considerable
before *Constantine,* but the houses and gardens where they
met, and thir places of burial: and I perswade me, that from
15 them the ancient *Waldenses,* whom deservedly I cite so often,
held, *that to endow churches is an evil thing;* and, that the
church then fell off and turnd whore sitting on that beast in
the *Revelation,* when under Pope *Sylvester* she receivd those
temporal donations. So the forecited tractate of thir doctrin
20 testifies. This also thir own traditions of that heavenly voice
witnesd, and som of the ancient fathers then living, foresaw
and deplor'd. And indeed, how could these endowments
thrive better with the church, being unjustly taken by those
emperors, without suffrage of the people, out of the tributes
25 and publick lands of each citie, whereby the people became
liable to be oppressd with other taxes. Being therefor given
for the most part by kings and other publick persons, and so
likeliest out of the publick, and if without the peoples con-

sent, unjustly, however to publick ends of much concernment to the good or evil of a commonwealth, and in that regard made publick though given by privat persons, or which
is worse, given, as the clergie then perswaded men, for thir
5 soul's health, a pious gift, but as the truth was, oft-times a
bribe to God or to Christ for absolution, as they were then
taught, from murders, adulteries, and other hainous crimes,
what shall be found heretofore given by kings or princes out
of the publick, may justly by the magistrate be recalld and
10 reappropriated to the civil revenue: what by privat or publick
persons out of thir own, the price of blood or lust, or to som
such purgatorious and superstitious uses, not only may but
ought to be taken off from Christ, as a foul dishonor laid
upon him, or not impiously given, nor in particular to any
15 one, but in general to the churches good, may be converted
to that use, which shall be judgd tending more directly to
that general end. Thus did the princes and cities of *Germany*
in the first reformation; and defended thir so doing by many
reasons, which are set down at large in *Sleidan, l.* 6, *an.* 1526,
20 and *l.* 11, *an.* 1537, and *l.* 13, *an.* 1540. But that the magistrate either out of that church revenue which remanes yet in
his hand, or establishing any other maintenance instead of
tithe, should take into his own power the stipendiarie maintenance of church-ministers, or compell it by law, can stand
25 neither with the peoples right nor with Christian liberty, but
would suspend the church wholly upon the state, and turn
her ministers into state-pensioners. And for the magistrate
in person of a nursing father to make the church his meer

ward, as alwaies in minoritie, the church, to whom he ought
as a magistrate, *Esa.* 49, 23, *To bow down with his face to-*
ward the earth, and lick up the dust of her feet, her to subject to his political drifts or conceivd opinions by mastring
5 her revenue, and so by his examinant committies to circum-
scribe her free election of ministers, is neither just nor pious;
no honor don to the church, but a plane dishonor: and upon
her, whose only head is in heaven, yea upon him, who is her
only head, sets another in effect, and, which is most mon-
10 strous, a human on a heavenly, a carnal on a spiritual, a political head on an ecclesiastical bodie; which at length by
such heterogeneal, such incestuous conjunction, transformes
her oft-times into a beast of many heads and many horns.
For if the church be of all societies the holiest on earth, and
15 so to be reverenc'd by the magistrate, not to trust her with her
own belief and integritie, and therefor not with the keeping,
at least with the disposing of what revenue shall be found
justly and lawfully her own, is to count the church not a
holy congregation, but a pack of giddy or dishonest persons,
20 to be rul'd by civil power in sacred affairs. But to proceed
further in the truth yet more freely, seeing the Christian
church is not national, but consisting of many particular congregations, subject to many changes, as well through civil
accidents as through schism and various opinions, not to be
25 decided by any outward judge, being matters of conscience,
whereby these pretended church-revenues, as they have bin
ever, so are like to continue endles matter of dissention both
between the church and magistrate, and the churches among

themselves, there will be found no better remedie to these
evils, otherwise incurable, then by the incorruptest councel
of those *Waldenses,* our first reformers, to remove them as a
pest, an apple of discord in the church, (for what els can be
5 the effect of riches and the snare of monie in religion?) and
to convert them to those more profitable uses above expressd
or other such as shall be judgd most necessarie; considering
that the church of Christ was founded in poverty rather then
in revenues, stood purest and prosperd best without them,
10 receivd them unlawfully from them who both erroneously
and unjustly, somtimes impiously, gave them, and so justly
was ensnar'd and corrupted by them. And least it be thought
that these revenues withdrawne and better imploid, the magistrate ought in stead to settle by statute som maintenance of
15 ministers, let this be considerd first, that it concerns every
mans conscience to what religion he contributes; and that the
civil magistrate is intrusted with civil rights only, not with
conscience, which can have no deputy or representer of it
self, but one of the same minde: next, that what each man
20 gives to the minister, he gives either as to God, or as to his
teacher; if as to God, no civil power can justly consecrate to
religious uses any part either of civil revenue, which is the
peoples, and must save them from other taxes, or of any
mans proprietie, but God by special command, as he did by
25 *Moses,* or the owner himself by voluntarie intention and the
perswasion of his giving it to God; forc'd consecrations out
of another mans estate are no better then forc'd vowes; hateful to God, who *loves a chearful giver;* but much more hate-

ful, wrung out of mens purses to maintaine a disapprov'd
ministerie against thir conscience; however, unholy, infamous and dishonorable to his ministers and the free gospel,
maintaind in such unworthy manner as by violence and ex-
5 tortion: If he give it as to his teacher, what justice or equitie
compells him to pay for learning that religion which leaves
freely to his choise whether he will learn it or no, whether of
this teacher or another, and especially to pay for what he
never learnd, or approves not; whereby, besides the wound of
10 his conscience, he becoms the less able to recompence his
true teacher? Thus far hath bin enquir'd by whom church-
ministers ought to be maintaind; and hath bin prov'd most
natural, most equal and agreeable with scripture, to be by
them who receive thir teaching; and by whom, if they be
15 unable. Which waies well observd, can discourage none but
hirelings, and will much lessen thir number in the church.

It remanes lastly to consider in what manner God hath
ordaind that recompence be given to ministers of the gospel:
and by all scripture it will appeer that he hath given it them
20 not by civil law and freehold, as they claim, but by the benevolence and free gratitude of such as receive them: *Luke*
10. 7, 8. *Eating and drinking such things as they give you.*
If they receive you, eate such things as are set before you.
Matth. 10. 7, 8. *As ye go, preach, saying, The kingdome of*
25 *God is at hand, &c. Freely ye have receivd, freely give.* If
God have ordaind ministers to preach freely, whether they
receive recompence or not, then certainly he hath forbidd
both them to compell it, and others to compell it for them.

But freely given, he accounts it as given to himself: *Phillip.*
4. 16, 17, 18. Ye sent once and again to my necessitie. Not
because I desire a gift; but I desire fruit that may abound to
your account. Having receivd of Epaphroditus *the things*
5 *which were sent from you, an odour of sweet smell, a sacrifice*
acceptable, well pleasing to God. Which cannot be from force
or unwillingnes. The same is said of almes, *Heb.* 13. 16. *To*
do good and to communicate, forgett not: for with such sac-
rifices God is well pleasd. Whence the primitive church
10 thought it no shame to receive all thir maintenance as the
almes of thir auditors. Which they who defend tithes, as if it
made for thir cause, when as it utterly confutes them, omitt
not to set down at large; proving to our hands out of *Origen,*
Tertullian, Cyprian, and others, that the clergie livd at first
15 upon the meer benevolence of thir hearers: who gave what
they gave, not to the clergie, but to the church; out of which
the clergie had thir portions given them in baskets; and were
thence calld *sportularii, basket-clerks:* that thir portion was a
very mean allowance, only for a bare livelihood; according
20 to those precepts of our Saviour, *Matth.* 10, 7, *&c;* the rest
was distributed to the poore. They cite also out of *Prosper,*
the disciple of St. *Austin,* that such of the clergie as had
means of thir own, might not without sin partake of church-
maintenance; not receiving thereby food which they abound
25 with, but feeding on the sins of other men: that the holy ghost
saith of such clergie men, they eat the sins of my people: and
that a councel at *Antioch,* in the year 340, sufferd not either
priest or bishop to live on church-maintenance without ne-

cessitie. Thus far tithers themselves have contributed to thir own confutation, by confessing that the church livd primitively on almes. And I add, that about the year 359, *Constantius* the emperor having summond a general councel of

5 bishops to *Ariminum* in *Italie,* and provided for thir subsistence there, the *British* and *French* bishops judging it not decent to live on the publick, chose rather to be at thir own charges. Three only out of *Britain* constraind through want, yet refusing offerd assistance from the rest, accepted the em-

10 peror's provision; judging it more convenient to subsist by publick then by privat sustenance. Whence we may conclude, that *bishops* then in this Iland had thir livelihood only from benevolence: in which regard this relater *Sulpitius Severus,* a good author of the same time, highly praises them. And

15 the *Waldenses,* our first reformers, both from the scripture and these primitive examples, maintaind those among them who bore the office of ministers, by almes only. Take thir very words from the historie written of them in *French, Part. 3. l. 2. c. 2. La nourriture & ce de quoy nous sommes*

20 *couverts &c. Our food & cloathing is sufficiently administerd & given to us by way of gratuitie and almes, by the good people whom we teach.* If then by almes and benevolence, not by legal force, not by tenure of freehold or copyhold: for almes, though just, cannot be compelld; and

25 benevolence forc'd, is malevolence rather, violent and inconsistent with the gospel; and declares him no true minister therof, but a rapacious hireling rather, who by force receiving it, eats the bread of violence and exaction, no holy or just

livelihood, no not civilly counted honest; much less beseeming such a spiritual ministry. But, say they, our maintenance is our due, tithes the right of Christ, unseparable from the priest, no where repeald; if then, not otherwise to be had, by
5 law to be recoverd: for though *Paul* were pleasd to forgoe his due, and not to use his power, 1 *Cor.* 9. 12, yet he had a power, *v.* 4, and bound not others. I answer first, because I see them still so loath to unlearn thir decimal arithmetic, and still grasp thir tithes as inseparable from a priest, that minis-
10 ters of the gospel are not priests; and therefor separated from tithes by thir own exclusion; being neither calld priests in the new testament, nor of any order known in scripture: not of *Melchisedec,* proper to Christ only; not of *Aaron,* as they themselves will confess; and the third priesthood, only re-
15 maining, is common to all the faithful. But they are ministers of our high priest. True; but not of his priesthood, as the Levites were to *Aaron:* for he performs that whole office himself incommunicably. Yet tithes remane, say they, still unreleasd, the due of Christ; and to whom payable, but to his
20 ministers? I say again, that no man can so understand them, unless Christ in som place or other so claim them. That example of *Abram* argues nothing but his voluntarie act; honor once only don, but on what consideration, whether to a priest or to a king, whether due the honor, arbitrarie that kinde of
25 honor or not, will after all contending be left still in meer conjecture: which must not be permitted in the claim of such a needy and suttle spiritual corporation pretending by divine right to the tenth of all other mens estates; nor can it

be allowd by wise men or the verdit of common law. And the tenth part, though once declar'd holy, is declar'd now to be no holier then the other nine, by that command to *Peter Act.* 10. 15. 28: whereby all distinction of holy and unholy
5 is remov'd from all things. Tithes therefor though claimd, and holy under the law, yet are now releasd and quitted both by that command to *Peter,* and by this to all ministers, above-cited *Luke* 10; *eating and drinking such things as they give you:* made holy now by thir free gift only. And therefor S.
10 *Paul,* 1 *Cor.* 9. 4, asserts his power, indeed; but of what? not of tithes, but, *to eat and drink such things as are given* in reference to this command: which he calls not holy things or things of the gospel, as if the gospel had any consecrated things in answer to things of the temple, *v.* 13, but he calls
15 them *your carnal things, v.* 11. without changing thir property. And what power had he? not the power of force but of conscience only, whereby he might lawfully and without scruple live on the gospel; receiving what was given him, as the recompence of his labor. For if Christ the master hath
20 professd his kingdom to be not of this world, it suits not with that profession either in him or his ministers to claim temporal right from spiritual respects. He who refus'd to be the divider of an inheritance between two brethren, cannot approve his ministers by pretended right from him to be di-
25 viders of tenths and freeholds out of other mens possessions, making thereby the gospel but a cloak of carnal interest, and, to the contradiction of thir master, turning his heavenly kingdom into a kingdom of this world, a kingdom of force and

rapin. To whom it will be one day thunderd more terribly then to *Gehazi,* for thus dishonoring a far greater master and his gospel, *is this a time to receive monie and to receive garments and olive-yards and vinyards and sheep and oxen?*
5 The leprosie of *Naaman* linkd with that apostolic curse of *perishing* imprecated on *Simon Magus,* may be feard will *cleave to* such *and to* thir *seed for ever.* So that when all is don, and bellie hath us'd in vain all her cunning shifts, I doubt not but all true ministers, considering the demonstra-
10 tion of what hath bin here prov'd, will be wise, and think it much more tolerable to hear, that no maintenance of ministers, whether tithes or any other, can be settl'd by statute; but must be given by them who receive instruction; and freely given, as God hath ordaind. And indeed what can be a more
15 honorable maintenance to them, then such whether almes or willing oblations as these, which being accounted both alike as given to God, the only acceptable sacrifices now remaining, must needs represent him who receives them much in the care of God and neerly related to him, when not by
20 worldly force and constraint, but with religious awe and reverence, what is given to God, is given to him, and what to him, accounted as given to God. This would be well anough, say they; but how many will so give? I answer, as many, doubtles, as shall be well taught; as many as God shall so
25 move. Why are ye so distrustful both of your own doctrin and of Gods promises, fulfilld in the experience of those disciples first sent: *Luke* 22. 35. *When I sent you without purse and scrip and shooes, lackd ye anything? And they said, Noth-*

ing. How then came ours, or who sent them thus destitute, thus poor and empty both of purse and faith? Who stile themselves embassadors of Jesus Christ, and seem to be his tithe-gatherers, though an office of thir own setting up to his
5 dishonor, his exacters, his publicans rather, not trusting that he will maintain them in thir embassy, unless they binde him to his promise by a statute law that we shall maintain them. Lay down for shame that magnific title, while ye seek maintenance from the people: it is not the manner of embassa-
10 dors to ask maintenance of them to whom they are sent. But he who is Lord of all things, hath so ordaind: trust him then; he doubtless will command the people to make good his promises of maintenance more honorably unaskd, unrak'd for. This they know, this they preach, yet beleeve not: but
15 think it as impossible without a statute law to live of the gospel, as if by those words they were bid go eat thir bibles, as *Ezechiel* and *John* did thir books; and such doctrins as these are as bitter to thir bellies: but will serve so much the better to discover hirelings, who can have nothing, though but in
20 appearance, just and solid to answer for themselves against what hath bin here spoken, unless perhaps this one remaning pretence, which we shall quickly see to be either fals or uningenuous. They pretend that thir education either at schoole or universitie hath bin very chargeable; and therefor
25 ought to be repar'd in future by a plentiful maintenance: whenas it is well known that the better half of them, and oft times poor and pittiful boyes of no merit or promising hopes that might intitle them to the publick provision but thir

povertie and the unjust favor of friends, have had the most of thir breeding both at schoole and universitie by schollarships, exhibitions and fellowships at the publick cost; which might ingage them the rather to give freely, as they have freely re-
5 ceivd. Or if they have missd of these helps at the latter place, they have after two or three years left the cours of thir studies there, if they ever well began them, and undertaken, though furnishd with little els but ignorance, boldnes and ambition, if with no worse vices, a chaplainship in som gentlemans
10 house, to the frequent imbasing of his sons with illiterate and narrow principles. Or if they have livd there upon thir own, who knows not that seaven years charge of living there, to them who fly not from the government of thir parents to the license of a universitie, but com seriously to studie, is no
15 more then may be well defraid and reimbours'd by one years revenue of an ord'nary good benifice? If they had then means of breeding from thir parents, 'tis likely they have more now; and if they have, it needs must be mechanique and uningenuous in them to bring a bill of charges for the
20 learning of those liberal arts and sciences, which they have learnd (if they have indeed learnd them, as they seldom have) to thir own benefit and accomplishment. But they will say, we had betaken us to som other trade or profession, had we not expected to finde a better livelihood by the min-
25 isterie. This is that which I lookd for, to discover them openly neither true lovers of learning, and so very seldom guilty of it, nor true ministers of the gospel. So long agoe out of date is that old *true saying,* 1 *Tim.* 3. 1. *if a man desire a bishop-*

rick, he desires a good work: for now commonly he who desires to be a minister, looks not at the work but at the wages;
and by that lure or loubel may be toald from parish to parish
all the town over. But what can be planer Simonie, then thus
5 to be at charges beforehand to no other end then to make thir
ministry doubly or trebly beneficial? to whom it might be
said as justly as to that *Simon, thy monie perish with thee,
because thou hast thought that the gift of God may be purchas'd with monie: thou hast neither part nor lot in this
10 matter.* Next, it is a fond error, though too much beleevd
among us, to think that the universitie makes a minister of
the gospel; what it may conduce to other arts and sciences, I
dispute not now: but that which makes fit a minister, the
scripture can best informe us to be only from above; whence
15 also we are bid to seek them; *Matth.* 9. 38. *Pray ye therefor
to the Lord of the harvest, that he will send forth laborers
into his harvest.* Acts 20. 28. *The flock, over which the holy
ghost hath made you over-seers.* Rom. 10. 15. *How shall
they preach, unless they be sent?* by whom sent? by the uni-
20 versitie, or the magistrate, or thir belly? no surely: but sent
from God only, and that God who is not thir belly. And
whether he be sent from God or from *Simon Magus,* the inward sense of his calling and spiritual abilitie will sufficiently
tell him; and that strong obligation felt within him, which
25 was felt by the apostle, will often exprcss from him the same
words: 1 *Cor.* 9. 16. *Necessity is laid upon me, yea, woe is
me, if I preach not the gospel.* Not a beggarly necessity, and
the woe feard otherwise of perpetual want, but such a neces-

sitie as made him willing to preach the gospel *gratis,* and to
embrace povertie rather then as a woe to fear it. 1 *Cor.* 12.
28. *God hath set som in the church, first apostles, &c.* Eph.
4. 11, *&c. He gave som apostles, &c. For the perfeting of*
5 *the saints, for the work of the ministerie, for the edifying of*
the body of Christ, till we all come to the unitie of the faith.
Whereby we may know that as he made them at the first, so
he makes them still, and to the worlds end. 2 *Cor.* 3. 6. *Who*
hath also made us fit or able ministers of the new testament.
10 1 Tim. 4. 14. *The gift that is in thee, which was given thee*
by prophesie and the laying on of the hands of the presby-
terie. These are all the means which we read of requir'd in
scripture to the making of a minister. All this is granted you
will say: but yet that it is also requisite he should be traind
15 in other learning; which can be no where better had then at
universities. I answer, that what learning either human or
divine can be necessary to a minister, may as easily and less
chargeably be had in any private house. How deficient els
and to how little purpose are all those piles of sermons, notes,
20 and comments on all parts of the bible, bodies and marrows
of divinitie, besides all other sciences, in our English tongue;
many of the same books which in Latine they read at the
universitie? And the small necessitie of going thether to learn
divinitie, I prove first from the most part of themselves, who
25 seldom continue there till they have well got through Logic,
thir first rudiments; though, to say truth, Logic also may
much better be wanting in disputes of divinitie, then in the
suttle debates of lawyers and statesmen, who yet seldom or

never deal with syllogisms. [And those theological disputations there held by Professors and graduates are such as tend
least of all to the edification or capacitie of the people, but
rather perplex and leaven pure doctrin with scholastical trash]
5 then enable any minister to the better preaching of the gospel.
Whence we may also compute, since they com to recknings,
the charges of his needful library: which, though som shame
not to value at 600 l, may be competently furnishd for 60 l.
If any man for his own curiositie or delight be in books fur-
10 ther expensive, that is not to be recknd as necessarie to his
ministerial either breeding or function. But Papists and other
adversaries cannot be confuted without fathers and councels,
immense volumes and of vast charges. I will shew them
therefor a shorter and a better way of confutation: *Tit.* 1. 9.
15 *Holding fast the faithful word, as he hath bin taught, that he*
may be able by sound doctrin, both to exhort and to convince
gain-sayers: who are confuted as soon as heard, bringing that
which is either not in scripture or against it. To persue them
further through the obscure and intangld wood of antiquitie,
20 fathers and councels fighting one against another, is needles,
endles, not requisite in a minister, and refus'd by the first
reformers of our religion. And yet we may be confident, if
these things be thought needful, let the state but erect in
publick good store of libraries, and there will not want men
25 in the church, who of thir own inclinations will become able
in this kinde against Papist or any other adversarie. I have
thus at large examind the usual pretences of hirelings, col-
ourd over most commonly with the cause of learning and

universities: as if with divines learning stood and fell; wherin
for the most part thir pittance is so small: and, to speak
freely, it were much better, there were not one divine in the
universitie; no schoole-divinitie known, the idle sophistrie of
5 monks, the canker of religion; and that they who intended
to be ministers, were traind up in the church only, by the
scripture and in the original languages therof at schoole;
without fetching the compas of other arts and sciences, more
then what they can well learn at secondary leasure and at
10 home. Neither speak I this in contempt of learning or the
ministry, but hating the common cheats of both; hating that
they who have preachd out bishops, prelats and canonists,
should, in what serves thir own ends, retain thir fals opinions, thir Pharisaical leaven, thir avarice and closely thir am-
15 bition, thir pluralities, thir nonresidences, thir odious fees,
and use thir legal and Popish arguments for tithes: that In-
dependents should take that name, as they may justly from
the true freedom of Christian doctrin and church-discipline
subject to no superior judge but God only, and seek to be
20 Dependents on the magistrate for thir maintenance; which
two things, independence and state-hire in religion, can never
consist long or certainly together. For magistrates at one time
or other, not like these at present our patrons of Christian
libertie, will pay none but such whom by thir committies of
25 examination, they find conformable to their interest and
opinions: and hirelings will soone frame themselves to that
interest and those opinions which they see best pleasing to
thir paymasters; and to seem right themselves, will force

others as to the truth. But most of all they are to be revil'd
and sham'd, who cry out with the distinct voice of notorious
hirelings, that if ye settle not our maintenance by law, farwell
the gospel: then which nothing can be utterd more fals, more
5 ignominious, and, I may say, more blasphemous against our
Saviour; who hath promisd, without this condition, both his
holy spirit and his own presence with his church to the
worlds end: nothing more fals (unless with thir own mouths
they condemne themselves for the unworthiest and most
10 mercenary of all other ministers) by the experience of 300.
years after Christ, and the churches at this day in *France,
Austria, Polonia,* and other places witnessing the contrary
under an advers magistrate not a favorable: nothing more
ignominious, levelling or rather undervaluing Christ beneath
15 *Mahomet.* For if it must be thus, how can any Christian object it to a Turk, that his religion stands by force only; and
not justly fear from him this reply, yours both by force and
monie in the judgment of your own preachers. This is that
which makes atheists in the land, whom they so much com-
20 plain of: not the want of maintenance or preachers, as they
alleage, but the many hirelings and cheaters that have the
gospel in thir hands; hands that still crave, and are never
satisfi'd. Likely ministers, indeed, to proclaim the faith or to
exhort our trust in God, when they themselves will not trust
25 him to provide for them in the message wheron, they say, he
sent them; but threaten for want of temporal means to desert it; calling that want of means, which is nothing els but
the want of thir own faith; and would force us to pay the hire

of building our faith to their covetous incredulitie. Doubtles, if God only be he who gives ministers to his church till
the worlds end; and through the whole gospel never sent us
for ministers to the schools of Philosophie, but rather bids us
5 beware of such *vain deceit, Col.* 2. 8. (which the primitive
church, after two or three ages not remembring, brought
herself quickly to confusion) if all the faithful be now *a holy
and a royal priesthood,* 1 *Pet.* 2. 5. 9, not excluded from the
dispensation of things holiest, after free election of the church
10 and imposition of hands, there will not want ministers,
elected out of all sorts and orders of men, for the Gospel
makes no difference from the magistrate himself to the
meanest artificer, if God evidently favor him with spiritual
gifts, as he can easily and oft hath don, while those batchelor
15 divines and doctors of the tippet have bin passd by. Heretofore in the first evangelic times (and it were happy for Christendom if it were so again) ministers of the gospel were by
nothing els distinguishd from other Christians but by thir
spiritual knowledge and sanctitie of life, for which the church
20 elected them to be her teachers and overseers, though not
thereby to separate them from whatever calling she then
found them following besides, as the example of S. *Paul* declares, and the first times of Christianitie. When once they
affected to be calld a clergie, and became as it were a peculiar
25 tribe of levites, a partie, a distinct order in the commonwealth, bred up for divines in babling schooles and fed at the
publick cost, good for nothing els but what was good for
nothing, they soone grew idle: that idlenes with fulnes of

bread begat pride and perpetual contention with thir feeders
the despis'd laitie, through all ages ever since; to the pervert-
ing of religion, and the disturbance of all Christendom. And
we may confidently conclude, it never will be otherwise
5 while they are thus upheld undepending on the church, on
which alone they anciently depended, and are by the magistrate publickly maintaind a numerous faction of indigent
persons, crept for the most part out of extream want and bad
nurture, claiming by divine right and freehold the tenth of
10 our estates, to monopolize the ministry as their peculiar,
which is free and open to all able Christians, elected by any
church. Under this pretence exempt from all other imploy-
ment, and inriching themselves on the publick, they last of
all prove common incendiaries, and exalt thir horns against
15 the magistrate himself that maintains them, as the priest of
Rome did soone after against his benefactor the emperor, and
the presbyters of late in *Scotland*. Of which hireling crew together with all the mischiefs, dissentions, troubles, warrs
meerly of their kindling, Christendom might soone rid her-
20 self and be happie, if Christians would but know thir own
dignitie, thir libertie, thir adoption, and let it not be wonderd if I say, thir spiritual priesthood, whereby they have all
equally access to any ministerial function whenever calld by
thir own abilities and the church, though they never came
25 neer commencement or universitie. But while Protestants,
to avoid the due labor of understanding thir own religion are
content to lodge it in the breast or rather in the books of a
clergie man, and to take it thence by scraps and mammocks

as he dispences it in his sundays dole, they will be alwaies learning and never knowing, alwaies infants, alwaies either his vassals, as lay-papists are to their priests, or at odds with him, as reformed principles give them som light to be not

5 wholly conformable, whence infinit disturbances in the state, as they do, must needs follow. Thus much I had to say; and, I suppose, what may be anough to them who are not avariciously bent otherwise, touching the likeliest means to remove hirelings out of the church; then which nothing can more

10 conduce to truth, to peace and all happines both in church and state. If I be not heard nor beleevd, the event will bear me witnes to have spoken truth: and I in the mean while have borne my witnes not out of season to the church and to my countrey.

The End.

A LETTER TO A FRIEND

A Letter to a Friend,

Concerning
the Ruptures of the Commonwealth.

SIR,

UPON the sad and serious Discourse which we
fell into last night, concerning these dangerous
Ruptures of the Commonwealth, scarce yet in
her Infancy, which cannot be without some inward flaw
5 in her Bowels; I began to consider more intensly theron
than hitherto I have bin wont, resigning my self to the
Wisdom and Care of those who had the Government; and
not finding that either God, or the Publick requir'd more
of me, than my Prayers for them that govern. And since
10 you have not only stir'd up my thoughts, by acquainting me
with the state of Affairs, more inwardly than I knew before; but also have desired me to set down my Opinion
therof, trusting to your Ingenuity, I shall give you freely
my apprehension, both of our present Evils, and what Ex-
15 pedients, if God in Mercy regard us, may remove them.
I will begin with telling you how I was over-joy'd, when
I heard that the Army, under the working of God's holy
Spirit, as I thought, and still hope well, had bin so far
wrought to Christian Humility, and Self-denial, as to con-
20 fess in publick thir backsliding from the good Old Cause,
and to shew the fruits of thir Repentance, in the righteous-

ness of thir restoring the old famous Parliament, which they
had without just Authority dissolved: I call it the famous
Parliament, tho not the harmles, since none well-affected,
but will confes, they have deserved much more of these Na-
5 tions, than they have undeserved. And I perswade me, that
God was pleas'd with thir Restitution, signing it, as he did,
with such a signal Victory, when so great a part of the Nation were desperately conspir'd to call back again thir Egyp-
tian Bondage. So much the more it now amazes me, that
10 they, whose Lips were yet scarce clos'd from giving Thanks
for that great Deliverance, should be now relapsing, and so
soon again backsliding into the same fault, which they con-
fest so lately, and so solemnly to God and the World, and
more lately punish'd in those *Cheshire* Rebels; that they
15 should now dissolve that Parliament, which they themselves
re-establish'd, and acknowledg'd for thir Supreme Power in
thir other days humble Representation: and all this, for no
apparent cause of publick Concernment to the Church or
Commonwealth, but only for discommissioning nine great
20 Officers in the Army; which had not bin don, as is reported,
but upon notice of thir Intentions against the Parliament. I
presume not to give my Censure on this Action, not knowing, as yet I do not, the bottom of it. I speak only what it
appears to us without doors, till better cause be declar'd, and
25 I am sure to all other Nations most illegal and scandalous, I
fear me barbarous, or rather scarce to be exampl'd among
any Barbarians, that a paid Army should, for no other cause,
thus subdue the Supream Power that set them up. This, I

say, other Nations will judg to the sad dishonour of that
Army, lately so renown'd for the civilest and best order'd in
the World, and by us here at home, for the most conscien-
tious. Certainly, if the great Officers and Souldiers of the
5 *Holland, French* or *Venetian* Forces, should thus sit in
Council, and write from Garison to Garison against their
Superiors, they might as easily reduce the King of *France,*
or Duke of *Venice,* and put the United Provinces in like
Disorder and Confusion. Why do they not, being most of
10 them held ignorant of true Religion? because the Light of
Nature, the Laws of Human Society, the Reverence of their
Magistrates, Covenants, Engagements, Loyalty, Allegiance,
keeps them in awe. How grievous will it then be? how
infamous to the true Religion which we profess? how dis-
15 honorable to the Name of God, that his Fear and the power
of his Knowledg in an Army professing to be his, should not
work that Obedience, that Fidelity to thir Supream Magistrates, that levied them, and paid them, when the Light of
Nature, the Laws of Human Society, Covenants, and Con-
20 tracts, yea common Shame works in other Armies, amongst
the worst of them? Which will undoubtedly pull down the
heavy Judgment of God among us, who cannot but avenge
these Hypocrisies, Violations of Truth and Holines; if they
be indeed so as they yet seem. For, neither do I speak this in
25 reproach to the Army, but as jealous of thir Honour, inciting
them to manifest and publish, with all speed, some better
cause of these thir late Actions, than hath hitherto appear'd,
and to find out the *Achan* amongst them, whose close Ambi-

tion in all likelihood abuses thir honest Natures against thir
meaning to these Disorders; thir readiest way to bring in
again the common Enemy, and with him the Destruction of
true Religion, and civil Liberty. But, because our Evils are
5 now grown more dangerous and extream, than to be rem-
edi'd by Complaints, it concerns us now to find out what
Remedies may be likeliest to save us from approaching Ruin.
Being now in Anarchy, without a counselling and governing
Power; and the Army, I suppose, finding themselves insuf-
10 ficient to discharge at once both Military and Civil Affairs,
the first thing to be found out with all speed, without which
no Commonwealth can subsist, must be a Senate, or General Council of State, in whom must be the Power, first, to
preserve the publick Peace, next the Commerce with Foreign
15 Nations; and lastly, to raise Monies for the Management of
these Affairs: this must either be the Parliament readmitted
to sit, or a Council of State allow'd of by the Army, since
they only now have the Power. The Terms to be stood on
are, Liberty of Conscience to all professing Scripture to be
20 the Rule of thir Faith and Worship; and the Abjuration of
a single Person. If the Parliament be again thought on, to
salve Honour on both sides, the well-affected Party of the
City, and the congregated Churches, may be induced to
mediate by publick Addresses, and brotherly beseechings,
25 which, if there be that Saintship among us which is talk'd
of, ought to be of highest and undeniable Perswasion to
Reconcilement. If the Parliament be thought well dissolv'd,
as not complying fully to grant Liberty of Conscience, and

the necessary Consequence therof, the removal of a forc'd
Maintenance from Ministers, then must the Army forthwith
choose a Council of State, wherof as many to be of the
Parliament, as are undoubtedly affected to these two Condi-
5 tions propos'd. That which I conceive only able to cement,
and unite for ever the Army, either to the Parliament recall'd, or this chosen Council, must be a mutual League and
Oath, private or publick, not to desert one another till Death:
That is to say, that the Army be kept up, and all these
10 Officers in thir places during Life, and so likewise the
Parliament, or Counsellors of State; which will be no way
unjust, considering thir known Merits on either side, in
Councel or in Field, unless any be found false to any of
these two Principles, or otherwise personally criminous in
15 the Judgment of both Parties. If such a Union as this be not
accepted on the Army's part, be confident there is a single
Person underneath. That the Army be upheld, the necessity
of our Affairs and Factions will constrain long enough
perhaps, to content the longest Liver in the Army. And
20 whether the Civil Government be an annual Democracy, or
a perpetual Aristocracy, is not to me a Consideration for the
Extremities wherin we are, and the hazard of our Safety
from our common Enemy, gaping at present to devour us.
That it be not an Oligarchy, or the Faction of a few, may be
25 easily prevented by the Numbers of thir own choosing, who
may be found infallibly constant to those two Conditions
forenam'd, full Liberty of Conscience, and the Abjuration
of Monarchy propos'd: and the well-order'd Committies of

thir faithfullest Adherents in every County may give this
Government the resemblance and effects of a perfect Democracy. As for the Reformation of Laws, and the places of
Judicature, whether to be here, as at present, or in every
5 County, as hath bin long aim'd at, and many such Proposals,
tending no doubt to publick good, they may be consider'd
in due time when we are past these pernicious Pangs, in a
hopeful way of Health, and firm Constitution. But unless
these things, which I have above propos'd, one way or other,
10 be once settl'd, in my fear, which God avert, we instantly
ruin; or at best become the Servants of one or other single
Person, the secret Author and Fomenter of these Disturbances. You have the sum of my present Thoughts, as much as
I understand of these Affairs freely imparted, at your request,
15 and the Perswasion you wrought in me, that I might chance
herby to be some way serviceable to the Commonwealth, in
a time when all ought to be endeavouring what good they
can, whether much, or but little. With this you may do
what you please, put out, put in, communicate or suppress:
20 you offend not me, who only have obey'd your Opinion, that
in doing what I have don, I might happen to offer somthing which might be of som use in this great time of need.
However, I have not bin wanting to the opportunity which
you presented before me, of shewing the readines which I
25 have in the midst of my Unfitnes, to what ever may be
requir'd of me, as a publick Duty.

October 20. 1659.

LETTER TO GENERAL MONK

The Present Means,

and brief Delineation of a Free Commonwealth, Easy to be put in Practice, and
without Delay. In a Letter to General Monk.

FIRST, all endeavours speedily to be us'd, that the
ensuing Election be of such as are already firm, or inclinable to constitute a free Commonwealth (according to the former qualifications decreed in Parlament, and
5 not yet repeal'd, as I hear) without single Person, or House
of Lords. If these be not such, but the contrary, who fore-
sees not, that our Liberties will be utterly lost in this next
Parlament, without some powerful course taken, of speediest
prevention? The speediest way will be to call up forthwith
10 the chief Gentlemen out of every County; to lay before them
(as your Excellency hath already, both in your publish'd
Letters to the Army, and your Declaration recited to the
Members of Parlament) the Danger and Confusion of readmitting Kingship in this Land; especially against the Rules
15 of all Prudence and Example, in a Family once ejected, and
therby not to be trusted with the power of Revenge: that you
will not longer delay them with vain expectation, but will
put into thir hands forthwith the possession of a free Commonwealth; if they will first return immediately and elect
20 them, by such at least of the People as are rightly qualifi'd, a

standing Council in every City, and great Town, which may
then be dignified with the name of City, continually to consult
the good and flourishing state of that Place, with a competent
Territory adjoin'd; to assume the judicial Laws, either these
5 that are, or such as they themselves shall new make severally,
in each Commonalty, and all Judicatures, all Magistracies,
to the Administration of all Justice between man and man,
and all the Ornaments of publick Civility, Academies, and
such like, in thir own hands. Matters appertaining to men of
10 several Counties, or Territories, may be determin'd, as they
are here at *London,* or in some more convenient Place, under
equal Judges.

Next, That in every such Capital Place, they will choose
them the usual number of ablest Knights and Burgesses,
15 engag'd for a Commonwealth, to make up the Parlament,
or (as it will from henceforth be better called) the Grand or
General Council of the Nation: whose Office must be, with
due Caution, to dispose of Forces, both by Sea and Land,
under the conduct of your Excellency, for the preservation
20 of Peace, both at home and abroad; must raise and manage
the publick Revenue, but with provided inspection of thir
Accompts; must administer all forein Affairs, make all
General Laws, Peace, or War, but not without Assent of the
standing Council in each City, or such other general Assem-
25 bly as may be call'd on such occasion, from the whole Territory, where they may without much trouble, deliberate on
all things fully, and send up thir Suffrages within a set time,
by Deputies appointed. Though this grand Council be per-

petual (as in that Book I prov'd would be best and most conformable to best examples) yet they will then, thus limited,
have so little matter in thir Hands, or Power to endanger
our Liberty; and the People so much in thirs, to prevent
5 them, having all Judicial Laws in thir own choice, and free
Votes in all those which concern generally the whole Commonwealth, that we shall have little cause to fear the per-
petuity of our general Senat; which will be then nothing else
but a firm foundation and custody of our Public Liberty,
10 Peace, and Union, through the whole Commonwealth, and
the transactors of our Affairs with forein Nations.

If this yet be not thought enough, the known Expedient
may at length be us'd, of a partial Rotation.

Lastly, if these Gentlemen convocated, refuse these fair
15 and noble Offers of immediate Liberty, and happy Condition, no doubt there be enough in every County who will
thankfully accept them, your Excellency once more declaring publickly this to be your Mind, and having a faithful
Veteran Army, so ready, and glad to assist you in the prose-
20 cution therof. For the full and absolute Administration of
Law in Every County, which is the difficultest of these Proposals, hath bin of most long desired; and the not granting it,
held a general Grievance. The rest when they shall see the be-
ginnings and proceedings of these Constitutions propos'd, and
25 the orderly, the decent, the civil, the safe, the noble Effects
therof, will be soon convinc'd, and by degrees come in of thir
own accord, to be partakers of so happy a Government.

THE READIE AND EASIE WAY

THE
READIE & EASIE
VV A Y·
TO
ESTABLISH
A
Free Commonwealth,
AND
The EXCELLENCE therof

Compar'd with

The inconveniences and dangers of
readmitting kingſhip in this nation.

The author J. M.

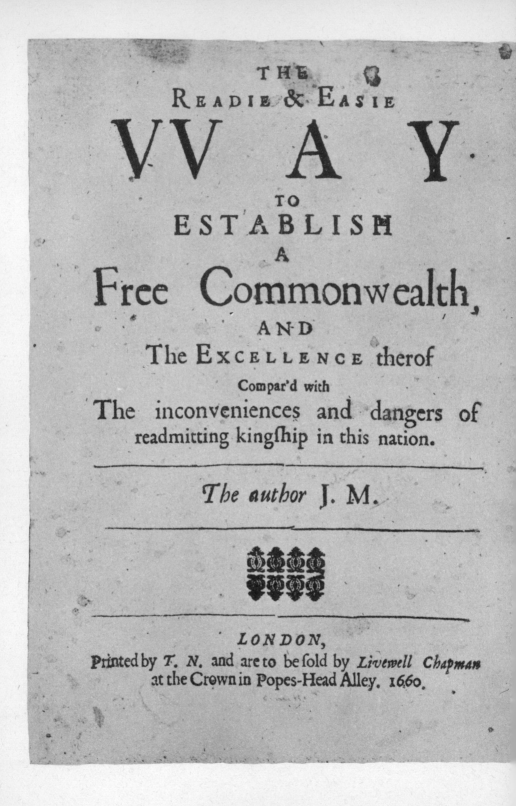

LONDON,

Printed by *T. N.* and are to be ſold by *Livewell Chapman*
at the Crown in Popes-Head Alley. 1660.

The readie and easie way to establish a free Commonwealth.

ALTHOUGH since the writing of this treatise, the face of things hath had som change, writs for new elections have bin recall'd, and the members at first chosen, readmitted from exclusion, yet not a little rejoicing
5 to hear declar'd the resolution of those who are in power, tending to the establishment of a free Commonwealth, and to remove, if it be possible, this noxious humor of returning to bondage, instilld of late by som deceivers, and nourishd from bad principles and fals apprehensions among too many
10 of the people, I thought best not to suppress what I had written, hoping that it may now be of much more use and concernment to be freely publishd, in the midst of our Elections to a free Parlament, or their sitting to consider freely of the Government; whom it behoves to have all things repre-
15 sented to them that may direct thir judgment therin; and I never read of any State, scarce of any tyrant grown so incurable, as to refuse counsel from any in a time of public deliberation; much less to be offended. If thir absolute determination be to enthrall us, before so long a Lent of Servitude, they
20 may permitt us a little Shroving-time first, wherin to speak freely, and take our leaves of Libertie. And because in the former edition through haste, many faults escap'd, and many books were suddenly dispersd, ere the note to mend them

could be sent, I took the opportunitie from this occasion to revise and somwhat to enlarge the whole discourse, especially that part which argues for a perpetual Senat. The treatise thus revis'd and enlarg'd, is as follows.

5   The Parliament of *England,* assisted by a great number of the people who appeerd and stuck to them faithfullest in defence of religion and thir civil liberties, judging kingship by long experience a government unnecessarie, burdensom and dangerous, justly and magnanimously abolishd it; turn-
10 ing regal bondage into a free Commonwealth, to the admiration and terrour of our emulous neighbours. They took themselves not bound by the light of nature or religion, to any former covnant, from which the King himself by many forfeitures of a latter date or discoverie, and our own longer
15 consideration theron had more & more unbound us, both to himself and his posteritie; as hath bin ever the justice and the prudence of all wise nations that have ejected tyrannie. They covnanted *to preserve the Kings person and autoritie in the preservation of the true religion and our liberties;* not in
20 his endeavoring to bring in upon our consciences a Popish religion, upon our liberties thraldom, upon our lives destruction, by his occasioning, if not complotting, as was after discoverd, the *Irish* massacre, his fomenting and arming the rebellion, his covert leaguing with the rebels against us, his
25 refusing more then seaven times, propositions most just and necessarie to the true religion and our liberties, tenderd him by the Parlament both of *England* and *Scotland.* They made

not thir covnant concerning him with no difference between
a king and a god, or promisd him as *Job* did to the Almightie,
to trust in him, though he slay us: they understood that the
solemn ingagement, wherin we all forswore kingship, was
5 no more a breach of the covnant, then the covnant was of the
protestation before, but a faithful and prudent going on both
in the words, well weighd, and in the true sense of the covnant, *without respect of persons,* when we could not serve
two contrary maisters, God and the king, or the king and
10 that more supreme law, sworn in the first place to maintain,
our safetie and our libertie. They knew the people of *England*
to be a free people, themselves the representers of that freedom; & although many were excluded, & as many fled (so
they pretended) from tumults to *Oxford,* yet they were left
15 a sufficient number to act in Parlament; therefor not bound
by any statute of preceding Parlaments, but by the law of
nature only, which is the only law of laws truly and properly
to all mankinde fundamental; the beginning and the end of
all Government; to which no Parlament or people that will
20 throughly reforme, but may and must have recourse; as
they had and must yet have in church reformation (If they
throughly intend it) to evangelic rules; not to ecclesiastical
canons, though never so ancient, so ratifi'd and establishd in
the land by Statutes, which for the most part are meer posi-
25 tive laws, neither natural nor moral, & so by any Parlament
for just and serious considerations, without scruple to be at
any time repeal'd. If others of thir number, in these things
were under force, they were not, but under free conscience;

if others were excluded by a power which they could not resist, they were not therefore to leave the helm of government
in no hands, to discontinue thir care of the public peace and
safetie, to desert the people in anarchie and confusion; no
5 more then when so many of thir members left them, as made
up in outward formalitie a more legal Parlament of three
estates against them. The best affected also and best principl'd of the people, stood not numbring or computing on
which side were most voices in Parlament, but on which side
10 appeerd to them most reason, most safetie, when the house
divided upon main matters: what was well motiond and advis'd, they examind not whether fear or perswasion carried
it in the vote; neither did they measure votes and counsels by
the intentions of them that voted; knowing that intentions
15 either are but guessd at, or not soon anough known; and although good, can neither make the deed such, nor prevent
the consequence from being bad: suppose bad intentions in
things otherwise welldon; what was welldon, was by them
who so thought, not the less obey'd or followd in the state;
20 since in the church, who had not rather follow *Iscariot* or
Simon the magician, though to covetous ends, preaching,
then *Saul,* though in the uprightness of his heart persecuting
the gospell? Safer they therefor judgd what they thought the
better counsels, though carried on by some perhaps to bad
25 ends, then the wors, by others, though endevord with best
intentions: and yet they were not to learn that a greater number might be corrupt within the walls of a Parlament as well
as of a citie; wherof in matters of neerest concernment all

men will be judges; nor easily permitt, that the odds of voices
in thir greatest councel, shall more endanger them by corrupt
or credulous votes, then the odds of enemies by open assaults;
judging that most voices ought not alwaies to prevail where
5 main matters are in question; if others hence will pretend to
disturb all counsels, what is that to them who pretend not,
but are in real danger; not they only so judging, but a great
though not the greatest, number of thir chosen Patriots, who
might be more in waight, then the others in number; there
10 being in number little vertue, but by weight and measure
wisdom working all things: and the dangers on either side
they seriously thus waighd: from the treatie, short fruits of
long labours and seaven years warr; securitie for twenty
years, if we can hold it; reformation in the church for three
15 years: then put to shift again with our vanquishd maister.
His justice, his honour, his conscience declar'd quite contrarie to ours; which would have furnishd him with many
such evasions, as in a book entitl'd *an inquisition for blood,*
soon after were not conceald: bishops not totally remov'd,
20 but left as it were in ambush, a reserve, with ordination in
thir sole powr; thir lands alreadie sold, not to be alienated,
but rented, and the sale of them call'd *sacrilege;* delinquents
few of many brought to condigne punishment; accessories
punishd; the chief author, above pardon, though after ut-
25 most resistance, vanquish'd; not to give, but to receive laws;
yet besought, treated with, and to be thankd for his gratious
concessions, to be honourd, worshipd, glorifi'd. If this we
swore to do, with what righteousness in the sight of God,

with what assurance that we bring not by such an oath the whole sea of blood-guiltiness upon our own heads? If on the other side we preferr a free government, though for the present not obtain, yet all those suggested fears and difficul-
5 ties, as the event will prove, easily overcome, we remain finally secure from the exasperated regal power, and out of snares; shall retain the best part of our libertie, which is our religion, and the civil part will be from these who deferr us, much more easily recoverd, being neither so suttle nor so awe-
10 full as a King reinthron'd. Nor were thir actions less both at home and abroad then might become the hopes of a glorious rising Commonwealth: nor were the expressions both of armie and people, whether in thir publick declarations or several writings other then such as testifi'd a spirit in this
15 nation no less noble and well fitted to the liberty of a Com-monwealth, then in the ancient *Greeks* or *Romans*. Nor was the heroic cause unsuccesfully defended to all Christendom against the tongue of a famous and thought invincible adver-sarie; nor the constancie and fortitude that so nobly vindi-
20 cated our liberty, our victory at once against two the most prevailing usurpers over mankinde, superstition and tyrannie unpraisd or uncelebrated in a written monument, likely to outlive detraction, as it hath hitherto convinc'd or silenc'd not a few of our detractors, especially in parts abroad. After our
25 liberty and religion thus prosperously fought for, gaind and many years possessd, except in those unhappie interruptions, which God hath remov'd, now that nothing remains, but in all reason the certain hopes of a speedie and immediat settle-

ment for ever in a firm and free Commonwealth, for this ex-
tolld and magnifi'd nation, regardless both of honour wonn
or deliverances voutsaf't from heaven, to fall back or rather
to creep back so poorly as it seems the multitude would to thir
5 once abjur'd and detested thraldom of Kingship, to be our
selves the slanderers of our own just and religious deeds,
though don by som to covetous and ambitious ends, yet not
therefor to be staind with their infamie, or they to asperse
the integritie of others, and yet these now by revolting from
10 the conscience of deeds welldon both in church and state, to
throw away and forsake, or rather to betray a just and noble
cause for the mixture of bad men who have ill manag'd and
abus'd it (which had our fathers don heretofore, and on the
same pretence deserted true religion, what had long ere this
15 become of our gospel and all protestant reformation so much
intermixt with the avarice and ambition of some reformers?)
and by thus relapsing, to verifie all the bitter predictions of
our triumphing enemies, who will now think they wisely
discernd and justly censur'd both us and all our actions as
20 rash, rebellious, hypocritical and impious, not only argues a
strange degenerate contagion suddenly spread among us
fitted and prepar'd for new slaverie, but will render us a
scorn and derision to all our neighbours. And what will they
at best say of us and of the whole *English* name, but scoff-
25 ingly as of that foolish builder, mentiond by our Saviour,
who began to build a tower, and was not able to finish it.
Where is this goodly tower of a Commonwealth, which the
English boasted they would build to overshaddow kings, and

be another *Rome* in the west? The foundation indeed they laid gallantly; but fell into a wors confusion, not of tongues, but of factions, then those at the tower of *Babel;* and have left no memorial of thir work behinde them remaining, but
5 in the common laughter of *Europ.* Which must needs redound the more to our shame, if we but look on our neighbours the United Provinces, to us inferior in all outward advantages; who notwithstanding, in the midst of greater difficulties, courageously, wisely, constantly went through
10 with the same work, and are setl'd in all the happie enjoiments of a potent and flourishing Republic to this day.

Besides this, if we returne to Kingship, and soon repent, as undoubtedly we shall, when we begin to finde the old encroachments coming on by little and little upon our con-
15 sciences, which must necessarily proceed from king and bishop united inseparably in one interest, we may be forc'd perhaps to fight over again all that we have fought, and spend over again all that we have spent, but are never like to attain thus far as we are now advanc'd to the recoverie of our
20 freedom, never to have it in possession as we now have it, never to be voutsaf't heerafter the like mercies and signal assistances from heaven in our cause, if by our ingratefull backsliding we make these fruitless; flying now to regal concessions from his divine condescensions and gratious answers
25 to our once importuning praiers against the tyrannie which we then groand under: making vain and viler then dirt the blood of so many thousand faithfull and valiant *English* men, who left us in this libertie, bought with thir lives;

losing by a strange aftergame of folly, all the battels we have wonn, together with all *Scotland* as to our conquest, hereby lost, which never any of our kings could conquer, all the treasure we have spent, not that corruptible treasure only, but
5 that far more precious of all our late miraculous deliverances; treading back again with lost labour all our happie steps in the progress of reformation; and most pittifully depriving our selves the instant fruition of that free government which we have so dearly purchasd, a free Commonwealth, not only
10 held by wisest men in all ages the noblest, the manliest, the equallest, the justest government, the most agreeable to all due libertie and proportiond equalitie, both human, civil, and Christian, most cherishing to vertue and true religion, but also (I may say it with greatest probabilitie) planely com-
15 mended, or rather enjoind by our Saviour himself, to all Christians, not without remarkable disallowance, and the brand of *gentilism* upon kingship. God in much displeasure gave a king to the *Israelites,* and imputed it a sin to them that they sought one: but *Christ* apparently forbids his disciples
20 to admitt of any such heathenish government: *the kings of the gentiles,* saith he, *exercise lordship over them; and they that exercise authoritie upon them, are call'd benefactors: but ye shall not be so; but he that is greatest among you, let him be as the younger; and he that is chief, as he that serveth.*
25 The occasion of these his words was the ambitious desire of *Zebede's* two sons, to be exalted above thir brethren in his kingdom, which they thought was to be ere long upon earth. That he speaks of civil government, is manifest by the for-

mer part of the comparison, which inferrs the other part to be alwaies in the same kinde. And what government coms neerer to this precept of Christ, then a free Commonwealth; wherin they who are greatest, are perpetual servants and
5 drudges to the public at thir own cost and charges, neglect thir own affairs; yet are not elevated above thir brethren; live soberly in thir families, walk the streets as other men, may be spoken to freely, familiarly, friendly, without adoration. Wheras a king must be ador'd like a Demigod, with
10 a dissolute and haughtie court about him, of vast expence and luxurie, masks and revels, to the debaushing of our prime gentry both male and female; not in thir passetimes only, but in earnest, by the loos imploiments of court service, which will be then thought honorable. There will be a queen
15 also of no less charge; in most likelihood outlandish and a Papist; besides a queen mother such alreadie; together with both thir courts and numerous train: then a royal issue, and ere long severally thir sumptuous courts; to the multiplying of a servile crew, not of servants only, but of nobility and
20 gentry, bred up then to the hopes not of public, but of court offices; to be stewards, chamberlains, ushers, grooms, even of the close-stool; and the lower thir mindes debas'd with court opinions, contrarie to all vertue and reformation, the haughtier will be thir pride and profuseness: we may well
25 remember this not long since at home; or need but look at present into the *French* court, where enticements and preferments daily draw away and pervert the Protestant Nobilitie. As to the burden of expence, to our cost we shall soon

know it; for any good to us, deserving to be termd no better
then the vast and lavish price of our subjection and their de-
bausherie; which we are now so greedily cheapning, and
would so fain be paying most inconsideratly to a single per-
5 son; who for any thing wherin the public really needs him,
will have little els to do, but to bestow the eating and drinking of excessive dainties, to set a pompous face upon the su-
perficial actings of State, to pageant himself up and down in
progress among the perpetual bowings and cringings of an
10 abject people, on either side deifying and adoring him for
nothing don that can deserve it. For what can hee more then
another man? who even in the expression of a late court-
poet, sits only like a great cypher set to no purpose before a
long row of other significant figures. Nay it is well and
15 happy for the people if thir King be but a cypher, being
oft times a mischief, a pest, a scourge of the nation, and
which is wors, not to be remov'd, not to be contrould, much
less accus'd or brought to punishment, without the danger of
a common ruin, without the shaking and almost subversion
20 of the whole land. Wheras in a free Commonwealth, any
governor or chief counselor offending, may be remov'd and
punishd without the least commotion. Certainly then that
people must needs be madd or strangely infatuated, that build
the chief hope of thir common happiness or safetie on a
25 single person: who if he happen to be good, can do no more
then another man, if to be bad, hath in his hands to do more
evil without check, then millions of other men. The happiness of a nation must needs be firmest and certainest in a full

and free Councel of thir own electing, where no single person, but reason only swaies. And what madness is it, for them who might manage nobly thir own affaires themselves, sluggishly and weakly to devolve all on a single person; and
5 more like boyes under age then men, to committ all to his patronage and disposal, who neither can performe what he undertakes, and yet for undertaking it, though royally paid, will not be thir servant, but thir lord? how unmanly must it needs be, to count such a one the breath of our nostrils, to
10 hang all our felicity on him, all our safetie, our well-being, for which if we were aught els but sluggards or babies, we need depend on none but God and our own counsels, our own active vertue and industrie; *Go to the Ant, thou sluggard,* saith *Solomon; consider her waies, and be wise; which*
15 *having no prince, ruler, or lord, provides her meat in the summer, and gathers her food in the harvest.* Which evidently shews us, that they who think the nation undon without a king, though they look grave or haughtie, have not so much true spirit and understanding in them as a pismire:
20 neither are these diligent creatures hence concluded to live in lawless anarchie, or that commended, but are set the examples to imprudent and ungovernd men, of a frugal and self-governing democratie or Commonwealth; safer and more thriving in the joint providence and counsel of many in-
25 dustrious equals, then under the single domination of one imperious Lord. It may be well wonderd that any Nation styling themselves free, can suffer any man to pretend hereditarie right over them as thir lord; when as by acknowledging

that right, they conclude themselves his servants and his vassals, and so renounce thir own freedom. Which how a people and thir leaders especially can do, who have fought so gloriously for liberty, how they can change thir noble words and
5 actions, heretofore so becoming the majesty of a free people, into the base necessitie of court flatteries and prostrations, is not only strange and admirable, but lamentable to think on. That a nation should be so valorous and courageous to winn thir liberty in the field, and when they have wonn it, should
10 be so heartless and unwise in thir counsels, as not to know how to use it, value it, what to do with it or with themselves; but after ten or twelve years prosperous warr and contestation with tyrannie, basely and besottedly to run their necks again into the yoke which they have broken, and prostrate
15 all the fruits of thir victorie for naught at the feet of the vanquishd, besides our loss of glorie, and such an example as kings or tyrants never yet had the like to boast of, will be an ignominie if it befall us, that never yet befell any nation possessd of thir libertie; worthie indeed themselves, whatsoever
20 they be, to be for ever slaves: but that part of the nation which consents not with them, as I perswade me of a great number, far worthier then by their means to be brought into the same bondage. Considering these things so plane, so rational, I cannot but yet furder admire on the other side, how any man
25 who hath the true principles of justice and religion in him, can presume or take upon him to be a king and lord over his brethren, whom he cannot but know whether as men or Christians, to be for the most part every way equal or su-

perior to himself: how he can display with such vanitie and
ostentation his regal splendor so supereminently above other
mortal men; or being a Christian, can assume such extraordinarie honour and worship to himself, while the kingdom
5 of Christ our common King and Lord, is hid to this world,
and such *gentilish* imitation forbid in express words by himself to all his disciples. All Protestants hold that Christ in his
church hath left no vicegerent of his power, but himself without deputie, is the only head therof, governing it from
10 heaven: how then can any Christian-man derive his kingship
from Christ, but with wors usurpation then the Pope his
headship over the church, since Christ not only hath not left
the least shaddow of a command for any such vicegerence
from him in the State, as the Pope pretends for his in the
15 Church, but hath expressly declar'd, that such regal dominion is from the gentiles, not from him, and hath strictly
charg'd us, not to imitate them therin.

I doubt not but all ingenuous and knowing men will easily
agree with me, that a free Commonwealth without single
20 person or house of lords, is by far the best government, if it
can be had; but we have all this while say they bin expecting
it, and cannot yet attain it. Tis true indeed, when monarchie
was dissolvd, the form of a Commonwealth should have
forthwith bin fram'd; and the practice therof immediatly
25 begun; that the people might have soon bin satisfi'd and de-
lighted with the decent order, ease and benefit therof: we had
bin then by this time firmly rooted past fear of commotions
or mutations, & now flourishing: this care of timely setling a

new government instead of ye old, too much neglected, hath
bin our mischief. Yet the cause therof may be ascrib'd with
most reason to the frequent disturbances, interruptions and
dissolutions which the Parlament hath had partly from the
5 impatient or disaffected people, partly from som ambitious
leaders in the Armie; much contrarie, I beleeve, to the mind
and approbation of the Armie it self and thir other Commanders, once undeceivd, or in thir own power. Now is the opportunitie, now the very season wherein we may obtain a free
10 Commonwealth and establish it for ever in the land, without
difficulty or much delay. Writs are sent out for elections, and
which is worth observing in the name, not of any king, but
of the keepers of our libertie, to summon a free Parlament:
which then only will indeed be free, and deserve the true
15 honor of that supreme title, if they preserve us a free people.
Which never Parlament was more free to do; being now
call'd, not as heretofore, by the summons of a king, but by
the voice of libertie: and if the people, laying aside prejudice
and impatience, will seriously and calmly now consider thir
20 own good both religious and civil, thir own libertie and the
only means thereof, as shall be heer laid before them, and
will elect thir Knights and Burgesses able men, and according to the just and necessarie qualifications (which for aught
I hear, remain yet in force unrepeald, as they were formerly
25 decreed in Parlament) men not addicted to a single person
or house of lords, the work is don; at least the foundation
firmly laid of a free Commonwealth, and good part also
erected of the main structure. For the ground and basis of

every just and free government (since men have smarted so
oft for commiting all to one person) is a general councel of
ablest men, chosen by the people to consult of public affairs
from time to time for the common good. In this Grand Coun-
5 cel must the sovrantie, not transferrd, but delegated only, and
at it were deposited, reside; with this caution they must have
the forces by sea and land committed to them for preservation of the common peace and libertie; must raise and manage the public revenue, at least with som inspectors deputed
10 for satisfaction of the people, how it is imploid; must make
or propose, as more expressly shall be said anon, civil laws;
treat of commerce, peace, or warr with forein nations, and
for the carrying on som particular affairs with more secrecie
and expedition, must elect, as they have alreadie out of thir
15 own number and others, a Councel of State.

And although it may seem strange at first hearing, by reason that mens mindes are prepossessd with the notion of successive Parlaments, I affirme that the Grand or General
Councel being well chosen, should be perpetual: for so thir
20 business is or may be, and oft times urgent; the opportunitie
of affairs gaind or lost in a moment. The day of counsel cannot be set as the day of a festival; but must be readie alwaies
to prevent or answer all occasions. By this continuance they
will become everie way skilfullest, best provided of intelli-
25 gence from abroad, best acquainted with the people at home,
and the people with them. The ship of the Commonwealth
is alwaies under sail; they sit at the stern; and if they stear
well, what need is ther to change them; it being rather dan-

gerous? Add to this, that the Grand Councel is both foundation and main pillar of the whole State; and to move pillars
and foundations, not faultie, cannot be safe for the building.
I see not therefor, how we can be advantag'd by successive
5 and transitorie Parlaments; but that they are much likelier
continually to unsettle rather then to settle a free government; to breed commotions, changes, novelties and uncertainties; to bring neglect upon present affairs and opportu-
nities, while all mindes are suspense with expectation of a
10 new assemblie, and the assemblie for a good space taken up
with the new setling of it self. After which, if they finde no
great work to do, they will make it, by altering or repealing
former acts, or making and multiplying new; that they may
seem to see what thir predecessors saw not, and not to have
15 assembld for nothing: till all law be lost in the multitude
of clashing statutes. But if the ambition of such as think
themselves injur'd that they also partake not of the government, and are impatient till they be chosen, cannot brook the
perpetuitie of others chosen before them, or if it be feard that
20 long continuance of power may corrupt sincerest men, the
known expedient is, and by som lately propounded, that an-
nually (or if the space be longer, so much perhaps the better)
the third part of Senators may go out according to the prece-
dence of thir election, and the like number be chosen in thir
25 places, to prevent the setling of too absolute a power, if it
should be perpetual: and this they call *partial rotation*. But
I could wish that this wheel or partial wheel in State, if it be
possible, might be avoided; as having too much affinitie with

the wheel of fortune. For it appeers not how this can be don, without danger and mischance of putting out a great number of the best and ablest: in whose stead new elections may bring in as many raw, unexperienc'd and otherwise affected,

5 to the weakning and much altering for the wors of public transactions. Neither do I think a perpetual Senat, especially chosen and entrusted by the people, much in this land to be feard, where the well-affected either in a standing armie, or in a setled militia have thir arms in thir own hands. Safest

10 therefor to me it seems and of least hazard or interruption to affairs, that none of the Grand Councel be mov'd, unless by death or just conviction of som crime: for what can be expected firm or stedfast from a floating foundation? however, I forejudge not any probable expedient, any tempera-

15 ment that can be found in things of this nature so disputable on either side. Yet least this which I affirme, be thought my single opinion, I shall add sufficient testimonie. Kingship it self is therefor counted the more safe and durable, because the king and, for the most part, his councel, is not chang'd

20 during life: but a Commonwealth is held immortal; and therin firmest, safest and most above fortune: for the death of a king, causeth ofttimes many dangerous alterations; but the death now and then of a Senator is not felt; the main bodie of them still continuing permanent in greatest and noblest

25 Commonwealths, and as it were eternal. Therefor among the *Jews,* the supreme councel of seaventie, call'd the *Sanhedrim,* founded by *Moses,* in *Athens,* that of *Areopagus,* in *Sparta,* that of the Ancients, in *Rome,* the Senat, consisted of mem-

bers chosen for term of life; and by that means remaind as it
were still the same to generations. In *Venice* they change indeed ofter then every year som particular councels of State,
as that of six, or such other; but the true Senat, which up-
5 holds and sustains the government, is the whole aristocracie
immovable. So in the United Provinces, the States General,
which are indeed but a councel of state deputed by the whole
union, are not usually the same persons for above three or
six years; but the States of every citie, in whom the sovran-
10 tie hath bin plac'd time out of minde, are a standing Senat,
without succession, and accounted chiefly in that regard the
main prop of thir liberty. And why they should be so in
every well orderd Commonwealth, they who write of policie,
give these reasons; "That to make the Senat successive, not
15 only impairs the dignitie and lustre of the Senat, but weak-
ens the whole Commonwealth, and brings it into manifest
danger; while by this means the secrets of State are frequently divulgd, and matters of greatest consequence committed to inexpert and novice counselors, utterly to seek in
20 the full and intimate knowledge of affairs past." I know not
therefor what should be peculiar in *England* to make successive Parlaments thought safest, or convenient here more
then in other nations, unless it be the fickl'ness which is attributed to us as we are Ilanders: but good education and
25 acquisit wisdom ought to correct the fluxible fault, if any
such be, of our watry situation. It will be objected, that in
those places where they had perpetual Senats, they had also
popular remedies against thir growing too imperious: as in

Athens, besides *Areopagus,* another Senat of four or five hunderd; in *Sparta,* the *Ephori;* in *Rome,* the Tribunes of the people. But the event tels us, that these remedies either little availd the people, or brought them to such a licentious 5 and unbridl'd democratie, as in fine ruind themselves with thir own excessive power. So that the main reason urg'd why popular assemblies are to be trusted with the peoples libertie, rather then a Senat of principal men, because great men will be still endeavoring to inlarge thir power, but the common 10 sort will be contented to maintain thir own libertie, is by experience found false; none being more immoderat and ambitious to amplifie thir power, then such popularities; which was seen in the people of *Rome;* who at first contented to have thir Tribunes, at length contended with the Senat that 15 one Consul, then both; soon after, that the Censors and Prætors also should be created Plebeian, and the whole empire put into their hands; adoring lastly those, who most were advers to the Senat, till *Marius* by fulfilling thir inordinat desires, quite lost them all the power for which they had so 20 long bin striving, and left them under the tyrannie of *Sylla:* the ballance therefor must be exactly so set, as to preserve and keep up due autoritie on either side, as well in the Senat as in the people. And this annual rotation of a Senat to consist of three hunderd, as is lately propounded, requires also another 25 other popular assembly upward of a thousand, with an answerable rotation. Which besides that it will be liable to all those inconveniencies found in the foresaid remedies, cannot but be troublesom and chargeable, both in thir motion and thir session, to the whole land; unweildie with thir own bulk, unable in so great a number to mature thir consultations as they ought, if any be allotted them, and that they meet not from so many parts remote to sit a whole year lieger in one

5   place, only now and then to hold up a forrest of fingers, or to convey each man his bean or ballot into the box, without reason shewn or common deliberation; incontinent of secrets, if any be imparted to them, emulous and always jarring with the other Senat. The much better way doubtless will be in

10 this wavering condition of our affairs, to deferr the changing or circumscribing of our Senat, more then may be done with ease, till the Commonwealth be throughly setl'd in peace and safetie, and they themselves give us the occasion. Militaric men hold it dangerous to change the form of battel in

15 view of an enemie: neither did the people of *Rome* bandie with thir Senat while any of the *Tarquins* livd, the enemies of thir libertie, nor sought by creating Tribunes to defend themselves against the fear of thir Patricians, till sixteen years after the expulsion of thir kings, and in full securitie of thir

20 state, they had or thought they had just cause given them by the Senat. Another way will be, to wel-qualifie and refine elections: not committing all to the noise and shouting of a rude multitude, but permitting only those of them who are rightly qualifi'd, to nominat as many as they will; and out of

25 that number others of a better breeding, to chuse a less number more judiciously, till after a third or fourth sifting and refining of exactest choice, they only be left chosen who are the due number, and seem by most voices the worthiest. To

make the people fittest to chuse, and the chosen fittest to govern, will be to mend our corrupt and faulty education, to teach the people faith not without vertue, temperance, modestie, sobrietie, parsimonie, justice; not to admire wealth or
5 honour; to hate turbulence and ambition; to place every one his privat welfare and happiness in the public peace, libertie and safetie. They shall not then need to be much mistrustfull of thir chosen Patriots in the Grand Councel; who will be then rightly call'd the true keepers of our libertie, though
10 the most of thir business will be in forein affairs. But to prevent all mistrust, the people then will have thir several ordinarie assemblies (which will henceforth quite annihilate the odious power and name of Committies) in the chief towns of every countie, without the trouble, charge, or time lost of
15 summoning and assembling from far in so great a number, and so long residing from thir own houses, or removing of thir families, to do as much at home in thir several shires, entire or subdivided, toward the securing of thir libertie, as a numerous assembly of them all formd and conven'd on pur-
20 pose with the wariest rotation. Wherof I shall speak more ere the end of this discourse: for it may be referrd to time, so we be still going on by degrees to perfection. The people well weighing and performing these things, I suppose would have no cause to fear, though the *Parlament,* abolishing that name,
25 as originally signifying but the *parlie* of our Lords and Commons with thir *Norman* king when he pleasd to call them, should, with certain limitations of thir power, sit perpetual, if thir ends be faithfull and for a free Commonwealth, under

the name of a Grand or General Councel. Till this be don, I
am in doubt whether our State will be ever certainly and
throughly setl'd; never likely till then to see an end of our
troubles and continual changes or at least never the true set-
5 tlement and assurance of our libertie. The Grand Councel
being thus firmly constituted to perpetuitie, and still, upon
the death or default of any member, suppli'd and kept in full
number, ther can be no cause alleag'd why peace, justice,
plentifull trade and all prosperitie should not thereupon en-
10 sue throughout the whole land; with as much assurance as
can be of human things, that they shall so continue (if God
favour us, and our wilfull sins provoke him not) even to the
coming of our true and rightfull and only to be expected
King, only worthie as he is our only Saviour, the Messiah, the
15 Christ, the only heir of his eternal father, the only by him
anointed and ordaind since the work of our redemption fin-
ishd, Universal Lord of all mankinde. The way propounded
is plane, easie and open before us; without intricacies, without the introducement of new or obsolete forms, or terms, or
20 exotic models; idea's that would effect nothing, but with a
number of new injunctions to manacle the native liberty of
mankinde; turning all vertue into prescription, servitude,
and necessitie, to the great impairing and frustrating of Christian libertie: I say again, this way lies free and smooth before
25 us; is not tangl'd with inconveniencies; invents no new incumbrances; requires no perilous, no injurious alteration or
circumscription of mens lands and proprieties; secure, that in
this Commonwealth, temporal and spiritual lords remov'd,

no man or number of men can attain to such wealth or vast
possession, as will need the hedge of an Agrarian law (never
succesful, but the cause rather of sedition, save only where
it began seasonably with first possession) to confine them
5 from endangering our public libertie; to conclude, it can have
no considerable objection made against it, that it is not practicable: least it be said hereafter, that we gave up our libertie
for want of a readie way or distinct form propos'd of a free
Commonwealth. And this facilitie we shall have above our
10 next neighbouring Commonwealth (if we can keep us from
the fond conceit of somthing like a duke of *Venice,* put lately
into many mens heads, by som one or other sutly driving on
under that notion his own ambitious ends to lurch a crown)
that our liberty shall not be hamperd or hoverd over by any
15 ingagement to such a potent familie as the house of *Nassaw*
of whom to stand in perpetual doubt and suspicion, but we
shall live the cleerest and absolutest free nation in the world.
On the contrarie, if ther be a king, which the inconsiderate
multitude are now so madd upon, mark how far short we are
20 like to com of all those happinesses, which in a free state we
shall immediatly be possessd of. First, the Grand Councel,
which, as I shewd before, should sit perpetually (unless thir
leisure give them now and then som intermissions or vacations, easilie manageable by the Councel of State left sitting)
25 shall be call'd, by the kings good will and utmost endeavor
as seldom as may be. For it is only the kings right, he will
say, to call a parlament; and this he will do most commonly
about his own affairs rather then the kingdom's, as will ap-

peer planely so soon as they are call'd. For what will thir
business then be and the chief expence of thir time, but an
endless tugging between petition of right and royal prerogative, especially about the negative voice, militia, or subsidies,
5 demanded and oft times extorted without reasonable cause
appeering to the Commons, who are the only true represen-
tatives of the people, and thir libertie, but will be then min-
gl'd with a court-faction; besides which within thir own
walls, the sincere part of them who stand faithfull to the
10 people, will again have to deal with two troublesom counter-
working adversaries from without, meer creatures of the
king, spiritual, and the greater part, as is likeliest, of temporal lords, nothing concernd with the peoples libertie. If
these prevail not in what they please, though never so much
15 against the peoples interest, the Parlament shall be soon dissolvd, or sit and do nothing; not sufferd to remedie the least
greevance, or enact aught advantageous to the people. Next,
the Councel of State shall not be chosen by the Parlament,
but by the king, still his own creatures, courtiers and favor-
20 ites; who will be sure in all thir counsels to set thir maister's
grandure and absolute power, in what they are able, far
above the peoples libertie. I denie not but that ther may be
such a king, who may regard the common good before his
own, may have no vitious favorite, may hearken only to the
25 wisest and incorruptest of his Parlament: but this rarely hap-
pens in a monarchie not elective; and it behoves not a wise
nation to committ the summ of thir welbeing, the whole state
of thir safetie to fortune. What need they; and how absurd

would it be, when as they themselves to whom his chief vertue will be but to hearken, may with much better management and dispatch, with much more commendation of thir
own worth and magnanimitie govern without a maister. Can
5 the folly be paralleld, to adore and be the slaves of a single
person for doing that which it is ten thousand to one whether
he can or will do, and we without him might do more easily,
more effectually, more laudably our selves? Shall we never
grow old anough to be wise to make seasonable use of gravest
10 autorities, experiences, examples? Is it such an unspeakable
joy to serve, such felicitie to wear a yoke? to clink our
shackles, lockt on by pretended law of subjection more intol-
erable and hopeless to be ever shaken off, then those which
are knockt on by illegal injurie and violence? *Aristotle,* our
15 chief instructer in the Universities, least this doctrine be
thought *Sectarian,* as the royalist would have it thought, tels
us in the third of his Politics, that certain men at first, for the
matchless excellence of thir vertue above others, or som great
public benifit, were created kings by the people; in small
20 cities and territories, and in the scarcitie of others to be found
like them: but when they abus'd thir power and governments grew larger, and the number of prudent men increasd,
that then the people soon deposing thir tyrants, betook them,
in all civilest places, to the form of a free Commonwealth.
25 And why should we thus disparage and prejudicate our own
nation, as to fear a scarcitie of able and worthie men united
in counsel to govern us, if we will but use diligence and im-
partiality to finde them out and chuse them, rather yoking

our selves to a single person, the natural adversarie and op-
pressor of libertie, though good, yet far easier corruptible by
the excess of his singular power and exaltation, or at best,
not comparably sufficient to bear the weight of government,
5 nor equally dispos'd to make us happie in the enjoyment
of our libertie under him.

But admitt, that monarchie of it self may be convenient to
som nations; yet to us who have thrown it out, receivd back
again, it cannot but prove pernicious. For kings to com,
10 never forgetting thir former ejection, will be sure to fortifie
and arm themselves sufficiently for the future against all such
attempts hereafter from the people: who shall be then so
narrowly watchd and kept so low, that though they would
never so fain and at the same rate of thir blood and treasure,
15 they never shall be able to regain what they now have purchasd and may enjoy, or to free themselves from any yoke
impos'd upon them: nor will they dare to go about it; utterly
disheartn'd for the future, if these thir highest attempts prove
unsuccesfull; which will be the triumph of all tyrants heer-
20 after over any people that shall resist oppression; and thir
song will then be, to others, how sped the rebellious *English?*
to our posteritie, how sped the rebells your fathers? This is
not my conjecture, but drawn from God's known denouncement against the gentilizing *Israelites;* who though they were
25 governd in a Commonwealth of God's own ordaining, he
only thir king, they his peculiar people, yet affecting rather
to resemble heathen, but pretending the misgovernment of
Samuel's sons, no more a reason to dislike thir Common-

wealth, then the violence of *Eli's* sons was imputable to that priesthood or religion, clamourd for a king. They had thir longing; but with this testimonie of God's wrath; *ye shall cry out in that day because of your king whom ye shall have* 5 *chosen, and the Lord will not hear you in that day.* Us if he shall hear now, how much less will he hear when we cry heerafter, who once deliverd by him from a king, and not without wondrous acts of his providence, insensible and unworthie of those high mercies, are returning precipitantly, 10 if he withhold us not, back to the captivitie from whence he freed us. Yet neither shall we obtain or buy at an easie rate this new guilded yoke which thus transports us: a new royal-revenue must be found, a new episcopal; for those are indi-vidual: both which being wholly dissipated or bought by 15 privat persons or assign'd for service don, and especially to the Armie, cannot be recoverd without a general detriment and confusion to mens estates, or a heavie imposition on all mens purses; benifit to none, but to the worst and ignoblest sort of men, whose hope is to be either the ministers of court 20 riot and excess, or the gainers by it: But not to speak more of losses and extraordinarie levies on our estates, what will then be the revenges and offences rememberd and returnd, not only by the chief person, but by all his adherents; accounts and reparations that will be requir'd, suites, inditements, in-25 quiries, discoveries, complaints, informations, who knows against whom or how many, though perhaps neuters, if not to utmost infliction, yet to imprisonment, fines, banishment, or molestation; if not these, yet disfavor, discountnance, dis-

regard and contempt on all but the known royalist or whom
he favors, will be plenteous: nor let the new royaliz'd presbyterians perswade themselves that thir old doings, though now
recanted, will be forgotten; what ever conditions be con-
5 triv'd or trusted on. Will they not beleeve this; nor remember
the pacification, how it was kept to the *Scots;* how other
solemn promises many a time to us? Let them but now read
the diabolical forerunning libells, the faces, the gestures that
now appeer foremost and briskest in all public places; as the
10 harbingers of those that are in expectation to raign over us;
let them but hear the insolencies, the menaces, the insultings
of our newly animated common enemies crept lately out of
thir holes, thir hell, I might say, by the language of thir in-
fernal pamphlets, the spue of every drunkard, every ribald;
15 nameless, yet not for want of licence, but for very shame of
thir own vile persons, not daring to name themselves, while
they traduce others by name; and give us to foresee that they
intend to second thir wicked words, if ever they have power,
with more wicked deeds. Let our zealous backsliders fore-
20 think now with themselves, how thir necks yok'd with these
tigers of Bacchus, these new fanatics of not the preaching but
the sweating-tub, inspir'd with nothing holier then the Ve-
nereal pox, can draw one way under monarchie to the establishing of church discipline with these new-disgorg'd athe-
25 ismes: yet shall they not have the honor to yoke with these, but
shall be yok'd under them; these shall plow on their backs.
And do they among them who are so forward to bring in the
single person, think to be by him trusted or long regarded?

So trusted they shall be and so regarded, as by kings are wont
reconcil'd enemies; neglected and soon after discarded, if not
prosecuted for old traytors; the first inciters, beginners, and
more then to the third part actors of all that followd; it will
5 be found also, that there must be then as necessarily as now
(for the contrarie part will be still feard) a standing armie;
which for certain shall not be this, but of the fiercest Cava-
liers, of no less expence, and perhaps again under *Rupert:*
but let this armie be sure they shall be soon disbanded, and
10 likeliest without arrear or pay; and being disbanded, not be
sure but they may as soon be questiond for being in arms
against thir king: the same let them fear, who have contributed monie; which will amount to no small number that
must then take thir turn to be made delinquents and com-
15 pounders. They who past reason and recoverie are devoted to
kingship, perhaps will answer, that a greater part by far of
the Nation will have it so; the rest therefor must yield. Not
so much to convince these, which I little hope, as to confirm
them who yield not, I reply; that this greatest part have both
20 in reason and the trial of just battel, lost the right of their
election what the government shall be: of them who have not
lost that right, whether they for kingship be the greater number, who can certainly determin? Suppose they be; yet of
freedom they partake all alike, one main end of government:
25 which if the greater part value not, but will degeneratly forgoe, is it just or reasonable, that most voices against the main
end of government should enslave the less number that would
be free? More just it is doubtless, if it com to force, that a less

number compell a greater to retain, which can be no wrong to them, thir libertie, then that a greater number for the pleasure of thir baseness, compell a less most injuriously to be thir fellow slaves. They who seek nothing but thir own just
5 libertie, have alwaies right to winn it and to keep it, when ever they have power, be the voices never so numerous that oppose it. And how much we above others are concernd to defend it from kingship, and from them who in pursuance therof so perniciously would betray us and themselves to most
10 certain miserie and thraldom, will be needless to repeat.

Having thus far shewn with what ease we may now obtain a free Commonwealth, and by it with as much ease all the freedom, peace, justice, plentie that we can desire, on the other side the difficulties, troubles, uncertainties, nay rather
15 impossibilities to enjoy these things constantly under a monarch, I will now proceed to shew more particularly wherin our freedom and flourishing condition will be more ample and secure to us under a free Commonwealth then under kingship.

20 The whole freedom of man consists either in spiritual or civil libertie. As for spiritual, who can be at rest, who can enjoy any thing in this world with contentment, who hath not libertie to serve God and to save his own soul, according to the best light which God hath planted in him to that pur-
25 pose, by the reading of his reveal'd will and the guidance of his holy spirit? That this is best pleasing to God, and that the whole Protestant Church allows no supream judge or rule in matters of religion, but the scriptures, and these to be inter-

preted by the scriptures themselves, which necessarily inferrs
liberty of conscience, I have heretofore prov'd at large in another treatise, and might yet furder by the public declarations, confessions and admonitions of whole churches and
5 states, obvious in all historie since the Reformation.

This liberty of conscience which above all other things
ought to be to all men dearest and most precious, no government more inclinable not to favor only but to protect, then a
free Commonwealth; as being most magnanimous, most
10 fearless and confident of its own fair proceedings. Wheras
kingship, though looking big, yet indeed most pusillani-
mous, full of fears, full of jealousies, startl'd at every om-
brage, as it hath bin observd of old to have ever suspected
most and mistrusted them who were in most esteem for ver-
15 tue and generositie of minde, so it is now known to have most
in doubt and suspicion them who are most reputed to be religious. Queen *Elizabeth* though her self accounted so good
a Protestant, so moderate, so confident of her Subjects love
would never give way so much as to Presbyterian reforma-
20 tion in this land, though once and again besought, as *Camden* relates, but imprisond and persecuted the very proposers
therof; alleaging it as her minde & maxim unalterable, that
such reformation would diminish regal autoritie. What liberty of conscience can we then expect of others, far wors
25 principl'd from the cradle, traind up and governd by *Popish*
and *Spanish* counsels, and on such depending hitherto for
subsistence? Especially what can this last Parlament expect,
who having reviv'd lately and publishd the covnant, have

reingag'd themselves, never to readmitt Episcopacie: which no son of *Charls* returning, but will most certainly bring back with him, if he regard the last and strictest charge of his father, *to persevere in not the doctrin only, but government*
5 *of the church of* England; *not to neglect the speedie and effectual suppressing of errors and schisms;* among which he accounted Presbyterie one of the chief: or if notwithstanding that charge of his father, he submitt to the covnant, how will he keep faith to us with disobedience to him; or regard
10 that faith given, which must be founded on the breach of that last and solemnest paternal charge, and the reluctance, I may say the antipathie which is in all kings against Presbyterian and Independent discipline? for they hear the gospel speaking much of libertie; a word which monarchie and her bish-
15 ops both fear and hate, but a free Commonwealth both favors and promotes; and not the word only, but the thing it self. But let our governors beware in time, least thir hard measure to libertie of conscience be found the rock wheron they shipwrack themselves as others have now don before them in the
20 cours wherin God was directing thir stearage to a free Commonwealth, and the abandoning of all those whom they call *sectaries,* for the detected falshood and ambition of som, be a wilfull rejection of thir own chief strength and interest in the freedom of all Protestant religion, under what abusive name
25 soever calumniated.

The other part of our freedom consists in the civil rights and advancements of every person according to his merit: the enjoyment of those never more certain, and the access to

these never more open, then in a free Commonwealth. Both
which in my opinion may be best and soonest obtaind, if
every countie in the land were made a kinde of subordinate
Commonaltie or Commonwealth, and one chief town or
5 more, according as the shire is in circuit, made cities, if they
be not so call'd alreadie; where the nobilitie and chief gentry
from a proportionable compas of territorie annexd to each
citie, may build, houses or palaces, befitting thir qualitie, may
bear part in the government, make thir own judicial laws, or
10 use these that are, and execute them by thir own elected judicatures and judges without appeal, in all things of civil government between man and man. So they shall have justice in
thir own hands, law executed fully and finally in thir own
counties and precincts, long wishd, and spoken of, but never
15 yet obtain; they shall have none then to blame but themselves, if it be not well administerd; and fewer laws to expect
or fear from the supreme autoritie; or to those that shall be
made, of any great concernment to public libertie, they may
without much trouble in these commonalties or in more gen-
20 eral assemblies call'd to thir cities from the whole territorie
on such occasion, declare and publish thir assent or dissent by
deputies within a time limited sent to the Grand Councel:
yet so as this thir judgment declar'd shal submitt to the
greater number of other counties or commonalties, and not
25 avail them to any exemption of themselves, or refusal of
agreement with the rest, as it may in any of the United Provinces, being sovran within it self, oft times to the great dis-
advantage of that union. In these imploiments they may

much better then they do now, exercise and fit themselves, till thir lot fall to be chosen into the Grand Councel, according as thir worth and merit shall be taken notice of by the people. As for controversies that shall happen between men
5 of several counties, they may repair, as they do now, to the capital citie, or any other more commodious, indifferent place and equal judges. And this I finde to have bin practisd in the old *Athenian* Commonwealth, reputed the first and ancientest place of civilitie in all *Greece;* that they had in thir
10 several cities, a peculiar; in *Athens,* a common government; and thir right, as it befell them, to the administration of both. They should have heer also schools and academies at thir own choice, wherin thir children may be bred up in thir own sight to all learning and noble education not in grammar only, but
15 in all liberal arts and exercises. This would soon spread much more knowledge and civilitie, yea religion through all parts of the land, by communicating the natural heat of government and culture more distributively to all extreme parts, which now lie numm and neglected, would soon make the
20 whole nation more industrious, more ingenuous at home, more potent, more honorable abroad. To this a free Commonwealth will easily assent; (nay the Parlament hath had alreadie som such thing in designe) for of all governments a Commonwealth aims most to make the people flourishing,
25 vertuous, noble and high spirited. Monarchs will never permitt: whose aim is to make the people, wealthie indeed perhaps and well fleec't, for thir own shearing and the supplie of regal prodigalitie; but otherwise softest, basest, vitiousest,

servilest, easiest to be kept under; and not only in fleece, but in minde also sheepishest; and will have all the benches of judicature annexd to the throne, as a gift of royal grace that we have justice don us; whenas nothing can be more essen-
5 tial to the freedom of a people, then to have the administration of justice and all public ornaments in thir own election and within thir own bounds, without long travelling or depending on remote places to obtain thir right or any civil accomplishment; so it be not supreme, but subordinate to the
10 general power and union of the whole Republic. In which happy firmness as in the particular above mentiond, we shall also far exceed the United Provinces, by having, not as they (to the retarding and distracting oft times of thir counsels or urgentest occasions) many Sovranties united in one Com-
15 monwealth, but many Commonwealths under one united and entrusted Sovrantie. And when we have our forces by sea and land, either of a faithful Armie or a setl'd Militia, in our own hands to the firm establishing of a free Commonwealth, publick accounts under our own inspection, general
20 laws and taxes with thir causes in our own domestic suffrages, judicial laws, offices and ornaments at home in our own ordering and administration, all distinction of lords and commoners, that may any way divide or sever the publick interest, remov'd, what can a perpetual senat have then wherin
25 to grow corrupt, wherin to encroach upon us or usurp; or if they do, wherin to be formidable? Yet if all this avail not to remove the fear or envie of a perpetual sitting, it may be easilie provided, to change a third part of them yearly or

every two or three years, as was above mentiond; or that it be
at those times in the peoples choice, whether they will change
them, or renew thir power, as they shall finde cause.

I have no more to say at present: few words will save us,
5 well considerd; few and easie things, now seasonably don.
But if the people be so affected, as to prostitute religion and
libertie to the vain and groundless apprehension, that nothing but kingship can restore trade, not remembring the frequent plagues and pestilences that then wasted this citie, such
10 as through God's mercie we never have felt since, and that
trade flourishes no where more then in the free Commonwealths of *Italie, Germanie,* and the Low-Countries before
thir eyes at this day, yet if trade be grown so craving and im-
portunate through the profuse living of tradesmen, that noth-
15 ing can support it, but the luxurious expences of a nation
upon trifles or superfluities, so as if the people generally
should betake themselves to frugalitie, it might prove a dangerous matter, least tradesmen should mutinie for want of
trading, and that therefor we must forgoe & set to sale re-
20 ligion, libertie, honor, safetie, all concernments Divine or
human to keep up trading, if lastly, after all this light among
us, the same reason shall pass for current to put our necks
again under kingship, as was made use of by the *Jews* to returne back to *Egypt* and to the worship of thir idol queen, be-
25 cause they falsly imagind that they then livd in more plentie
and prosperitie, our condition is not sound but rotten, both in
religion and all civil prudence; and will bring us soon, the
way we are marching, to those calamities which attend al-

waies and unavoidably on luxurie, all national judgments under forein or domestic slaverie: so far we shall be from mending our condition by monarchizing our government, whatever new conceit now possesses us. However with all
5 hazard I have ventur'd what I thought my duty to speak in season, and to forewarne my countrey in time: wherin I doubt not but ther be many wise men in all places and degrees, but am sorrie the effects of wisdom are so little seen among us. Many circumstances and particulars I could have
10 added in those things wherof I have spoken; but a few main matters now put speedily in execution, will suffice to recover us, and set all right: and ther will want at no time who are good at circumstances; but men who set thir mindes on main matters and sufficiently urge them, in these most difficult
15 times I finde not many. What I have spoken, is the language of that which is not call'd amiss *the good Old Cause:* if it seem strange to any, it will not seem more strange, I hope, then convincing to backsliders. Thus much I should perhaps have said though I were sure I should have spoken only to
20 trees and stones; and had none to cry to, but with the Prophet, *O earth, earth, earth!* to tell the very soil it self, what her perverse inhabitants are deaf to. Nay though what I have spoke, should happ'n (which Thou suffer not, who didst create mankinde free; nor Thou next, who didst redeem us
25 from being servants of men!) to be the last words of our expiring libertie. But I trust I shall have spoken perswasion to abundance of sensible and ingenuous men: to som perhaps whom God may raise of these stones to become children of

reviving libertie; and may reclaim, though they seem now
chusing them a captain back for *Egypt,* to bethink themselves a little and consider whether they are rushing; to exhort this torrent also of the people, not to be so impetuos,
5 but to keep thir due channell; and at length recovering and
uniting thir better resolutions, now that they see alreadie how
open and unbounded the insolence and rage is of our common enemies, to stay these ruinous proceedings; justly and
timely fearing to what a precipice of destruction the deluge
10 of this epidemic madness would hurrie us through the general defection of a misguided and abus'd multitude.

The End.

BRIEF NOTES
UPON A LATE SERMON

Brief Notes

upon a late Sermon, Titl'd, the Fear of God
and the King, &c.

I AFFIRMD in the Preface of a late discourse, Entitl'd,
*The ready way to establish a free Commonwealth, and
the dangers of readmitting Kingship in this Nation,*
that *the humor of returning to our old bondage, was in-*
5 *stilld of late by some deceivers;* and to make good, that what
I then affirmd, was not without just ground, one of those deceivers I present here to the people: and if I prove him not
such, refuse not to be so accounted in his stead.

He begins in his Epistle to the General; and moves cun-
10 ningly for a licence to be admitted Physitian both to Church
and State; then sets out his practice in Physical terms, *an
wholsom Electuary to be taken every morning next our
hearts:* tells of the opposition which he met with from the
Colledge of State-Physitians, then laies before you his drugs
15 and ingredients; *Strong purgatives in the Pulpit, contem-
perd of the myrrhe of mortification, the aloes of confession
and contrition, the rubarb of restitution and satisfaction;* a
pretty fantastic dos of Divinity from a Pulpit-Mountibanck,
not unlike the Fox, that turning Pedler, opend his pack
20 of ware before the Kid; though he now would seem to *per-
sonate the good Samaritan,* undertaking to *describe the rise
and progress of our national malady, and to prescribe the*

onely remedy: which how he performs, we shall quickly see.

First, he would suborn Saint *Luke* as his spokesman to the General, presuming, it seems, *to have had as perfect understanding of things from the very first,* as the Evangelist had
5 of his Gospel; that the General who hath so eminently born his part in the whole action, *might know the certainty of those things* better from him a partial Sequesterd enemy: for so he presently appears, though covertly and like the tempter; commencing his address with an impudent calumnie and
10 affront to his Excellence, that he would be pleasd *to carry on what he had so happily begun in the name and cause* not of God onely, which we doubt not, but *of his anointed,* meaning the late Kings son: which is to charge him most audaciously and falsly with the renouncing of his own public
15 promises and declarations both to the Parlament and the Army, and we trust his actions ere long will deterr such insinuating slanderers from thus approaching him for the future. But the General may well excuse him; for the *Comforter* himself scapes not his presumption, avouchd as fals-
20 ly, to have *impowrd* to those designs *him and him only,* who hath solemnly declar'd the contrary. What *Phanatique* against whom he so often inveighs, could more presumptuously affirm whom the Comforter hath impowrd, then this Antifanatic, as he would be thought?

The Text.

25 Prov. 24. 21. *My son, fear God and the King, and meddle not with them that be seditious, or desirous of change,* &c.

Letting pass matters not in controversie, I come to the main drift of your Sermon, *the King;* which word here is either to signifie any supreme Magistrate, or else your latter object of fear is not universal, belongs not at all to many parts
5 of Christendom, that have no King; and in particular, not to us. That we have no King since the putting down of Kingship in this Commonwealth, is manifest by this last Parlament, who to the time of thir dissolving not onely made no address at all to any King, but summond this next to come
10 by the Writ formerly appointed of a free Commonwealth, without restitution or the least mention of any Kingly right or power; which could not be, if there were at present any King of *England.* The main part therefore of your Sermon, if it mean a King in the usual sense, is either impertinent and
15 absurd, exhorting your auditory to fear that which is not, or if King here be, as it is, understood for any supreme Magistrate, by your own exhortation they are in the first place not to *meddle* with you, as being your self most of all the *seditious* meant here, and the *desirous of change,* in stirring them
20 up to *fear* a *King,* whom the present Government takes no notice of.

You begin with a vain vision, *God and the King at the first blush* (which will not be your last blush) *seeming to stand in* your *text like those two Cherubims on the mercy-*
25 *seat, looking on each other.* By this similitude, your conceited Sanctuary, worse then the Altar of *Ahaz,* patternd from *Damascus,* degrades God to a Cherub, and raises your King to be his collateral in place, notwithstanding the other

differences you put: which well agrees with the Court-letters, lately publishd from this Lord to tother Lord, that cry him up for no less then Angelical and Celestial.

Your first observation, *pag.* 8. is, *That God and the King*
5 *are coupl'd in the text, and what the Holy Ghost hath thus firmely combin'd, we may not, we must not dare to put asunder;* and your self is the first man who puts them asunder by the first proof of your doctrine immediately following, *Iudg.* 7. 20. which *couples the sword of the Lord and Gid-*
10 *eon,* a man who not only was no King, but refus'd to be a King or Monarch, when it was offered him, in the very next chapter, *vers.* 22, 23. *I will not rule over you, neither shall my son rule over you; the Lord shall rule over you.* Here we see that this worthy heroic deliverer of his Country thought
15 it best governd, if the Lord governd it in that form of a free Commonwealth, which they then enjoid without a single person. And this is your first Scripture, abus'd and most impertinently cited, nay against your self, to prove that *Kings at thir Coronation have a sword given them,* which you in-
20 terpret *the Militia, the power of life and death put into thir hands,* against the declar'd judgement of our Parlaments, nay of all our Laws, which reserve to themselves only the power of life and death, and render you in thir just resentment of this boldness, another Doctor *Manwaring.*
25 Your next proof is as false and frivolous, *The King,* say you, *is Gods sword-bearer;* true, but not the King only, for *Gideon* by whom you seek to prove this, neither was, nor would be a King; and as you your self confess, *pag.* 40. *there*

be divers forms of government. He bears not the sword in vain, Rom. 13. 4. this also is as true of any lawful rulers, especially supreme, so that *rulers, vers.* 3. and therefor this present government, without whose authority you excite the
5 people to a King, bear the sword as well as Kings, and as little in vain. *They fight against God, who resist his Ordinance, and go about to wrest the sword out of the hands of his Anointed.* This is likewise granted: but who is *his Anointed?* not every King, but they only who were anointed
10 or made Kings by his special command; as *Saul, David,* and his race, which ended in the Messiah, (from whom no Kings at this day can derive thir rule) *Iehu, Cyrus,* and if any other were by name appointed by him to some particular service: as for the rest of Kings, all other supreme Magistrates are as
15 much the Lords anointed as they; and our obedience commanded equally to them all; *For there is no power but of God, Rom.* 13. 1. and we are exhorted in the Gospell to obey Kings, as other Magistrates, not that they are call'd any where the Lord's anointed, but as they are *the ordinance of*
20 *man,* 1 *Pet.* 2. 13. You therefor and other such false Doctors, preaching Kings to your auditory, as the Lord's only anointed, to withdraw people from the present Government, by your own text are self condemnd, and not to be followd, not to be *medl'd with,* but to be noted, as most of all others the
25 *seditious and desirous of change.*

Your third proof is no less against your self. *Psal.* 105. 15. *touch not mine anointed.* For this is not spoken in behalf of Kings, but spoken to reprove Kings, that they should not

touch his anointed Saints and Servants, the seed of *Abraham*, as the verse next before might have taught you: *he reproved Kings for their sakes; saying, touch not mine anointed, and do my Prophets no harm;* according to that 2 *Cor.* 1. 21. *He*
5 *who hath anointed us, is God.* But how well you confirme one wrested Scripture with another: 1 *Sam.* 8. 7. *They have not rejected thee, but me:* grossly misapplying these words, which were not spoken to any who had *resisted or rejected* a King, but to them who much against the will of God had
10 sought a King, and rejected a Commonwealth, wherin they might have livd happily under the Raign of God only, thir King. Let the words interpret themselves: *v.* 6. 7. *But the thing displeased Samuel, when they said, give us a King to judge us: and Samuel prayed unto the Lord. And the Lord*
15 *said unto Samuel, hearken unto the voice of the people in all that they say unto thee; for they have not rejected thee, but they have rejected me, that I should not reign over them.* Hence you conclude, *so indissoluble is the Conjunction of God and the King.* O notorious abuse of Scripture! whenas
20 you should have concluded, So unwilling was God to give them a King, So wide was the disjunction of God from a King. Is this the doctrin you boast of to be *so clear in it self, and like a Mathematical principle, that needs no farther demonstration.* Bad Logic, bad Mathematics (for principles
25 can have no demonstration at all) but wors Divinitie. O people of an implicit faith no better then *Romish,* if these be thy prime teachers; who to thir credulous audience dare thus jugle with Scripture, to alleage those places for the

proof of thir doctrin, which are the plane refutation: and
this is all the Scripture which he brings to confirm his point.

The rest of his preachment is meer groundless chat, save
heer and there a few granes of corn scatterd to intice the silly
fowl into his net, interlac't heer and there with som human
reading; though slight, and not without Geographical and
Historical mistakes: as page 29, *Sucvia* the German dukedom, for *Suecia* the Northern Kingdom: *Philip of Macedon,*
who is generally understood of the great *Alexanders* father
only, made contemporanie, page 31, with *T. Quintus the
Roman commander,* instead of *T. Quintius* and the latter
Philip: and page 44, *Tully* cited *in his third oration against
Verres,* to say of him, *that he was a wicked Consul,* who
never was a Consul: nor Trojan *sedition ever portraid* by that
verse of *Virgil,* which you cite page 47, as *that* of *Troy:*
school-boyes could have tould you, that ther is nothing of
Troy in that whole portraiture, as you call it, of *sedition.*
These gross mistakes may justly bring in doubt your other
loos citations; and that you take them up somwhere at the
second or third hand rashly and without due considering.

Nor are you happier in the relating or the moralizing your
fable. *The frogs* (𝔟𝔢𝔦𝔫𝔤 𝔬𝔫𝔠𝔢 𝔞 𝔣𝔯𝔢𝔢 𝔑𝔞𝔱𝔦𝔬𝔫 saith the fable)
*petitioned Jupiter for a King: he tumbl'd among them a log.
They found it insensible: they petitioned then for a King
that should be active: he sent them a Crane* (a 𝔖𝔱𝔬𝔯𝔨 saith the
fable) *which straight fell to pecking them up.* This you apply
to the reproof of them who desire change: wheras indeed the
true moral shews rather the folly of those, who being free

seek a King; which for the most part either as a log lies heavie
on his Subjects, without doing ought worthie of his dignitie
and the charge to maintain him, or as a Stork is ever pecking
them up and devouring them.

5   *But by our fundamental Laws, the King is the highest
power,* page 40. If we must hear mooting and law-lectures
from the Pulpit, what shame is it for a Dr. of Divinitie, not
first to consider, that no law can be *fundamental,* but that
which is grounded on the light of nature or right reason,
10 commonly call'd *moral law:* which no form of Government
was ever counted; but arbitrarie, and at all times in the choice
of every free people, or thir representers. This choice of Government is so essential to thir freedom, that longer then they
have it, they are not free. In this land not only the late King
15 and his posteritie, but kingship it self hath bin abrogated by
a law; which involves with as good reason the posteritie of a
King forfeited to the people, as that Law heretofore of Treason against the King, attainted the children with the father.
This Law against both King and Kingship they who most
20 question, do no less question all enacted without the King
and his Antiparlament at *Oxford,* though call'd Mungrell by
himself. If no Law must be held good, but what passes in
full Parlament, then surely in exactness of legalitie, no member must be missing: for look how many are missing, so
25 many Counties or Cities that sent them, want thir representers. But if being once chosen, they serve for the whole Nation, then any number which is sufficient, is full, and most
of all in times of discord, necessitie and danger. The King

himself was bound by the old Mode of Parlaments, not to be absent, but in case of sickness, or som extraordinary occasion, and then to leave his substitute; much less might any member be allowd to absent himself. If the King then and many
5 of the members with him, without leaving any in his stead, forsook the Parlament upon a meer panic fear, as was at that time judg'd by most men, and to leavie Warr against them that sat, should they who were left sitting, break up, or not dare enact aught of neerest and presentest concernment to
10 public safety, for the punctilio wanting of a full number, which no Law book in such extraordinary cases hath determind? Certainly if it were lawfull for them to fly from thir charge upon pretence of privat safety, it was much more lawfull for these to sit and act in thir trust what was necessary
15 for public. By a Law therefor of Parlament, and of a Parlament that conquerd both *Ireland, Scotland,* & all thir enemies in *England,* defended thir friends, were generally acknowledgd for a Parlament both at home & abroad, kingship was abolishd: this Law now of late hath bin negatively re-
20 peald; yet Kingship not positively restor'd; and I suppose never was establishd by any certain Law in this Land, nor possibly could be: for how could our forefathers binde us to any certain form of Government, more then we can binde our posteritie? If a people be put to warre with thir King
25 for his misgovernment, and overcome him, the power is then undoubtedly in thir own hands how they will be governd. The warr was granted *just* by the King himself at the beginning of his last treatie; and still maintaind to be so by this

last Parlament, as appears by the qualification prescrib'd to the members of this next ensuing, That none shall be elected, who have born arms against the Parlament since 1641. If the warr were *just,* the conquest was also just by the Law of Na-
5 tions. And he who was the chief enemie, in all right ceasd to be the King, especially after captivitie, by the deciding verdit of warr; and royaltie with all her Laws and pretentions, yet remains in the victors power, together with the choice of our future Government. Free Commonwealths have bin ever
10 counted fittest and properest for civil, vertuous and industrious Nations, abounding with prudent men worthie to govern: monarchie fittest to curb degenerate, corrupt, idle, proud, luxurious people. If we desire to be of the former, nothing better for us, nothing nobler then a free Common-
15 wealth: if we will needs condemn our selves to be of the latter, desparing of our own vertue, industrie and the number of our able men, we may then, conscious of our own unworthiness to be governd better, sadly betake us to our befitting thraldom: yet chusing out of our own number one who hath
20 best aided the people, and best merited against tyrannie, the space of a raign or two we may chance to live happily anough, or tolerably. But that a victorious people should give up themselves again to the vanquishd, was never yet heard of; seems rather void of all reason and good policie, and will in
25 all probabilitie subject the subduers to the subdu'd, will expose to revenge, to beggarie, to ruin and perpetual bondage the victors under the vanquishd: then which what can be more unworthie?

From misinterpreting our Law, you return to do again the same with Scripture; and would prove the supremacy of *English* Kings from 1 *Pet.* 2. 13. as if that were the Apostles work: wherin if he saith that *the king is supreme,* he speaks 5 so of him but as an *ordinance of man,* and in respect of those *Governours that are sent by him,* not in respect of Parlaments, which by the Law of this Land are his bridle; in vain his bridle, if not also his rider: and therefor hath not only *co-ordination* with him, which you falsly call *seditious,* but hath 10 superioritie above him, and that neither *against religion,* nor *right reason:* no nor against Common Law; for our Kings reignd only by Law: but the Parlament is above all positive Law, whether civil or common, makes or unmakes them both, & still the latter Parlament above the former, above all 15 the former Lawgivers, then certainly above all precedent Laws, entaild the Crown on whom it pleasd; and, as a great Lawyer saith, *is so transcendent and absolute, that it cannot be confin'd either for causes or persons, within any bounds.* But your cry is, no Parlament without a King. If this be so, 20 we have never had lawfull Kings, who have all bin created Kings either by such Parlaments, or by conquest: if by such Parlaments, they are in your allowance none: if by conquest, that conquest we have now conquerd. So that as well by your own assertion as by ours, there can at present be no King. 25 And how could that person be absolutely supreme, who reignd, not under Law only, but under oath of his good demeanour given to the people at his coronation, ere the people gave him his Crown? and his principal oath was to maintain

those Laws which the people should chuse? If then the Law
it self, much more he who was but the keeper and minister
of Law, was in thir choice; and both he subordinat to the
performance of his duty sworn, and our sworn allegiance in
5 order only to his performance.

You fall next on the *Consistorian Schismatics;* for so you
call Presbyterians, page 40; and judge them to have *enervated
the Kings Supremacie by thir opinions and practice, differing in many things only in terms from Poperie;* though some
10 of those principles which you there cite concerning Kingship,
are to be read in *Aristotles* Politics, long ere Popery was
thought on. The Presbyterians therefor it concerns to be well
forewarnd of you betimes; and to them I leave you.

As for your examples of seditious men, page 54, &c. *Cora,
15 Absalom, Zimri, Sheba,* to these you might with much more
reason have added your own name, who *blow the Trumpet
of sedition* from your Pulpit against the present Government:
in reward wherof they have sent you by this time, as I hear,
to your *own place,* for preaching open sedition, while you
20 would seem to preach against it.

As for your appendix annext of the *Samaritan reviv'd,*
finding it so foul a libell against all the well-affected of this
land, since the very time of *Ship-money,* against the whole
Parlament, both Lords and Commons, except those that fled
25 to *Oxford,* against the whole reformed Church, not only in
England and *Scotland,* but all over *Europ* (in comparison
wherof you and your Prelatical partie are more truly schismatics and sectarians, nay more properly *fanatics* in your

fanes and guilded temples, then those whom you revile by those names) and meeting with no more Scripture or solid reason in your *Samaritane wine and oyle,* then hath already bin found sophisticated and adulterate, I leave your malig-
5 nant narrative, as needing no other confutation, then the just censure already pass'd upon you by the Councel of State.

OF TRUE RELIGION,
HERESIE, SCHISM AND
TOLERATION

OF

True Religion,
HÆRESIE,
SCHISM,
TOLERATION,

And what beſt means may be
uſ'd againſt the growth of

POPERY

The Author J. M.  (John Milton)

LONDON
Printed in the Year, 1673.

Of True Religion,

Heresie, Schism, and Toleration.

IT is unknown to no man, who knows ought of concernment among us, that the increase of Popery is at this day
no small trouble and offence to greatest part of the Nation; and the rejoycing of all good men that it is so; the more
5 their rejoycing, that God hath giv'n a heart to the people to
remember still their great and happy deliverance from Popish
Thraldom, and to esteem so highly the precious benefit of his
Gospel, so freely and so peaceably injoy'd among them. Since
therefore some have already in Publick with many considera-
10 ble Arguments exhorted the people to beware the growth of
this Romish Weed; I thought it no less then a common duty
to lend my hand, how unable soever, to so good a Purpose. I
will not now enter into the Labyrinth of Councels and Fathers, an intangl'd wood which the Papist loves to fight in, not
15 with hope of Victory, but to obscure the shame of an open
overthrow: which yet in that kind of Combate, many heretofore, and one of late, hath eminently giv'n them. And such
manner of dispute with them, to Learned Men, is useful and
very commendable: But I shall insist now on what is plainer
20 to Common apprehension, and what I have to say, without
longer introduction.

True Religion is the true Worship and Service of God,
learnt and believed from the Word of God only. No Man or

Angel can know how God would be worshipt and serv'd unless God reveal it: He hath Reveal'd and taught it us in the holy Scriptures by inspir'd Ministers, and in the Gospel by his own Son and his Apostles, with strictest command to reject all
5 other traditions or additions whatsoever. According to that of St. *Paul, Though wee or an Angel from Heaven preach any other Gospel unto you, than that which wee have preacht unto you, let him be Anathema, or accurst.* And *Deut.* 4. 2. *Ye shall not add to the word which I command you, neither shall you*
10 *diminish ought from it.* Rev. 22. 18, 19. *If any man shall add,* &c. *If any man shall take away from the Words,* &c. With good and Religious Reason therefore all Protestant Churches with one consent, and particularly the Church of *England* in Her thirty nine Articles, Artic. 6*th,* 19*th,* 20*th,* 21*st,* and
15 elsewhere, maintain these two points, as the main Principles of true Religion: that the Rule of true Religion is the Word of God only: and that their Faith ought not to be an implicit faith, that is, to believe, though as the Church believes, against or without express authority of Scripture. And if all Protes-
20 tants as universally as they hold these two Principles, so attentively and Religiously would observe them, they would avoid and cut off many Debates and Contentions, Schisms and Persecutions, which too oft have been among them, and more firmly unite against the common adversary. For hence
25 it directly follows, that no true Protestant can persecute, or not tolerate his fellow Protestant, though dissenting from him in som opinions, but he must flatly deny and Renounce these two his own main Principles, whereon true Religion is

founded; while he compels his Brother from that which he believes as the manifest word of God, to an implicit faith (which he himself condemns) to the endangering of his Brothers soul, whether by rash belief, or outward Conform-
5 ity: for *whatsoever is not of Faith, is Sin.*

I will now as briefly show what is false Religion or Heresie, which will be done as easily: for of contraries the definitions must needs be contrary. Heresie therefore is a Religion taken up and believ'd from the traditions of men and additions to
10 the word of God. Whence also it follows clearly, that of all known Sects or pretended Religions at this day in Christendom, Popery is the only or the greatest Heresie: and he who is so forward to brand all others for Hereticks, the obstinate Papist, the only Heretick. Hence one of their
15 own famous Writers found just cause to stile the Romish Church *Mother of Error, School of Heresie.* And whereas the Papist boasts himself to be a Roman Catholick, it is a meer contradiction, one of the Popes Bulls, as if he should say, universal particular a Catholic Schismatic. For Catholic in Greek
20 signifies universal: and the Christian Church was so call'd, as consisting of all Nations to whom the Gospel was to be preach't, in contradistinction to the Jewish Church, which consisted for the most part of Jews only.

Sects may be in a true Church as well as in a false, when
25 men follow the Doctrin too much for the Teachers sake, whom they think almost infallible; and this becomes, through Infirmity, implicit Faith; and the name Sectary, pertains to such a Disciple.

Schism is a rent or division in the Church, when it comes to the separating of Congregations; and may also happen to a true Church, as well as to a false; yet in the true needs not tend to the breaking of Communion; if they can agree in the
5 right administration of that wherein they Communicate, keeping their other Opinions to themselves, not being destructive to Faith. The Pharisees and Saduces were two Sects, yet both met together in their common worship of God at *Jerusalem*. But here the Papist will angrily demand, what!
10 Are Lutherans, Calvinists, Anabaptists, Socinians, Arminians, no Hereticks? I answer, all these may have some errors, but are no Hereticks. Heresie is in the Will and choice profestly against Scripture; error is against the Will, in misunderstanding the Scripture after all sincere endeavours to understand it rightly: Hence it was said well by one of the Ancients, *Err I may, but a Heretick I will not be.* It is a humane frailty to err, and no man is infallible here on earth. But so long as all these profess to set the Word of God only before them as the Rule of faith and obedience; and use all diligence
20 and sincerity of heart, by reading, by learning, by study, by prayer for Illumination of the holy Spirit, to understand the Rule and obey it, they have done what man can do: God will assuredly pardon them, as he did the friends of *Job,* good and pious men, though much mistaken, as there it appears, in
25 some Points of Doctrin. But some will say, with Christians it is otherwise, whom God hath promis'd by his Spirit to teach all things. True, all things absolutely necessary to salvation: But the hottest disputes among Protestants calmly and char-

itably enquir'd into, will be found less then such. The Luther-
an holds Consubstantiation; an error indeed, but not mortal.
The Calvinist is taxt with Predestination, and to make God
the Author of sin; not with any dishonourable thought of
5 God, but it may be over zealously asserting his absolute power,
not without plea of Scripture. The Anabaptist is accus'd of
Denying Infants their right to Baptism; again they say, they
deny nothing but what the Scripture denies them. The Arian
and Socinian are charg'd to dispute against the Trinity: they
10 affirm to believe the Father, Son, and Holy Ghost, according
to Scripture, and the Apostolic Creed; as for terms of Trinity,
Triniunity, Coessentiality, Tripersonality, and the like, they
reject them as Scholastic Notions, not to be found in Scripture,
which by a general Protestant Maxim is plain and perspicuous
15 abundantly to explain its own meaning in the properest words,
belonging to so high a Matter and so necessary to be known;
a mystery indeed in their Sophistic Subtilties, but in Scripture
a plain Doctrin. Their other Opinions are of less Moment.
They dispute the satisfaction of Christ, or rather the word
20 *Satisfaction,* as not Scriptural: but they acknowledge him
both God and their Saviour. The *Arminian* lastly is condemn'd for setting up free will against free grace; but that Imputation he disclaims in all his writings, and grounds himself largly upon Scripture only. It cannot be deny'd that the
25 Authors or late Revivers of all these Sects or Opinions, were
Learned, Worthy, Zealous, and Religious Men, as appears by
their lives written, and the same of their many Eminent and
Learned followers, perfect and powerful in the Scriptures,

holy and unblameable in their lives: and it cannot be imagin'd that God would desert such painful and zealous labourers in his Church, and ofttimes great sufferers for their Conscience, to damnable Errors & a Reprobate sense, who had so
5 often implor'd the assistance of his Spirit; but rather, having made no man Infallible, that he hath pardon'd their errors, and accepts their Pious endeavours, sincerely searching all things according to the rule of Scripture, with such guidance and direction as they can obtain of God by Prayer. What
10 Protestant then who himself maintains the same Principles, and disavowes all implicit Faith, would persecute, and not rather charitably tolerate such men as these, unless he mean to abjure the Principles of his own Religion? If it be askt how far they should be tolerated? I answer doubtless equally, as
15 being all Protestants; that is on all occasions to give account of their Faith, either by Arguing, Preaching in their several Assemblies, Publick writing, and the freedom of Printing. For if the *French* and *Polonian* Protestants injoy all this liberty among Papists, much more may a Protestant justly expect it
20 among Protestants; and yet some times here among us, the one persecutes the other upon every slight Pretence.

But he is wont to say he enjoyns only things indifferent. Let them be so still; who gave him authority to change their nature by injoyning them? If by his own Principles, as is prov'd,
25 he ought to tolerate controverted points of Doctrine not slightly grounded on Scripture, much more ought he not impose things indifferent without Scripture. In Religion nothing is indifferent, but, if it come once to be Impos'd, is either

a command or a Prohibition, and so consequently an addition
to the word of God, which he professes to disallow. Besides,
how unequal, how uncharitable must it needs be, to Impose
that which his conscience cannot urge him to impose, upon
5 him whose conscience forbids him to obey? What can it be
but love of contention for things not necessary to be done, to
molest the conscience of his Brother, who holds them necessary to be not done? To conclude, let such a one but call to
mind his own Principles above mention'd, and he must nec-
10 essarily grant, that neither he can impose, nor the other believe or obey ought in Religion, but from the Word of God
only. More amply to understand this, may be read the 14*th.*
and 15*th.* Chapters to the Romans, and the Contents of
the 14*th,* set forth no doubt but with full authority of the
15 Church of *England;* the Gloss is this. *Men may not con-
temn, or condemn one the other for things indifferent.* And
in the 6*th* Article above mentioned, *Whatsoever is not read
in Holy Scripture, nor may be proved thereby, is not to be
required of any man as an article of Faith, or necessary to
20 salvation.* And certainly what is not so, is not to be required
at all; as being an addition to the Word of God expressly
forbidden.

Thus this long and hot Contest, whether Protestants ought
to tolerate one another, if men will be but Rational and not
25 Partial, may be ended without need of more words to com-
pose it.

Let us now enquire whether Popery be tolerable or no.
Popery is a double thing to deal with, and claims a twofold

Power, Ecclesiastical, and Political, both usurpt, and the one supporting the other.

But Ecclesiastical is ever pretended to Political. The Pope by this mixt faculty, pretends right to Kingdoms and States, and especially to this of *England,* Thrones and Unthrones Kings, and absolves the people from their obedience to them; sometimes interdicts to whole Nations the Publick worship of God, shutting up their Churches: and was wont to dreign away greatest part of the wealth of this then miserable Land, as part of his Patrimony, to maintain the Pride and Luxury of his Court and Prelates: and now since, through the infinite mercy and favour of God, we have shaken off his *Babylonish* Yoke, hath not ceas'd by his Spyes and Agents, Bulls and Emissaries, once to destroy both King and Parliament; perpetually to seduce, corrupt, and pervert as many as they can of the People. Whether therefore it be fit or reasonable, to tolerate men thus principl'd in Religion towards the State, I submit it to the consideration of all Magistrates, who are best able to provide for their own and the publick safety. As for tolerating the exercise of their Religion, supposing their State activities not to be dangerous, I answer, that Toleration is either public or private; and the exercise of their Religion, as far as it is Idolatrous, can be tolerated neither way: not publicly, without grievous and unsufferable scandal giv'n to all consciencious Beholders; not privately, without great offence to God, declar'd against all kind of Idolatry, though secret. *Ezekiel* 8. 7, 8. *And he brought me to the door of the Court, and when I looked, behold a hole in the wall. Then said he*

*unto me, Son of Man, digg now in the wall; and when I had
digged, behold a Door, and he said unto me, go in, and behold the wicked Abominations that they do here.* And verse
12. *Then said he unto me, Son of Man, hast thou seen what
the Antients of the house of* Israel *do in the dark?* &c. And it
appears by the whole Chapter, that God was no less offended
with these secret Idolatries, then with those in public; and no
less provokt, then to bring on and hasten his Judgements on
the whole Land for these also.

Having shown thus, that Popery, as being Idolatrous, is not
to be tolerated either in Public or in Private; it must be now
thought how to remove it and hinder the growth thereof, I
mean in our Natives, and not Forreigners, Privileg'd by the
Law of Nations. Are we to punish them by corporal punishment, or fines in their Estates, upon account of their Religion?
I suppose it stands not with the Clemency of the Gospel, more
then what appertains to the security of the State: But first we
must remove their Idolatry, and all the furniture thereof,
whether Idols, or the Mass wherein they adore their God
under Bread and Wine: for the Commandment forbids to
adore, not only *any Graven Image, but the likeness of any
thing in Heaven above, or in the Earth beneath, or in the
Water under the Earth, thou shalt not bow down to them nor
worship them, for I the Lord thy God am a Jealous God.* If
they say that by removing their Idols we violate their Consciences, we have no warrant to regard Conscience which is
not grounded on Scripture: and they themselves confess in
their late defences, that they hold not their Images necessary

to salvation, but only as they are enjoyn'd them by tradition.

Shall we condescend to dispute with them? The Scripture is our only Principle in Religion; and by that only they will not be Judg'd, but will add other Principles of their own, which, forbidden by the Word of God, we cannot assent to. And the common Maxim also in *Logic* is, *against them who deny Principles, we are not to dispute.* Let them bound their disputations on the Scripture only, and an ordinary Protestant, well read in the Bible, may turn and wind their Doctors. They will not go about to prove their Idolatries by the Word of God, but run to shifts and evasions, and frivolous distinctions: Idols they say are *Laymens* Books, and a great means to stir up pious thoughts and Devotion in the Learnedst. I say they are no means of Gods appointing, but plainly the contrary: Let them hear the Prophets; *Jerem.* 10. 8. *The stock is a Doctrin of Vanities.* Habakkuk 2. 18. *What profiteth the graven Image that the maker thereof hath graven it: The Molten Image and a teacher of Lyes?* But they alleadge in their late answers, that the Laws of *Moses* giv'n only to the Jews, concern not us under the Gospel: and remember not that Idolatry is forbidden as expressly, [in several places of the Gospel,] But with these wiles and fallacies *compassing Sea and Land, like the Pharisees of old, to make one Proselite,* they lead away privily many simple and ignorant Souls, men or women, *and make them twofold more the Children of Hell then themselves,* Matt. 23. 15. But the Apostle hath well warn'd us, I may say, from such Deceivers as these, for their Mystery was then working. *I beseech you Brethren,* saith he,

mark them which cause divisions and offences, contrary to the
doctrin which ye have learned, and avoid them; for they that
are such serve not our Lord Jesus Christ, but their own belly,
and by good words and fair speeches deceive the heart of the
5 *simple,* Rom. 16. 17, 18.

The next means to hinder the growth of Popery will be to
read duly and diligently the Holy Scriptures, which as St. *Paul*
saith to *Timothy,* who had known them from a child, *are*
able to make wise unto salvation. And to the whole Church
10 of *Colossi; Let the word of Christ dwell in you plentifully,*
with all wisdome, Coloss. 3. 16. The Papal Antichristian
Church permits not her Laity to read the Bible in their own
tongue. Our Church on the contrary hath proposd it to all
men, and to this end translated it into English, with profitable
15 Notes on what is met with obscure, though what is most necessary to be known be still plainest: that all sorts and degrees
of men, not understanding the Original, may read it in their
Mother Tongue. Neither let the Countryman, the Trades-
man, the Lawyer, the Physician, the Statesman, excuse him-
20 self by his much business from the studious reading thereof.
Our Saviour saith, Luke 10. 41, 42. *Thou art careful and*
troubled about many things, but one thing is needful. If they
were ask't, they would be loath to set earthly things, wealth,
or honour before the wisdom of salvation. Yet most men in
25 the course and practice of their lives are found to do so; and
through unwillingness to take the pains of understanding
their Religion by their own diligent study, would fain be sav'd

by a Deputy. Hence comes implicit faith, ever learning and never taught, much hearing and small proficience, till want of Fundamental knowledg easily turns to superstition or Popery: Therefore the Apostle admonishes, Eccles. 4. 14.

5 *That we henceforth be no more children tossed to and fro and carried about with every wind of Doctrine, by the sleight of men, and cunning craftiness whereby they lye in wait to deceive.* Every member of the Church, at least of any breeding or capacity, so well ought to be grounded in spiritual knowl-

10 edg, as, if need be, to examine their Teachers themselves, Acts. 17. 11. *They searched the Scriptures dayly, whether those things were so.* Rev. 2. 2. *Thou hast tryed them which say they are Apostles, and are not.* How should any private Christian try his Teachers unless he be well grounded himself

15 in the Rule of Scripture, by which he is taught. As therefore among Papists, their ignorance in Scripture cheifly upholds Popery; so among Protestant People, the frequent and serious reading thereof will soonest pull Popery down.

Another means to abate Popery arises from the constant

20 reading of Scripture, wherein Beleivers who agree in the main, are every where exhorted to mutual forbearance and charity one towards the other, though dissenting in some opinions. It is written that the Coat of our Saviour was without seame: whence some would infer that there should be no

25 division in the Church of Christ. It should be so indeed; Yet seams in the same cloath, neither hurt the garment, nor misbecome it; and not only seams, but Schisms will be while men are fallible: But if they who dissent in matters not essential to

belief, while the common adversary is in the field, shall stand
jarring and pelting at one another, they will be soon routed
and subdued. The Papist with open mouth makes much advantage of our several opinions; not that he is able to confute
5 the worst of them, but that we by our continual jangle among
our selves make them worse then they are indeed. To save our
selves therefore, and resist the common enemy, it concerns us
mainly to agree within our selves, that with joynt forces we
may not only hold our own, but get ground; and why should
10 we not? The Gospel commands us to tolerate one another,
though of various opinions, and hath promised a good and
happy event thereof, *Phil. 3. 15. Let us therefore as many as
be perfect be thus minded; and if in any thing ye be otherwise
minded, God shall reveal even this unto you.* And we are bid,
15 1 *Thess. 5. 21. Prove all things, hold fast that which is good.*
St. *Paul* judg'd that not only to tolerate, but to examine and
prove all things, was no danger to our holding fast of that
which is good. How shall we prove all things, which includes
all opinions at least founded on Scripture, unless we not only
20 tolerate them, but patiently hear them, and seriously read
them? If he who thinks himself in the truth professes to have
learnt it, not by implicit faith, but by attentive study of the
Scriptures & full perswasion of heart, with what equity can
he refuse to hear or read him, who demonstrates to have gained
25 his knowledge by the same way? is it a fair course to assert
truth by arrogating to himself the only freedome of speech,
and stopping the mouths of others equally gifted? This is the
direct way to bring in that Papistical implicit faith which we

all disclaim. They pretend it would unsettle the weaker sort: the same groundless fear is pretended by the Romish Clergy in prohibiting the Scripture. At least then let them have leave to write in Latin which the common people understand not; that what they hold may be discust among the Learned only. We suffer the Idolatrous books of Papists, without this fear, to be sold & read as common as our own. Why not much rather of Anabaptists, Arians, Arminians, & Socinians? There is no Learned man but will confess he hath much profited by reading Controversies, his Senses awakt, his Judgement sharpn'd, and the truth which he holds more firmly establish't. If then it be profitable for him to read; why should it not at least be tolerable and free for his Adversary to write? In *Logic* they teach, that contraries laid together more evidently appear: it follows then that all controversies being permitted, falshood will appear more false, and truth the more true: which must needs conduce much, not only to the confounding of Popery, but to the general confirmation of unimplicit truth.

The last means to avoid Popery, is to amend our lives: it is a general complaint that this Nation of late years, is grown more numerously and excessively vitious then heretofore; Pride, Luxury, Drunkenness, Whoredom, Cursing, Swearing, bold and open Atheism every where abounding: Where these grow, no wonder if Popery also grow a pace. There is no man so wicked, but at somtimes his conscience will wring him with thoughts of another world, & the Peril of his soul: the trouble and melancholy which he conceives of true Repentance and amendment he endures not; but enclines rather

to some carnal Superstition, which may pacify and lull his Conscience with some more pleasing Doctrin. None more ready and officious to offer her self then the *Romish,* and opens wide her Office, with all her faculties to receive
5 him; easy Confession, easy Absolution, Pardons, Indulgences, Masses for him both quick and dead, *Agnus Dei's,* Reliques, and the like: and he, instead of *Working out his salvation with fear and trembling,* strait thinks in his heart (like another kind of fool then he in the Psalmes) to bribe God as a
10 corrupt judge; and by his Proctor, some Priest or Fryer, to buy out his Peace with money, which he cannot with his repentance. For God, when men sin outragiously, and will not be admonisht, gives over chastizing them, perhaps by Pestilence, Fire, Sword, or Famin, which may all turn to their good, and
15 takes up his severest punishments, hardness, besottedness of heart, and Idolatry, to their final perdition. Idolatry brought the Heathen to hainous Transgressions, *Romans* 2 d. And hainous Transgressions oft times bring the slight professors of true Religion, to gross Idolatry: 1 Thess. 2. 11, 12. *For*
20 *this cause, God shall send them strong delusion that they should believe a lye, that they all might be damnd who believe not the truth, but had pleasure in unrighteousness.* And Isaiah 44. 18. Speaking of Idolaters. *They have not known nor understood, for he hath shut their Eyes that they cannot*
25 *see, and their hearts that they cannot understand.* Let us therefore using this last means, last here spoken of, but first to be done, amend our lives with all speed; least through impenitency we run into that stupidly, which we now seek all means

so warily to avoid, the worst of superstitions, and the heaviest of all Gods Judgements, Popery.

FINIS.

OBSERVATIONS
ON THE ARTICLES OF PEACE

BY

The Lord Lieutenant Generall, and Generall Governour of the Kingdome of IRELAND.

ORMOND:

WHEREAS Articles of Peace, are made, concluded, accorded, and agreed upon, by and between Us, JAMES Lord Marquesse of OR-
MOND, Lord Lieut. Generall, and Generall Governor of his
5 Majesties Kingdome of *Ireland,* by vertue of the Authority
wherewith We are intrusted, for, and on the behalfe of His
Most Excellent Majesty of the one part, and the Generall
Assembly of the Roman Catholickes of the said Kingdome,
for and on the behalfe of his Majesties Roman Catholick Sub-
10 jects of the same, on the other part; A true Copy of which
Articles of Peace is hereunto annexed. We the Lord Lieut.
do by this Proclamation, in His Majesties name publish the
same, and do in his Majest. name strictly charge and command al His Majesties Subjects, and all others inhabiting or
15 residing within his Majesties said Kingdome of *Ireland* to
take notice thereof, and to render due obedience to the same
in all the parts thereof.

And as his Majesty hath been induced to this peace, out of
a deep sence of the miseries and calamities brought upon this

His Kingdome, and People, and out of a hope conceived by His Majesty, that it may prevent the further effusion of His Subjects blood, redeem them out of all the miseries and calamities under which they now suffer, restore them to all
5 quietnesse and happinesse, under His Majesties most Gracious Government, deliver the Kingdome in generall, from those slaughters, depredations, rapines, and spoyles which always accompany a war encourage the Subjects and others with comfort to betake themselves to trade, traffique, comerce,
10 manufacture, and all other things, which un-interrupted, may increase the wealth and strength of the Kingdome, beget in all his Majesties Subjects of this Kingdome, a perfect unity amongst themselves, after the too long continued division amongst them; So His Majesty assures himselfe, that all his
15 Subjects of this his Kingdom (duely considering the great and inestimable benefits which they may find in this Peace) will with all duty render due obedience thereunto. And We in his Majesties name, doe hereby declare, that all persons so rendering due obedience to the said Peace, shall be protected,
20 cherished, countenanced, and supported by his Majesty, and his Royall Authority, according to the true intent and meaning of the said Articles of Peace.

Given at our Castle of *Kilkenny*   God Save The
    17 *January*, 1648.   King.

---

25 Articles of Peace, made, concluded, accorded and agreed upon, by and between his Excellency *James* Lord Marquesse of *Ormond,* Lord Lieutenant General, and Generall

of his Majesties Kingdome of *Ireland,* for and on the behalfe of His most Excellent Majesty, by vertue of the authority wherewith the said Lord Lieutenant is intrusted,
on the one part; And the Generall Assembly of the Roman
5 Catholickes of the said Kingdome, for and on the behalfe
of His Majesties Roman Catholicke Subjects of the same,
on the other part.

*HIS Majesties Roman Catholique Subjects, as thereunto
bound by allegiance, duty and nature, doe most hum-*
10 *bly and freely acknowledge and recognize their Soveraigne
Lord King* Charles *to be lawfull and undoubted King of this
Kingdom of* Ireland, *and other his Highnesse Realms and
Dominions; And his Majesties said Roman Catholicke Subjects, apprehending with a deep sence, the sad condition*
15 *whereunto His Majesty is reduced. As a further testimony of
their Loyalty: Doe declare, that they and their posterity for
ever, to the utmost of their power, even to the expence of their
blood and fortunes will maintaine and uphold His Majesty,
His Heires and lawfull Successors their Rights, Prerogatives,*
20 *Government and Authority, and thereunto freely and heartily will render all due obedience.*

*Of which faithfull and loyall recognition and declaration
so seasonably made by the said Roman Catholickes; His Majesty is graciously pleased to accept, and accordingly to owne*
25 *them His loyall and dutifull Subjects; And is further graciously pleased to extend unto them the following graces and
securities.*

1. In primis, It is concluded, accorded, and agreed upon, by and between the said Lord Lieutenant, for, and on the behalfe of His most Excellent Majesty; And the said General Assembly, for and on the behalf of the said Roman Catholick

5 Subjects, and His Majestie is graciously pleased, that it shall be enacted by act to be passed in the next Parliament to be held in this Kingdome, that all and every the professors of the Roman Catholicke Religion within the said Kingdom, shall be free and exempt from all mulctes, penalties, restraints and

10 inhibitions that are, or may be imposed upon them by any law, declaration of law, Statute, Custome or usage whatso-the free exercise of the Roman Catholick Religion: And that it shall be likewise enacted that the said Roman Catholicks or any of them shall not be questioned or molested in their per-

15 sons, goods or estates, for any matter or cause whatsoever for, concerning, or by reason of the free exercise of their Religion, by vertue of any power, authority, statute, law, or useage whatsoever; And that it shall be further enacted, that no Roman Catholique in this Kingdome shall be compelled to

20 exercise any Religion, forme of devotion or Divine service other then such as shall be agreeable to their Conscience, and that they shall not be prejudiced or molested in their persons, goods or estates for not observing, using or hearing the Booke of Common-Prayer or any other forme of devotion or divine

25 service by vertue of any coulor or Statute made in the second yeare of Queen *Elizabeth,* or by vertue or coullor of any other law; statute useage or custome whatsoever, for or concerning ever made or declared, or to be made or declared; And that

it shall be further enacted, that the Professors of the Roman Catholicke Religion, or any of them be not bound or oblieged to take the Oath commonly called, the Oath of *Supremacy* expressed in the Statute of 2 *Elizabeth c.* 1 or in any other Statute or Statutes; And that the said Oath shall not be tendered unto them, and that the refusall of the said oath shall not redound to the prejudice of them, or any of them, they taking the oath of Allegiance *in hæc verba, viz.* I A. B. *Doe hereby acknowledge, professe, testifie and declare in my conscience, before God and the world, that our Soveraigne Lord King* Charles, *is lawfull and rightfull King of this Realme, and of other His Majesties Dominions and Countries; and I will beare Faith and true Allegiance to His Majesty, and His Heires and Successors, and Him and them will defend to the uttermost of my power against all Conspiracies and Attempts whatsoever which shall be made against His or Their Crowne and Dignitie, and do my best endeavour to disclose and make knowne to His Majesty, His Heires and Successors, or to the Lord Deputy, or other His Majesties cheife Governour or Governors for the time being, all Treason or Traiterous conspiracies which I shall know or heare to be entended against His Majesty or any of them, And I doe make this Recognition and acknowledgment, heartily, willingly and truly, upon the true faith of a Christian, so helpe me God, &c.* Neverthelesse the said Lord Lieutenant doth not hereby intend that any thing in these concessions contained shall extend, or be construed to extend to the granting of Churches, Church-livings, or the exercise of Jurisdiction, the authority of the said Lord

Lieutenant not extending so far, yet the said Lord Lieutenant is authorized to give the said Roman Catholicks full assurance as hereby the said Lord Lieutenant doth give unto the
said Roman Catholicks full assurance that they or any of them
5 shall not be molested in the possession which they have at present of the Churches and Church-livings, or of the Exercise of
their respective Jurisdictions as they now exercise the same
untill such time as His Majesty upon a ful consideration of the
desires of the said Roman Catholicks in a free Parliament to
10 be held in this Kingdome shall declare his further pleasure.

2. Item, it is concluded, accorded, and agreed upon, by
and between the said parties, and His Majestie is further graciously pleased, that a free Parliament shall be held in this
Kingdome within six months after the date of these Articles
15 of Peace, or as soon after as *Thomas* Lord Viscount *Dillon* of
Costologh Lord President of *Connaght, Donnogh* Lord Viscount *Muskery, Francis* Lord Baron of *Athunry, Allexander
Mac Donnell* Esquire, Sir *Lucas Dillon* Knight, Sir *Nicholas
Plunket* Knight, Sir *Richard Barnewall* Baronet, *Jefferey
20 Browne, Donnogh O Callaghan, Tyrlagh O Neile, Miles
Reily,* and *Gerrald Fennell* Esquires, or the major part of
them will desire the same, so that by possibility it may be held,
and that in the mean time, and untill the Articles of these
presents, agreed to be passed in Parliament be accordingly
25 passed, the same shall be inviolably observed as to the matters
therein conteined, as if they were enacted in Parliament; And
that in case a Parliament be not called and held in this Kingdom within two yeares next after the date of these Articles of

peace, Then His Majesties Lord Lieutenant, or other His
Majesties cheif Governour or Governours of this Kingdome
for the time being, will at the request of the said *Thomas* Lord
Viscount *Dillon* of *Costollogh* Lord President of *Connaght,*
5 *Donnogh* Lord Viscount *Muskery, Francis* Lord Baron of
Athunry, Allexander Mac Donnell Esquires, Sir *Lucas Dillon*
Knight, Sir *Nicholas Plunket* Knight, Sir *Richard Barnewall*
Baronet, *Geffery Browne, Donnogh O Callaghan, Tyrlagh
O Neile, Miles Reily, and Gerrald Fennell* Esquires, or the
10 major part of them, call a Generall Assembly of the Lords
and Commons of this Kingdom, to attend upon the said
Lord Lieutenant or other his Majesties cheife Governour or
Governours of this Kingdom for the time being, in some convenient place, for the better setling of the affairs of the King-
15 dome; And it is further concluded, accorded and agreed by,
and between the said parties, that all matters that by these
Articles are agreed upon to be passed in Parliament, shall be
transmitted into *England,* according to the usuall forme, to be
passed in the said Parliament, and that the said Acts so agreed
20 upon, and so to be passed, shall receive no dis-junction or alteration here, or in *England;* Provided that nothing shall be concluded by both, or either of the said Houses of Parliament,
which may bring prejudice to any of his Majesties Protestant
party; or their adherents or to his Majest. Roman Catholicke
25 subjects or their adherents, other then such things as upon this
Treaty are concluded to be done, or such things as may be
proper for the Committee of priviledges of either or both
Houses to take cognizance of, as in such cases heretofore hath

been accustomed, and other then such matters as his Majesty
will be graciously pleased to declare his further pleasure in,
to be passed in Parliament for the satisfaction of his Subjects,
and other then such things as shall be propounded to either or
5 both houses by his Majesties Lord Lieut. or other cheif Governor or Governors of this Kingdome for the time being, during the said Parliament, for the advancement of his Majesties
service, and the Peace of the Kingdom, which clause is to
admit no construction which may trench upon the Articles
10 of peace or any of them and that both houses of Parliament
may consider what they shall thinke convenient touching the
repeale or suspension of the Statute commonly called *Poynings* Act, entitled an Act, That no Parliament be holden in
that land, untill the Acts be certified into *England*.

15   3. Item, It is further concluded, accorded and agreed upon,
by, and between the said parties, and his Majesty is graciously
pleased; that all Acts, Ordinances, and Orders made by both,
or either houses of Parliament, to the blemish, dishonour or
prejudice of his Majesties Roman Catholicke Subjects of this
20 Kingdome, or any of them, sithence the seventh of *August*
1641. shall be vacated; and that the same and all Exemplifi-
cations and other Acts which continue the memory of them
be made voide by Act to be past in the next Parliament to be
held in this Kingdome, and that in the meane time the said
25 Acts or Ordinances, or any of them shall bee no prejudice to
the said Roman Catholickes or any of them.

    4. Item, It is also concluded and agreed upon, and his Maj-
esty is likewise graciously pleased, that all indictments, at-

tainders, outlawries in this Kingdome, and all the processes
and other proceedings thereupon, and all Letters, Pattents,
Grants, Leases, Customes, Bonds, Recognizances, and all
Records, Act or Acts, Office or Offices, Inquisitions, and all
5 other things depending upon, or taken by reason of the said
Indictments, Attainders or outlawries, sithence the seventh
day of *August,* 1641. in prejudice of the said Catholickes,
their Heirs, Executors, Administrators or Assignes, or any
of them, or the widdowes of them, or any of them shall
10 be vacated and made void in such sort as no memory shall
remain thereof, to the blemish, dishonour or prejudice of the
said Catholikes, their heires, executors, administrators, or assignes, or any of them, or the widows of them, or any of
them; and that to be done when the said *Thomas* Lord Vis-
15 count *Dillon of Costologh* Lord President of *Connaght, Don
nogh* Lord Visc. *Muskerry, Francis* Lord Baron of *Athunry,
Alexander Mac Donnell* Esquire, Sir *Lucas Dillon* Knight,
Sir *Nicholas Plunket* Knight, Sir *Richard Barnwell* Baronet,
Jeffery Brown, Donnogh O Callaghan, Tyrlagh O Neal, Miles
20 *Reilie* and *Gerrald Fennell* Esquires, or the major part of
them shall desire the same, so that by possibilitie it may be
done, and in the mean time that no such inditements, attainders, outlawries, processes, or any other proceeding thereupon, or any letters, patents, grants, leases, custodiums, bonds,
25 recognizances, or any Record or acts, office or offices, inquisitions, or any other thing depending upon, or by reason of
the said indictments, attainders, or outlawries, shall in any
sort prejudice the said Roman Catholikes, or any of them, but

that they and every of them shall bee forthwith upon perfection of these Articles, restored to their respective possessions,
and hereditaments respectively, provided that no man shall
be questioned by reason hereof, for measne rates, or wastes,
5 saving wilfull wastes committed after the first day of *May*
last past.

5. Item, It is likewise concluded, accorded, and agreed, and
his Majesty is graciously pleased, that as soon as possible may
be, all impediments which may hinder the said Roman Cath-
10 olikes, to sit or vote in the next intended Parliament, or to
choose, or to be chosen Knights, and Burgesse, to sit or vote
there, shall be removed, and that before the said Parliament.

6. Item, it is concluded accorded, and agreed upon, and
his Majestie is further graciously pleased, that all debts shall
15 remain as they were upon the 23. of *October* 1641. Notwithstanding any disposition made, or to be made, by vertue or
colour of any attainder, outlawrie, fugacie, or other forfeiture,
and that no disposition or grant made, or to be made of any
such debts, by vertue of any attainder, outlawrie, fugacie, or
20 other forfeiture shall be of force, and this to be passed as an
act in the next Parliament.

7. Item, It is further concluded, accorded, and agreed upon, and his Majesty is graciously pleased; that for the securing
of the Estates or reputed estates of the Lords, Knights, gen-
25 tlemen and freeholders, or reputed freeholders, as well of
Connaght, and county of *Clare,* or country of Thomond as of
the counties of *Limerick* and *Tipperary,* the same to be secured
by Act of Parliament, according to the intent of the 25. Ar-

ticle, of the graces granted in the fourth year of his Majesties
Reign the tenor whereof for so much as concerneth the same
doth ensue in these words, *viz.* Wee are graciously pleased,
that for the Inhabitants of *Connaght,* and country of *Tho-*
5 *mond,* and county of *Clare,* that their several estates shall be
confirmed unto them, and their heires against us, and our
heires and successors, by Act to be passed in the next Parliament to be holden in *Ireland,* to the end the same may never
hereafter be brought into any further question, by Us or our
10 Heires and Successors. In which Act of Parliament so to be
passed, you are to take care, that all tenures *in capite,* and all
rents and services as are now due, or which ought to be
answered unto us out of the said lands and premises, by any
letters pattents, past thereof, since the first year of King *Henry*
15 *the eight.* or found by any office taken from the said first
year of King *Henry the eight,* untill the 21. of *July* 1645.
whereby our late dear father or any his Predecessors, actually
received any profit, by wardship, liveries, primer-seisins,
measne, rates, ousterlemains or fines of alienations without
20 licence, be again reserved unto us, or Heires and successors,
and all the rest of the premises to be holden of our Castle of
Athlone by Knights service, according to our said late Fathers
letters, notwithstanding any tenures *in capite* found for Us
by office, since the 21. of *July* 1615. and not appearing in any
25 such letters patents, or offices, within which rule, his Majesty
is likewise graciously pleased, that the said lands in the Counties of *Limerick* and *Tipperarie* be included, but to be held by
such rents and tenures only, as they were in the fourth year

of his Majesties Reign; Provided alwaies that the said Lords,
Knights, Gentlemen and Freeholders of the said Province of
Connaght, county of *Clare,* and Countrey of *Thomond,* and
Counties of *Tipperarie* and *Limerick* shall have and enjoy the
5 full benefit of such composition and agreement which shall
be made with his most Excellent Majestie, for the Court of
Wards, tenures, respits, and issues of homage, any clause in
this Article to the contrary notwithstanding; and as for the
lands within the counties of *Kilkennie* and *Wickloe;* unto
10 which his Majestie was intituled by offices, taken or found in
the time of the Earl of *Straffords* government in this Kingdom, His Majestie is further graciously pleased that the State
thereof, shall be considered in the next intended Parliament,
where his Majestie will assent unto that which shall be just
15 and honourable, and that the like act of limitation of his Majesties Titles, for the securitie of the estates of his Subjects of
this Kingdome be passed in the said Parliament as was enacted in the 21. year of his late Majestie *King James* his Reign
in England.

20   8. Item, it is further concluded, accorded, and agreed upon, and His Majestie is further graciously pleased, That all
incapacities imposed upon the Natives of this Kingdome or
any of them, as Natives, by any Act of Parliament, Provisoes
in Patents or otherwise, be taken away by Act to be passed in
25 the said Parliament; and that they may be enabled to erect one
or more Innes of Court in or neer the city of *Dublin* or elsewhere, as shall be thought fit by his Majesties Lord Lieutenant, or other chief Governour or Governours of this Kingdom

for the time being; and in case the said Innes of Court shall be
erected before the first day of the next Parliament, then the
same shall be in such place as his Majesties Lord Lieutenant,
or other chief Governor or Governors of this Kingdom for
5 the time being, by and with the advice and consent of the said
Thomas Lord Viscount *Dillon* of *Costologh*, Lord President
of *Connaght, Donnogh* Lord Viscount *Muskerrie, Francis*
Lord Baron of *Athunrie, Alexander Mac Donnell* Esquire,
Sir *Lucas Dillon* Knight, Sir *Nicholas Plunket* Knight, Sir
10 *Richard Barnwall* Baronet, *Jefferie Brown, Donnogh O Callaghan, Tyrlagh O Neal, Miles Reily, Gerrald Fennell* Esquires, or any seven or more of them shall thinke fit; And
that such students natives of this Kingdom as shall be therein,
may take and receive the usuall degrees accustomed in any
15 Innes of court, they taking the insuing oath, *viz.* I A. B. *Doe
hereby acknowledge professe, testifie and declare in my conscience, before God and the world that our Soveraign Lord
K.* Charles, *is lawful and rightful King of this Realm, and of
other His Majesties Dominions and Countries; and I will
20 bear Faith and true Allegiance to His Majesty, and His Heirs
and Successors, and Him and them will defend to the uttermost of my power against all conspiracies and attempts whatsoever, which shall be made against his or their Crown and
Dignity, and do my best endeavour to disclose and make
25 known to His Majesty, His Heires and Successors, or to the
Lord Deputy, or other His Majesties cheife Governour or
Governors for the time being, all Treason or Traiterous conspiracies which I shall know or heare to be entended against*

His Majesty or any of them, And I doe make this Recognition
and acknowledgment, heartily, willingly and truly, upon the
true faith of a Christian, so help me God, &c. And his Majestie is further graciously pleased that his Majesties Roman
5 Catholike Subjects may erect and keep free schools for education of youths in this Kingdom, any law or statute to the contrarie notwithstanding; and that all the matters assented unto
in this Article be passed as Acts of Parliament in the said next
Parliament.

10   9. Item, It is further concluded, accorded, and agreed
upon, by, and between the said parties, and his Majestie is
graciously pleased; That places of command, honour, profit
and trust in his Majesties Armies in this Kingdom shall be
upon perfection of these Articles actually and by particular
15 instances conferred upon his Roman Catholike subjects of
this Kingdom, and that upon the distribution conferring and
disposing of the places of command, honour, profit, and trust
in his Majesties Armies in this Kingdome, for the future no
difference shall be made between the said Roman Catholikes,
20 and other his Majesties Subjects. But that such distribution
shall be made with equall indifferency according to their
respective merits and abilities; and that all His Majesties Subjects of this Kingdom, as well Roman Catholikes as others,
may for his Majesties service, and their own security, arme
25 themselves the best they may, wherein they shall have all fit-
ting incouragement; And it is further concluded, accorded
and agreed upon, by and between the said parties, and his
Majestie is further graciously pleased; That places of com-

mand, honour, profit, and trust in the civill government in
this Kingdome, shall be upon passing of the Bills in these
Articles mentioned in the next Parliament, actually and by
particular instances conferred upon his Majesties Roman
5 Catholike subjects of this Kingdome, and that in the distribution, conferring and disposall of the places of command,
honour, profit, and trust, in the civill government; for the
future no difference shall be made between the said Roman
Catholikes, and other his Majesties Subjects, but that such
10 distribution shall bee made with equall indifferencie, according to their respective merits and abilities, and that in the
distribution of ministeriall officers or places which now are,
or hereafter shall be void in this Kingdom, equalitie shall be
used to the Roman Catholike Natives of this Kingdom, as to
15 other his Majesties Subjects; and that the command of Forts,
Castles, Garrison Towns, and other places of importance in
this Kingdom, shall be conferred upon his Majesties Roman
Catholike Subjects of this Kingdom upon perfection of these
Articles actually and by particular instances, and that in the
20 distribution conferring and disposall of Forts, Castles, Garrison Towns, and other places of importance in this Kingdome, no difference shall be made between his Majesties
Roman Catholike Subjects of this Kingdom, and other his
Majesties Subjects, but that such distribution shall be made
25 with equall indifferencie, according to their respective merits
and abilities, and that untill full settlement in Parliament
fifteen thousand foot, and two thousand and five hundred
Horse of the Roman Catholikes of this Kingdom shall be of

the standing Armie of this Kingdome: and that untill full
settlement in Parliament as aforesaid, the said Lord Lieutenant or other chief Governour or Governours of this Kingdom
for the time being, and the said *Thomas* Lord Viscount *Dillon*
5 of *Costologh* Lord President of *Connaght, Donnogh* Lord
Visc. *Muskerry, Francis* Lord Baron of *Athunry, Alexander
Mac Donnell* Esquire, Sir *Lucas Dillon* Knight, Sir *Nicholas Plunket* Knight; Sir *Richard Barnwall* Baronet, *Jeffery
Brown, Donnogh O Callaghan, Tyrlagh O Neal, Miles Reilie*
10 and *Gerrald Fennell* Esquires, or any seven or more of them,
the said *Thomas* Lord Viscount *Dillon* of *Costologh,* Lord
President of *Connaght, Donnogh* Lord Viscount *Muskerie,
Francis* Lord Baron of *Athunry, Alexander Mac Donnell*
Esquire, Sir *Lucas Dillon* Knight, Sir *Nicholas Plunket*
15 Knight, Sir *Richard Barnwall, Jefferie Brown, Donnogh
O Callaghan, Tyrlagh O Neal, Miles Reily.* and *Gerrald
Fennell* Esquires, shall diminish or adde unto the said num-
ber, as they shall see cause from time to time.

10. Item, it is further concluded, accorded and agreed
20 upon, by and between the said parties, and his Majesty is
further graciously pleased, that his Majestie will accept of
the yeerly rent, or annuall fum of twelve thousand pounds
sterling, to be applotted with indifferencie and equalitie, and
consented to be paid to his Majestie, his heires and successors
25 in Parliament, for and in lieu of the Court of Wards in this
Kingdom, tenures in Capite, Common Knights-service, and
all other tenures within the cognizance of that Court, and for
and in lieu of all Wardships, primer seizins, fines, ouster-

lemains, liveries, intrusions, alienations, measne rates, re-
leases, and all other profits, within the cognizance of the
said Court, or incident to the said tenures or any of them, or
fines to accrew to his Majestie by reason of the said tenures
5 or any of them, and for and in lieu of the respits and issues of
homage, and fines for the same. And the said yearly rent
being so applotted and consented unto in Parliament as aforesaid, then a Bill to be agreed on in the said Parliament to
be passed as an Act for the securing of the said yeerly Rent,
10 or annuall sum of twelve thousand pounds to be applotted as
aforesaid, and for the extinction and taking away of the said
Court, and other matters aforesaid in this Article contained.
And it is further agreed, that reasonable compositions shall
bee accepted for Wardships fallen since the 23. of *October*
15 1641. and already granted, and that no wardships fallen and
not granted or that shall fall, shall be passed untill the successe of this Article shall appear; and if his Majesty be secured
as aforesaid, then all Wardships fallen since the said 23. of
Octob. are to be included in the agreement aforesaid, upon
20 composition to be made with such as have grants as aforesaid,
which composition to be made with the grantees since the
time aforesaid, is to be left to indifferent persons, and the
umpirage to the said Lord Lieutenant.

11. Item. It is further concluded, accorded, and agreed
25 upon, by and between the said parties, and his Majesty is
further graciously pleased, That no Nobleman or Peer of this
Realm in Parliament shall be hereafter capable of more Proxies then two, and that blanck Proxies shall be hereafter totally

dis-allowed; and that if such Noble Men or Peers of this Realm
as have no Estates in this Kingdom do not within five yeares,
to begin from the conclusion of these Articles purchase in this
Kingdom as followeth, *viz.* A Lord Baron 200 *l. per annum,*
5 a Lord Viscount 400 *li. per annum* and an Earl 600 *l. per
annum,* a Marquesse 800 *l. per annum,* a Duke 1000 *l. per
annum,* shall loose their votes in Parliament untill such time
as they shall afterwards acquire such estates respectively; and
that none be admitted in the House of Commons, but such
10 as shall bee estated, and resident within this Kingdome.

12 Item, It is further concluded, accorded and agreed
upon, by and between the said parties, and his Majesty is
further graciously pleased; that as for and concerning the
independency of the Parliament of *Ireland* on the Parliament
15 of *England,* his Majesty will leave both houses of Parliament
in this Kingdom to make such declaration therein as shall be
agreeable to the Laws of the Kingdome of *Ireland.*

13 Item, It is further concluded and agreed upon, by and
between the said parties, and his Majesty is further graciously
20 pleased, that the Councel-Table shall containe it selfe within
its proper bounds in handling matters of State and weight fit
for that place, amongst which the Pattents of Plantation and
the offices whereupon those Grants are founded to be handled
as matters of State, and to be heard and determined by his Maj-
25 esties Lord Lieutenant, or other chiefe Governour or Governours for the time being, and the Councell publickly at the
Councell-Board, and not otherwise, But titles between party
and party grown after these patents granted, are to be left to

the ordinary course of Law, and that the Councel-Table do
not hereafter intermedle with common businesse, that is,
within the cognizance of the ordinary Courts, nor with the
altering of possessions of Lands, nor make, nor use private
5 Orders, hearings or references, concerning any such matter,
nor grant any injunction or order for stay of any suites in any
civill cause; And that parties grieved for or by reason of any
proceedings formerly had there, may commence their suites
and prosecute the same in any of his Majestics Courts of Jus-
10 tice or Equity for remedy of their pretended rights, without
any restraint or interruption from his Majesty; or otherwise
by the cheife Governour or Governours, and Councell of this
Kingdome; And that the proceedings in the respective Presi-
dency Courts, shall be pursuant, and according to his Maj-
15 esties printed Book of Instructions, and that they shall containe themselves within the limits prescribed by that Book,
when the Kingdom shall be restored to such a degree of quietnesse, as they be not necessarily enforced to exceed the same.

14 Item it is further concluded, accorded and agreed
20 upon, by and between the said parties and his Majesty is
further graciously pleased: That as for and concerning one
Statute made in this Kingdome, in the eleventh year of the
Reigne of Queene *Elizabeth* intituled, an Act for staying of
Wooll, Flockes, Tallow, and other necessaries within this
25 Realme; And another Statute made in the said Kingdome, in
the twelfth year of the Reign of the said Queen, intituled an
Act

and one other Statute made in the said Kingdome, in the 13
year of the Reign of the said late Queen, intituled An Exem-
planation of the Act made in a Session of this Parliament for
the staying of Wooll, Flocks, Tallow; and other wares and
5 commodities mentioned in the said Act, and certaine Articles
added to the same Act, all concerning staple or native commodities of this Kingdom shall be repealed, if it shal be so
thought fit in the Parliament (excepting for Wooll and Wooll-
fells, and that such indifferent persons as shall be agreed on
10 by the said Lord Lieutenant, and the said *Thomas* Lord Viscount *Dillon* of *Costollogh* Lord President of *Connaght,*
Donnogh Lord Viscount *Muskery, Francis* Lord Baron of
Athunry, Allexander Mac Donnell Esquires, Sir *Lucas Dillon*
Knight, Sir *Nicholas Plunket* Knight, Sir *Richard Barnewall*
15 Baronet, *Geffery Browne, Donnogh O Callaghan, Tyrlagh*
O Neile, Miles Reily, and Gerrald Fennell Esquires, or any
seven or more of them shall be authorized by Commission
under the great Seal, to moderate and ascertain the rates of
merchandize to be exported or imported out of, or into this
20 Kingdome, as they shall think fit.

15 Item, It is concluded, accorded, and agreed, by and
between the said parties, and his Majesty is graciously pleased,
that all and every person and persons within this Kingdome
pretending to have suffered by offices found of several Coun-
25 tries, Territories, Lands and Hereditaments in the Province
of *Ulster,* and other Provinces of this Kingdome in or since the
first year of King *James* his Reign, or by attainders or forfeitures, or by pretence and coulor thereof, since the said first

year of King *James* or by other Acts depending on the said
offices, attainders and forfeitures may petition his Majesty in
Parliament for reliefe and redresse; and if after examination
it shal appeare to His Majesty, the said persons, or any of
5 them have been injured, then His Majesty will prescribe a
course to repaire the person or persons so suffering according
to Justice and honor.

16 Item, It is further concluded, accorded and agreed
upon by, and between the said parties, and His Majesty is
10 graciously pleased; that as to the particular cases of *Maurice*
Lord Viscount de *Rupe & Fermoy, Arthur* Lord Viscount
Iveagh, Sir *Edward Fitz* Gerrald of *Cloanglish* Baronet,
*Charles mac Carty Reag, Roger Moore, Anthony Mare, Wil-
liam Fitz* Gerrald, *Anthony Linch, John Lacy, Collo mac*
15 *Brienmac Mahowne, Daniel Castigni, Edmond Fitz* Gerrald
of *Ballimartir, Lucas Keating, Theobald Roch Fitz Miles,
Thomas Fitz* Gerrald of the *Vally, John Bourke* of *Logh-
maske, Edmond Fitz* Gerrald of *Ballimalloe, James Fitz
William* Gerrald of *Glinane,* and *Edward Sutton,* they may
20 petition His Majesty in the next Parliament, whereupon His
Majesty will take such consideration of them as shall be just
and fit.

17 Item it is likewise concluded, accorded, and agreed
upon, by and between the said parties, and his Majesty is
25 graciously pleased, That the Citizens, Free-men, Burgesses
and former Inhabitants of the City of *Corke,* Townes of
Youghall and *Downegarven* shall be forthwith upon perfection of these Articles, restored to their respective possessions

and Estates in the said City and Townes, respectively where
the same extends not to the endangering of the said Garrisons
in the said City and Townes. In which case so many of the
said Citizens and Inhabitants as shall not be admitted to the
5 present possession of their houses within the said City and
Towns, shall be afforded a valuable annuall rent for the same
untill settlement in Parliament, at which time they shall bee
restored to those their possessions. And it is further agreed,
and his Majesty is graciously pleased, that the said Citizens,
10 Free-men, Burgesses, and Inhabitants of the said City of
Corke, and Townes of *Youghall* and *Downegraven* respectively shall be enabled in convenient time before the next
Parliament to be held in this Kingdome to chuse and returne
Burgesses into the same Parliament.

15   18. Item it is further concluded, accorded and agreed
upon, by and between the said parties, and his Majesty is
further graciously pleased that an Act of oblivion be past in
the next Parliament, to extend to all his Majesties Subjects
of this Kingdom and their adherents, of all Treasons and
20 offences, capitall, criminall and personall, and other offences
of what nature, kind, or quality soever, in such manner as if
such Treasons or offences had never been committed, perpe-
trated or don; That the said Act do extend to the Heires,
Children, Kindred, Executors, Administrators, Wives, Wid-
25 owes, Dowagers or Assignes of such of the said Subjects and
their adherents who dyed on, before, or since the 23 of *October*
1641. that the said Act doe relate to the first day of the next
Parliament, that the said Act doe extend to all bodies Politicke

and Corporate, and their respective successors, and unto all
Cities, Burroughs, Counties, Baronies, Hundreds, Townes,
Villages, Thitlings and every of them within this Kingdom,
for and concerning all and every of the said offences, or any
5 other offence or offences, in them, or any of them committed,
or done by his Majesties said Subjects, or their adherents, or
any of them, before, in, or since the 23 of *October,* 1641. Provided this Act shall not extend to be construed to pardon any
offence or offences, for which any person or persons have been
10 convicted or attainted of Record at any time before the 23 day
of *October* in the year of our Lord 1641. That this Act shall
extend to Piracies, and all other offences committed upon the
Sea, by His Majesties said Subjects, or their adherents, or any
of them, That in this Act of oblivion, words of release, ac-
15 quittall and discharge be incerted, that no person or persons,
bodies Politicke, or Corporate, Counties, Cities, Burroughs,
Baronnies, Hundreds, Townes, Villages, Thitlings, or any of
them within this Kingdom, included within the said Act be
troubled, impeached, sued, inquieted, or molested, for, or by
20 reason of any offence, matter or thing whatsoever, comprised
within the said Act: and the said Act shall extend to all rents,
goods, and chattles, taken, detained or growne due to the Subjects of the one party from the other since the 23 of *October*
1641 to the date of these Articles of Peace; and also to all
25 customes, rents, arrears of rents, prizes, recognizances, bonds,
fines, forfeitures, penalties and to all other profits, perquisits
and dues which were due, or did or should accrew to His
Majesty on, before, or since the 23 of *October* 1641 untill the

perfection of these Articles, and likewise to all measne, rates, fines, of what nature soever, recognizances, Judgements, Executions thereupon, and penalties whatsoever, and to all other profit due to his Majesty since the said 23 of *October* and be-
5 fore, untill the perfection of these Articles, for by reason, or which lay within the Survey or recognizance of the Court of Wards; and also to all respits, issues of homage and fines for the same; provided this shall not extend to discharge or remit any of the Kings debts or subsidies due before the said 23 of
10 *October* 1641 which were then or before levyed, or taken by the Sheriffes, Commissioners, Receivers, or Collectors, and not then or before accounted for, or since disposed to the publick use of the said Roman Catholick subjects, but that such persons may be brought to account for the same after full
15 settlement in Parliament, and not before, unlesse by, and with the advice and consent of the said *Thomas* Lord Viscount *Dillon* of *Costologh* Lord President of *Connaght, Donnogh* Lord Viscount *Muskery, Francis* Lord Baron of *Athunry, Allexander Mac Donnell* Esquire, Sir *Lucas Dillon* Knight,
20 Sir *Nicholas Plunket* Knight, Sir *Richard Barnewall* Baronet, *Jefferey Browne, Donnogh O Callaghan, Tyrlagh O Neile, Miles Reily,* and *Gerrald Fennell* Esquires, or any seaven or more of them, as the said Lord Lieut. otherwise shall thinke fit; Provided that such barrowys and inhumain crimes as
25 shal be particularized and agreed upon by the said Lord Lieutenant, and the said *Thomas* Lord Viscount *Dillon* of *Costollogh* Lord President of *Connagh* Lord Viscount *Muskery, Francis* Lord Baron of *Athunry, Allexander Mac Don-*

nell Esquire, Sir *Lucas Dillon* Knight, Sir *Nicholas Plunket*
Knight, Sir *Richard Barnewall* Baronet, *Jeffry Browne, Don-*
nogh O Callaghan, Tirlagh O Neile, Miles Reily, and *Gerrald*
Fennell Esquires, or any seven or more of them, as to the actors
5 and procurers thereof bee left to bee tryed and adjudged by
such indifferent Commissioners as shall be agreed upon by
the said Lord Lieutenant, and the said *Thomas* Lord Viscount
Dillon of *Costollogh* Lord President of *Connaght, Donnogh*
Lord Viscount *Muskery, Francis* Lord Baron of *Athunry, Al-*
10 *lexander Mac Donnell* Esq. Sir *Lucas Dillon* Kt. Sir *Nicholas*
Plunket Kt. Sir *Richard Barnewal* Baronet, *Jeffrey Browne,*
Donnogh O Callaghan, Tyrlagh O Neile, Miles Reily and
Gerrald Fennell Esquires, or any seven or more of them; And
that the power of the said Commissioners shall continue onely
15 for two yeares next ensuing the date of their commission,
which commission is to issue within six months after the date
of these Articles; Provided also, that the commissioners to
bee agreed on for tryall of the said particular crimes to be excepted; shall hear, order and determine all cases of trust where
20 reliefe may or ought in equity to be afforded against all manner of persons according to the equity and circumstances of
every such cases, and His Majesties cheife Governor or Governours and other Magistrats for the time being, in all His
Majesties Courts of Justice and other his Majesties Officers of
25 what condition or quality soever be bound and required to
take notice of, and pursue the said Act of oblivion without
pleading or suite to bee made for the same, and that no Clerke
or other Officers doe make out or write out any manner of

writs, processes, summons or other precept for, concerning,
or by reason of any matter, cause, or thing whatsoever released, forgiven, discharged, or to be forgiven by the said Act
under pain of 20 *li.* sterling, And that no Sheriffe or other
5 Officer, do execute any such writ, processe, summons or precept; and that no Record, writing or memory, do remain of
any offence or offences, released or forgiven, or mentioned to
be forgiven by this Act; and that all other clauses usually inserted in Acts of generall pardon or oblivion, enlarging His
10 Majesties grace and mercy, nor herein particularised, bee incerted and comprised in the said Act when the Bill shall be
drawn up with the exceptions already expressed and none
other. Privided always that the said Act of oblivion shall not
extend to any treason, felony, or other offence or offences
15 which shall be committed or don from or after the date of
these Articles untill the first day of the before mentioned next
Parliament, to be held in this Kingdome; Provided also that
any Act or Acts which shall be done by vertue, pretence, or
in pursuance of these Articles of peace agreed upon, or any
20 Act or Acts which shall be don by vertue, coulor or pretence
of the power or authority used, or exercised by and amongst
the Confederate Roman Catholicks after the date of the said
Articles, and before the said publication, shall not be accounted, taken, construed, or to be, Treason, Felony, or other
25 offence to be excepted out of the said Act of oblivion; Provided
likewise that the said Act of oblivion shall not extend unto any
person or persons that will not obey and submit unto the peace
concluded and agreed on by these Articles; Provided further

that the said Act of oblivion or any thing in this Article con-
tained shall not hinder or interrupt the said *Tho.* Lord Visc.
Dillon of *Costologh* Lord Presid. of *Connaght, Donnogh*
Lord Viscount *Muskery, Francis* Lord Baron of *Athunry,*
5 *Allexander Mac Donnell* Esquire, Sir *Lucas Dillon* Knight,
Sir *Nicholas Plunket* Knight, Sir *Richard Barnewall* Baronet,
*Jeffrey Browne, Donnogh O Callaghan, Tyrlagh O Neile,
Miles Reily,* and *Gerrald Fennell* Esquires, or any seven or
more of them, to call to an account, and proceed against the
10 Councell and Congregation, and the respective Supream
Councells Commissioners generall, appointed hitherto from
time to time by the Confederate Catholickes to manage their
affaires, or any other person or persons accomptable to an accompt for their respective receipts and disbursements, since
15 the beginning of their respective imployments under the said
Confederate Catholickes, or to acquit or release any arrears of
excises, customes, or publicke taxes to be accounted for, since
the 23 of *Octo.* 1641. and not disposed of hitherto, to the publicke use, but that the parties therein concerned may be called
20 to an account for the same as aforesaid, by the said *Thomas*
Lord Viscount *Dillon* of *Costologh* Lord President of *Connaght, Donnogh* Lord Viscount *Muskery, Francis* Lord Baron
of *Athunry, Allexander Mac Donnell* Esquire, Sir *Lucas
Dillon* Knight, Sir *Nicholas Plunket* Knight, Sir *Richard
25 Barnewall* Baronet, *Jeffrey Browne, Donnogh O Callaghan,
Tyrlagh O Neile, Miles Reily* and *Gerrald Fennell* Esquires,
or any seaven or more of them, the said Act or any thing
therein contained to the contrary notwithstanding.

19 Item, it is further concluded, accorded and agreed upon, by and between the said parties, and his Majestie is graciously pleased, That an Act be passed in the next Parliament, prohibiting that neither the Lord Deputy, or other chief Governor, or Governors, Lord Chancellor, Lord High Treasurer, Vice-Treasurer, Chancellor, or any of the Barons of the Exchequer, Privie Councel or Judges of the foure courts be farmers of his Majesties customes within this Kingdom.

20. Item, It is likewise concluded, accorded and agreed, and his Majestie is graciously pleased, that an Act of Parliament passe in this Kingdom against Monopolies, such as was enacted in *England* 21. *Jacobi Regis,* with a further clause of repealing of all grants of Monopolies in this Kingdom, and that Commissioners be agreed upon by the said Lord lieutenant, and the said *Thomas* Lord Viscount *Dillon* of *Costologh* Lord president of *Connaght, Donnogh* Lord Viscount *Muskerrie, Francis* Lord Baron of *Athunrie, Alexander Mac Donnell* Esquire, Sir *Lucas Dillon* Knight, Sir *Nicholas Plunket* Knight, Sir *Richard Barnwall* Baronet, *Jeffry Brown, Donnogh O Callaghan, Tyrlagh O Neal, Miles Reily,* and *Gerrald Fennell* Esquires, or any seven or more of them, to set down the rates for the custome and imposition to be laid on *Aquavitæ, Wine, Oile, Yarne* and *Tobacco.*

21. Item, it is concluded, accorded, and agreed, and his Majestie is graciously pleased, that such persons as shall be agreed on by the said Lord lieutenant, and the said *Thomas* Lord Viscount *Dillon* of *Costologh,* Lord president of *Connaght, Donnogh* Lord Viscount *Muskerie, Francis* Lord

Baron of *Athunrie, Alexander Mac Donnell* Esquire, Sir *Lucas Dillon* Knight, Sir *Nicholas Plunket* Knight, Sir *Richard Barnwell* Baronet, *Jeffery Brown, Donnogh O Callaghan, Tirlagh O Neal, Miles Reilie,* and *Gerrald Fennell* Esquires,
5 or any seven or more of them shall be as soon as may be authorized by Commission under the great Seal, to regulate the Court of Castle-chamber, and such causes as shall be brought into, and censured in the said Court.

22. Item, It is concluded, accorded, and agreed upon, and
10 his Majesty is graciously pleased, that two acts lately passed in this Kingdom, one prohibiting the plowing with Horses by the tail, and the other prohibiting the burning of Oates in the straw bee repealed.

23. Item, it is further concluded, accorded, and agreed
15 upon by, and between the said parties, and his Majestie is further graciously pleased, for as much as upon application of Agents from this Kingdome unto his Majestie in the fourth yeer of his Reign, and lately upon humble suit made unto his Majestie, by a Committee of both houses of the Parliament of
20 this Kingdom, order was given his Majestie for redresse of severall grievances, and for so many of those as are not expressed in the Articles, whereof both Houses in the next insuing Parliament shall desire the benefit of his Majesties said former directions for redresse therein, that the same be af-
25 forded them, yet so, as for prevention of inconveniences to his Majesties service, that the warning mentioned in the 24. Article of the graces in the 4. yeer of his Majesties Reign be so understood, that the warning being left at the persons

dwelling houses be held sufficient warning, and as to the 22
Article of the said graces, the proces hitherto used in the Court
of Wards doe still continue, as hitherto it hath done in that,
and hath beene used in other English Courts, but the Court
5 of Wards being compounded for so much of the aforesaid
answer as concernes warning and processe shall be omitted.

24. Item, it is further concluded, accorded, and agreed
upon by, and between the said parties, and his Majesty is
further graciously pleased, that Maritine causes may be de-
10 termined in this Kingdome, without driving of Merchants
or others to appeal and seek Justice elsewhere; and if it shall
fall out that there bee cause of an appeal, the party grieved
is to appeal to his Majestie in the Chancerie of *Ireland,* and
the sentence thereupon to be given by the deligates, to be
15 definitive and not to be questioned upon any further appeal
except it be in the Parliament of this Kingdome, if the Parliament shall then be sitting, otherwise not, this to be by Act
of Parliament, and untill the said Parliament, the Admiraltie
and Maritine causes shall be ordered and setled by the said
20 Lord lieutenant, or other chief Governor or Governors of this
Kingdome for the time being, by and with the advice and
consent of the said *Thomas* Lord Viscount *Dillon* of *Costologh,* Lord President of *Connaght, Donnogh* Lord Viscount
Muskerie, Francis Lord Baron of *Athunrie, Alexander Mac*
25 *Donnel* Esquire, Sir *Lucas Dillon* Knight, Sir *Nicholas Plunket* Knight, Sir *Richard Barnwall* Baronet, *Jeffery Brown,
Donnogh O Callaghan, Tyrlagh O Neal, Miles Reily* and
Gerrald Fennell Esquires, or any seven or more of them.

25. Item, it is further concluded, accorded, and agreed upon, by and between the said parties, and his Majestie is graciously pleased, that his Majesties Subjects of this Kingdom be eased of all rents and increase of rents lately raised on the commission or defective titles in the Earl of *Staffords* government, this to be by Act of Parliament; and that in the mean time the said rents or increase of rents shall not be written for, by any processe, or the payment thereof in any sort procured.

26. Item, it is further concluded, accorded, and agreed upon, by and between the said parties, and his Majestie is further graciously pleased, that by Act to be passed in the next Parliament, all the arrears of interest mony, which did accrue and grow due by way of debt, mortgage or otherwise, and yet not so satisfied since the 23. of *October* 1641. untill the perfection of these Articles, shall be fully forgiven and be released, and that for and during the space of three yeeres next ensuing, no more shall be taken for use or interest of money then five pounds *per centum*. And in cases of equitie arising through dis-abilitie, occasioned by the distempers of the times, the considerations of equitie to be like unto both parties; but as for mortgages contracted between his Majesties Roman Catholike Subjects and others of that partie, where entry hath been made by the mortgagers against Law, and the condition of their mortgages, and detained wrongfully by them without giving any satisfaction to the mortgages, or where any such mortgagers have made profit of the lands morgaged above countrey charges, yet answer no rent, or other consideration

to the mortgagees, the parties grieved respectively to be left for releife to a course of equitie therein.

27. Item, it is further concluded, accorded, and agreed upon, and His Majestie is further graciously pleased, That
5 immediatly upon perfection of these Articles, the said *Thomas* Lord Viscount *Dillon* of *Costologh,* Lord President of *Connaght, Donnogh* Lord Viscount *Muskerrie, Francis* Lord Baron of *Athunrie, Alexander Mac Donnell* Esquire, Sir *Lucas Dillon* Knight, Sir *Nicholas Plunket* Knight, Sir
10 *Richard Barnwall* Baronet, *Jefferie Brown, Donnogh O Callaghan, Tyrlagh O Neal, Miles Reily, Gerrald Fennell* Esquires, shall be authorized by the said Lord lieutenant to proceed in, hear, determine, and execute in, and throughout this Kingdom, the ensuing particulars, and all the matters there-
15 upon depending, and that such authoritie and other the authorities hereafter mentioned shall remain of force without revocation, alteration or diminution, untill Acts of Parliament be passed, according to the purport and intent of these Articles, and that in case of death, miscarriage, disabilitie to
20 serve, by reason of sicknesse or otherwise of any the said *Thomas* Lord Viscount *Dillon* of *Costologh* Lord president of *Connaght, Donnogh* Lord Viscount *Muskerie, Francis* Lord Baron of *Athunrie, Alexander Mac Donnel* Esquire, Sir *Lucas Dillon* Knight, Sir *Nicholas Plunket* Knight, Sir *Rich-*
25 *ard Barnwall* Baronet, *Jeffery Brown, Donnogh O Callaghan Tirlagh O Neal, Miles Reily,* and *Gerrald Fennell* Esquires, and his Majesties Lord Lieutenant or other chief Governor or

Governors of this Kingdom for the time being, shall name and authorize another in the place of such as shall be so dead, or shall miscarrie himselfe, or be so disabled, and that the same shall be such person, as shall bee allowed of by the said

5 *Thomas* Lord Viscount *Dillon* of *Costologh* Lord President of *Connaght, Donnogh* Lord Viscount *Muskerry, Francis* Lord Baron of *Athunry, Alexander Mac Donnell* Esquire, Sir *Lucas Dillon* Knight, Sir *Nicholas Plunket* Knight, Sir *Richard Barnwall* Baronet, *Jeffery Brown, Donnogh O Callaghan,*

10 *Tyrlagh O Neal, Miles Reilie* and *Gerrald Fennell* Esquires, or any seven or more of them then living. And that the said *Thomas* Lord Viscount *Dillon* of *Costologh*, Lord President of *Connaght, Donnogh* Lord Viscount *Muskerie, Francis* Lord Baron of *Athunry, Alexander Mac Donnell* Esquire,

15 Sir *Lucas Dillon* Knight, Sir *Nicholas Plunket* Kt. Sir *Richard Barnwal* Baronet, *Jeffery Brown, Donnogh O Callaghan, Tyrlagh O Neal, Miles Reily,* and *Gerrald Fennell* Esquires, or any seven or more of them shall have power to applot, raise and leavie meanes with indifferencie and equalitie by way of

20 Excise or otherwise, upon all his Majesties Subjects within the said Kingdom, their persons, Estates and goods, towards the maintenance of such Armie or Armies as shall be thought fit to continue, and be in pay for his Majesties service, the defence of the Kingdom, and other the necessary publike charges

25 thereof, and towards the maintenance of the Forts, Castles, Garrisons, and Towns of both or either partie, other then such of the said Forts, Garrisons and Castles, as from time to time, untill there shall bee a settlement in Parliament shall be

thought fit, by his Majesties chief Governor or Governours of
this Kingdom for the time being, by and with the advice and
consent of the said *Thomas* Lord Viscount *Dillon* of *Costologh* Lord President of *Connaght, Donnogh* Lord Viscount
5 *Muskerie, Francis* Lord Baron of *Athunrie, Alexander Mac
Donnel* Esquire, Sir *Lucas Dillon* Knight, Sir *Nicholas Plunket* Knight, Sir *Richard Barnwal* Baronet, *Jefferie Brown,
Donnogh O Callaghan, Tyrlagh O Neal, Miles Reily,* and
Gerrald Fennel Esquires, or any seven or more of them, not
10 to be maintained at the charge of the publike, provided that
his Majesties Lord Lieutenant or other chief Governor or Governors of this Kingdome for the time being, be first made
acquainted with such taxes, levies, and excises as shall be
made, and the manner of leavying thereof, and that he ap-
15 prove the same; and to the end that such of the Protestant
party, as shall submit to the Peace may in the severall Counties
where any of their estates lyeth, have equallitie and indifferencie in the Assessements and levies that shall concern their
estates in the said severall Counties.

20   It is concluded, accorded, and agreed upon, and his Majestie is graciously pleased, That in the directions which shall
issue to any such County, for the applotting, subdeviding, and
levying of the said publike assessements, some of the said
Protestant party shall be joyned with others of the Roman
25 Catholike party to that purpose, and for effecting that service;
and the said *Thomas* Lord Viscount *Dillon* of *Costologh*
Lord President of *Connaght, Donnogh* Lord Viscount *Muskerie, Francis* Lord Baron of *Athunrie, Alexander Mac Don-*

nel Esquire, Sir *Lucas Dillon* Knight, Sir *Nicholas Plunket* Knight, Sir *Richard Barnwell* Baronet, *Jeffery Brown, Donnogh O Callaghan, Tyrlagh O Neil, Miles Reily,* and *Gerrald Fennell* Esquires, or any seven or more of them shall have
5 power to leavie the arrears of all excises and other publike taxes imposed by the Confederate Roman Catholikes, and yet unpaid, and to call Receivers and other accomptants of all former taxes and all publike dues to a just and strict account either by themselves, or by such as they or any seven or more
10 of them shall name or appoint; and that the said Lord Lieutenant, or any other chief Governor or Governors of this Kingdom for the time being, shall from time to time issue Commissions to such person and persons as shall be named and appointed by the said *Thomas* Lord Viscount *Dillon* of *Costo-*
15 *logh,* Lord President of *Connaght, Donnogh* Lord Viscount *Muskerie, Francis* Lord Baron of *Athunrie, Alexander Mac Donnel* Esquire, Sir *Lucas Dillon* Knight, Sir *Nicholas Plunket* Knight, Sir *Richard Barnwall* Baronet, *Jefferie Brown, Donnogh O Callaghan, Tyrlagh O Neal, Miles Reily* and *Ger-*
20 *rald Fennell* Esquires, or any seven or more of them, for letting, setting and improving the estates of all such person and persons, as shall adhere to any partie opposing his Majesties Authority and not submitting to the Peace; and that the profits of such estates shall be converted by the said Lord lieutenant,
25 or other chief Governor or Governors of this Kingdom for the time being, to the maintenance of the Kings Armie, and other necessary charges, untill settlement by Parliament; and that the said *Thomas* Lord Viscount *Dillon* of *Costologh* Lord

President of *Connaght, Donnogh* Lord Viscount *Muskerie,*
Francis Lord Baron of *Athunry, Alexander Mac Donnel* Esquire, Sir *Lucas Dillon* Knight, Sir *Nicholas Plunket* Knight,
Sir *Richard Barnwal* Baronet, *Jefferie Brown, Donnogh*
5 *O Callaghan, Tirlagh O Neal, Miles Reily,* and *Gerrald Fen-*
nel Esquires, or any seven or more of them shall have power
to applot, raise and leavie meanes with indifferencie and
equalitie for the buying of Armes and Ammunition, and for
the entertaining of Frigots in such proportion as shall be
10 thought fit by his Majesties Lord Lieutenant, or other chief
Governors of this Kingdom for the time being, by and with
the advice and consent of the said *Thomas* Lord Viscount
Dillon of *Costologh,* Lord President of *Connaght, Donnogh*
Lord Viscount *Muskerie, Francis* Lord Baron of *Athunrie,*
15 *Alexander Mac Donnell* Esquire, Sir *Lucas Dillon* Knight,
Sir *Nicholas Plunket* Knight, Sir *Richard Barnwall* Baronet,
Jefferie Brown, Donnogh O Callaghan, Tirlagh O Neal,
Miles Reily, and *Gerrald Fennel* Esquires, or any seven or
more of them, the said Armes and Ammunition, to be laid up
20 in such Magazines, and under the charge of such persons as
shall be agreed on, by the said Lord lieutenant, and the said
Thomas Lord Viscount *Dillon* of *Costologh* Lord President
of *Connaght, Donnogh* Lord Viscount *Muskerie, Francis*
Lord Baron of *Athunrie, Alexander Mac Donnel* Esquire, Sir
25 *Lucas Dillon* Knight, Sir *Nicholas Plunket* Knight, Sir *Rich-*
ard Barnwal Baronet, *Jefferie Brown, Donnogh O Callaghan*
Tirlagh O Neal, Miles Reily, and *Gerrald Fennel* Esquires, or
any seven or more of them, and to be disposed of, and the said

Frigots to be imployed for his Majesties service, and the publike use and benefit of this Kingdom of *Ireland;* and that
the said *Thomas* Lord Viscount *Dillon* of *Costologh* Lord
president of *Connaght, Donnogh* Lord Viscount *Muskerrie,*
5 *Francis* Lord Baron of *Athunrie, Alexander Mac Donnell*
Esquire, Sir *Lucas Dillon* Knight, Sir *Nicholas Plunket*
Knight, Sir *Richard Barnwall* Baronet, *Jeffery Brown, Don-*
nogh O Callaghan, Tyrlagh O Neal, Miles Reily, and *Gerrald*
Fennell Esquires, or any seven or more of them, shall have
10 power to applot, raise, and levie meanes with indifferencie
and equallitie, by way of Excise or otherwise, in the severall
Cities, corporate Towns, Counties, and part of Counties, now
within the Quarters, and only upon the Estates of the said
confederate Roman Catholikes, all such sum and summes of
15 money as shall appear to the said *Thomas* Lord Viscount
Dillon of *Costologh,* Lord president of *Connaght, Donnogh*
Lord Viscount *Muskerie, Francis* Lord Baron of *Athunrie,*
Alexander Mac Donnell Esquire, Sir *Lucas Dillon* Knight,
Sir *Nicholas Plunket* Knight, Sir *Richard Barnwell* Baronet,
20 *Jeffery Brown, Donnogh O Callaghan, Tirlagh O Neal, Miles*
Reilie, and *Gerrald Fennell Esquires,* or any seven or more of
them to be really due for and in the discharge of the publike
ingagements of the said confederate Catholikes, incurred or
grown due before the conclusion of these Articles; and that
25 the said *Thomas* Lord Viscount *Dillon* of *Costologh,* Lord
President of *Connaght, Donnogh* Lord Viscount *Muskerie,*
Francis Lord Baron of *Athunrie, Alexander Mac Donnel* Esquire, Sir *Lucas Dillon* Knight, Sir *Nicholas Plunket* Knight,

Sir *Richard Barnwall* Baronet, *Jeffery Brown, Donnogh O Callaghan, Tyrlagh O Neal, Miles Reily,* and *Gerrald Fennell* Esquires, or any seven or more of them shall be authorized to appoint Receivers, Collectors, and all other Officers,

5 for such monies as shall bee assessed, taxed, or applotted, in pursuance of the authorities mentioned in this Article, and for the arrears of all former applotments, taxes, and other publike dues yet unpaid; And that the said *Thomas* Lord Viscount *Dillon* of *Costologh* Lord President of *Connaght, Don-*

10 *nogh* Lord Viscount *Muskerie, Francis* Lord Baron of *Athunrie, Alexander Mac Donnel* Esquire, Sir *Lucas Dillon* Knight, Sir *Nicholas Plunket* Knight, Sir *Richard Barnwell* Baronet, *Jeffery Brown, Donnogh O Callaghan, Tyrlagh O Neil, Miles Reily,* and *Gerrald Fennell* Esquires, or any

15 seven or more of them, in case of refractories, or delinquencie may distrain and imprison, and cause such delinquents to be distrained and imprisoned. And the said *Thomas* Lord Viscount *Dillon* of *Costologh* Lord President of *Connaght, Donnogh* Lord Viscount *Muskerie, Francis* Lord Baron of *Ath-*

20 *unrie, Alexander Mac Donnel* Esquire, Sir *Lucas Dillon* Knight, Sir *Nicholas Plunket* Knight, Sir *Richard Barnwal* Baronet, *Jefferie Brown, Donnogh O Callaghan, Tyrlagh O Neal, Miles Reily,* and *Gerrald Fennel* Esquires, or any seven or more of them, make perfect books of all such monies

25 as shall be applotted, raised, or levied, out of which books they are to make severall and respective abstracts to be delivered under their hands or the hands of any seven or more of them to the severall and respective collectors which shall be

appointed to levy and receive the same. And that a duplicate
of the said books under the hands of the said *Thomas* Lord
Visc. *Dillon* of *Costologh,* Lord President of *Connaght, Don-*
nogh Lord Visc. *Muskerie, Francis* Lord Baron of *Athunrie,*
5 *Alexander Mac Donnell* Esq. Sir *Lucas Dillon* Knight, Sir
Nicholas Plunket Knight, Sir *Richard Barnwall* Baronet,
Jefferie Brown, Donnogh O Callaghan, Tyrlagh O Neal,
Miles Reily, Gerrald Fennell Esquires, or any seven or more
of them be delivered unto his Majesties Lord lieutenant, or
10 other chief Governor or Governors of this Kingdom for the
time being, whereby a perfect account may be given; and that
the said *Thomas* Lord Viscount *Dillon* of *Costologh* Lord
president of *Connaght, Donnogh* Lord Viscount *Muskerie,*
Francis Lord Baron of *Athunrie, Alexander Mac Donnel* Es-
15 quire, Sir *Lucas Dillon* Knight, Sir *Nicholas Plunket* Knight,
Sir *Richard Barnwall* Baronet, *Jeffery Brown, Donnogh*
O Callaghan Tirlagh O Neal, Miles Reily, and *Gerrald Fen-*
nell Esq. or any seven or more of them shall have power to
call the Councell and Congregation, and the respective su-
20 pream Councells, and Commissioners Generall, appointed
hitherto from time to time by the said Confederate Roman
Catholickes, to mannage their publick affaires, and all other
persons accountable to an account for all their receipts and
disbursments since the beginning of their respective imploy-
25 ments under the Confederate Roman Catholicks.

    28 Item it is concluded, accorded, and agreed, by and be-
tween the said parties, and his Majesty is graciously pleased,
that for the preservation of the peace and tranquility of the

Kingdome, the said Lord Lieutenant, and the said *Thomas* Lord Viscount *Dillon* of *Costollogh* Lord President of *Connaght, Donnogh* Lord Viscount *Muskery, Francis* Lord Barron of *Athunry, Allexander Mac Donnell* Esquire, Sir

5 *Lucas Dillon* Knight, Sir *Nicholas Plunket* Knight, Sir *Richard Barnewall* Baronet, *Jeffrey Browne, Donnogh O Callaghan, Tyrlagh O Neile, Miles Reily,* and *Gerrald Fennell* Esquires, or any seaven or more of them shall for the present agree upon such persons who are to be authorized by commis-

10 sion under the great Seale to be Commissioners of the Peace, Oyer and Terminer, Assises and Goale Delivery, in, and throughout the Kingdome, to continue during pleasure, with such power as Justices of the Peace, Oyer and Terminer, Assizes and Goale delivery in former time of Peace, have usually

15 had, which is not to extend unto any crime or offence committed before the first of *May* last past, and to be quallified with power to hear and determin al civil causes coming before them, not exceeding ten pounds; Provided that they shall not intermeddle with titles of Lands; provided likewise the

20 authority of such Commissioners shall not extend to question any person or persons, for any shipping, cattle or goods heretofore taken by either party from the other, or other injuries done contrary to the Articles of cessation, concluded by and with the said Roman Catholicke party, in, or since *May* last,

25 but that the same shall bee determined by such indifferent persons as the Lord Lieutenant, by the advice and consent of the said *Thomas* Lord Visc. *Dillon* of *Costollogh* Lord Presi. of *Connagh, Donnogh* Lord Viscount *Muskery, Francis* Lord

Baron of *Athunry, Allexander Mac Donnell* Esquire, Sir
Lucas Dillon Knight, Sir *Nicholas Plunket* Knight, Sir *Rich-*
ard Barnewall Baronet, *Jeffry Browne, Donnogh O Callaghan,*
Tirlagh O Neile, Miles Reily, and *Gerrald Fennell* Esquires,
5 or any seven or more of them shall think fit, to the end, that
speedy and equall justice may be done to all parties grieved;
And the said Commissioners are to make their Estreats as
accustomed of peace, and shall take the ensuing Oath, *viz.*
You shall sweare, that as Justice of the Peace, Oyer and Ter-
10 miner, Assizes, and Goale delivery in the Counties of A. B
in all articles to the commission to you directed. You shall do
equall right to the poore, and to the Rich after your cunning,
and wit and power, and after the Lawes and Customes of the
Realme, and in pursuance of these Articles; And you shall not
15 be of councell of any quarrell hanging before you; And the
issues, fines and amerciaments which shall happen to be made,
and all forfeitures which shall happen before you, you shall
cause to bee entred without any concealment or imbeazling,
and send to the Court of Exchequer, or to such other place as
20 his Majesties Lord Lieut. or other cheif Governor or Governors of his Kingdome shall appoint, untill there may be ac-
cesse unto the said Court of Exchequer; You shall not let for
gift or other cause, but well and truly; you shall doe your
office of Justice of the Peace, Oyer and Terminer, Assises and
25 Goale delivery in that behalfe, and that you take nothing for
your office of Justice of the Peace, Oyer and Terminer, Assizes and Goale delivery to be done, but of the King, and Fees
accustomed; and you shall not direct, or cause to be directed

any warrant by you, to be made to the parties, but you shall
direct them to the Sheriffs and Bayliffs of the said counties
respectively, or other the Kings Officers or Ministers, or
other indifferent persons to doe execution thereof, so helpe me
5 God, *&c.*

And that as well in the said Commission, as in all other commissions and authorities to be issued in pursuance of the present Articles, this clause shall be incerted *viz.* That all officers,
civill and martiall, shall be required to be aiding and assist-
10 ing, and obedient unto the said Commissioners, and other
persons to be authorized as above said in the execution of their
respective powers.

29 Item, It is further concluded, accorded and agreed
upon, by and between the said parties, and his Majesty is
15 further graciously pleased that his Majesties Roman Catholicke Subjects, do continue the possession of such of his Majesties Cities, Garrisons, Townes, Forts and Castles which are
within their now Quarters, untill settlement by Parliament,
and to be commanded, ruled and governed in cheife, upon
20 occasion of necessity (as to the Martiall and Military affairs,
by such as his Majesty, or his cheife Governour or Governours
of this Kingdom for the time being, shall appoint; and the
said appointment to be by, and with the advice and consent
of the said *Thomas* Lord Viscount *Dillon* of *Costologh* Lord
25 President of *Connaght, Donnogh* Lord Viscount *Muskery,*
Francis Lord Baron of *Athunry, Allexander Mac Donnell*
Esquire, Sir *Lucas Dillon* Knight, Sir *Nicholas Plunket*
Knight, Sir *Richard Barnewall* Baronet, *Jefferey Browne,*

Donnogh O Callaghan, Tyrlagh O Neile, Miles Reily, and
Gerrald Fennell Esquires, or any seaven or more of them, and
His Majestyes cheife Governour or Governours is to issue
Commissions accordingly, to such persons as shall be so named
5 and appointed, as aforsaid, for the executing of such comand,
rule, or Government, to continue untill all the particulars in
these present Articles agreed on to passe in Parliament, shall
be accordingly passed, only in case of death or misbehaviour,
such other person or persons to be appointed for the said com-
10 mand, rule and Government to be named and appointed in
the place or places, of him or them, who shall so dye, or mis-
behave themselves as the cheife Governor or Governors for
the time being, by the advice and consent of the said *Thomas*
Lord Visc. *Dillon* of *Costologh* Lord President of *Connaght,*
15 *Donnogh* Lord Viscount *Muskery, Francis* Lord Baron of
Athunry, Allexander Mac Donnell Esquire, Sir *Lucas Dillon*
Knight, Sir *Nicholas Plunket* Knight, Sir *Richard Barnewall*
Baronet, *Jeffrey Browne, Donnogh O Callaghan, Tyrlagh
O Neile, Miles Reily* and *Gerrald Fennell* Esquires, or any
20 seaven or more of them, shall thinke fit, and to bee continued
untill a settlement in Parliament as aforesaid.

30 Item, It is further concluded, accorded and agreed
upon by, and between the said parties, and his Majesty is
further graciously pleased, that all customes and tenths of
25 prizes belonging to his Majesty, which from the perfection of
these Articles, shall fall due within this Kingdome, shall be
paid unto his Majesties receipt, or until recourse may be had
thereunto in the ordinary legal way, unto such person or per-

sons, and in such place or places, and under such Controls as the Lord Lieutenant shall appoint to be disposed of, in order to the defence and safety of the Kingdome, and the defraying of other the necessary publicke charges thereof,

5 for the ease of the Subjects in other their levyes, charges and applotments. And that all, and every person or persons who are at present intrusted and imployed by the said Roman Catholicks, in the entries, receipts, collections, or otherwise, concerning the said customes and tenths of Prizes, doe continue

10 their respective imployments in the same, untill full settlement in Parliament accountable to His Majesties receipts, or untill recourse may be had thereunto; as the said Lord Lieutenant shall appoint as aforesaid, other then to such, and so many of them, as to the cheife Governour or Governours for

15 the time being, by, and with the advice and consent of the said *Tho.* Lord Visc. *Dillon* of *Costologh* Lord Pres. of *Connaght, Donnogh* Lord Visc. *Muskery, Francis* Lord Baron of *Athunry, Allexander Mac Donnell* Esquire, Sir *Lucas Dillon* Knight, Sir *Nicholas Plunket* Knight, Sir *Richard Barnewall*

20 Baronet, *Jeffrey Browne, Donnogh O Callaghan, Tyrlagh O Neile, Miles Reily,* and *Gerrald Fennell* Esquires, or any seven or more of them shall be thought fit to be altered; and then, and in such case, or in case of death, fraud or misbehavior, or other alteration of any such person or persons, then

25 such other person or persons to be imployed therein, as shall be thought fit by the cheife Governour or Governours for the time being, by, and with the advice and consent of the said *Tho.* Lord Visc. *Dillon* of *Costollogh* Lord President of *Con-*

naght, Donnogh Lord Viscount *Muskery, Francis* Lord
Baron of *Athunry, Allexander Mac Donnell* Esq. Sir *Lucas
Dillon* Kt. Sir *Nicholas Plunket* Kt. Sir *Richard Barnewal*
Baronet, *Jeffrey Browne, Donnogh O Callaghan, Tyrlagh*
5 *O Neile, Miles Reily* and *Gerrald Fennell* Esquires, or any
seven or more of them; And when it shall appeare, that any
person or persons who shall be found faithfull to his Majesty,
hath right to any of the offices or places about the said customes wherunto he or they, may not be admitted untill set-
10 tlement in Parliament as aforesaid, that a reasonable compen-
sation shall be afforded to such person or persons for the same.

    31. Item, as for and concerning his Majesties rents, payable
at Easter next, and from thenceforth to grow due, untill a settlement in Parliament. It is concluded, accorded, and agreed
15 upon, by and between the said parties, and his Majestie is
graciously pleased, that the said rents be not written for, or
levied untill a full settlement in Parliament, and in due time
upon application to be made to the said Lord Lieutenant, or
other chief Governor or Governors of this Kingdome by the
20 said *Thomas* Lord Viscount *Dillon* of *Costologh* Lord President of *Connaght, Donnogh* Lord Viscount *Muskerie, Francis* Lord Baron of *Athunry, Alexander Mac Donnell* Esquire,
Sir *Lucas Dillon* Knight, Sir *Nicholas Plunket* Knight, Sir
Richard Barnwal Baronet, *Jeffery Brown, Donnogh O Cal-
25 laghan, Tyrlagh O Neal, Miles Reily,* and *Gerrald Fennell*
Esquires, or any seven or more of them for remittall of those
rents, the said Lord Lieutenant, or any other chief Governor
or Governors of this Kingdome for the time being, shall inti-

mate their desires, and the reason thereof to his Majestie, who upon consideration of the present condition of this Kingdome will declare his gracious pleasure therein, as shall be just and honorable, and satisfactorie to the reasonable desires of his
5 Subjects.

32. Item, It is concluded, accorded, and agreed, by and between the said parties, and his Majestie is graciously pleased, that the Commissioners of Oyer and Terminer, and Goal de-liverie to be named as aforesaid, shall have power to hear and
10 determine all Murthers, Man-slaughters, Rapes, Stealths, burning of houses and corn in Rick, or Stack, Robberies, bur-glaries, forcible entries, detainers of possessions and other of-fences committed or done, and to be committed and done since the first day of *May* last past, untill the first day of the next
15 Parliament, these present Articles or any thing therein con-tained to the contrary notwithstanding; Provided that the Authority of the said Commissioners shall not extend to ques-tion any person or persons, for doing or committing any act whatsoever, before the conclusion of this Treaty, by vertue or
20 colour of any warrant or direction from those in publike au-thoritie among the confederate Roman Catholikes, nor unto any act which shall be done after the perfecting and conclud-ing of these Articles, by vertue or pretence of any authority which is now by these Articles agreed on; Provided also that
25 the said Commission shall not continue longer then the first day of the next Parliament.

33. Item, it is concluded, accorded by and between the said parties, and his Majestie is further graciously pleased, that

for the determining such differences which may arise between
his Majesties Subjects within this Kingdome, and the prevention of inconvenience and disquiet, which through want of
due remedie in severall causes may happen, there shall be judi-
5 catures established in this Kingdome, and that the persons to
be authorized in them shall have power to do all such things
as shall be proper and necessary for them to doe; and the said
Lord lieutenant by and with the advice and consent of the said
Thomas Lord Viscount *Dillon* of *Costollogh* Lord President
10 of *Connaght, Donnogh* Lord Viscount *Muskerry, Francis*
Lord Baron of *Athunry, Alexander Mac Donnell* Esquire, Sir
Lucas Dillon Knight, Sir *Nicholas Plunket* Knight, Sir *Richard Barnwall* Baronet, *Jeffery Brown, Donnogh O Callaghan,
Tyrlagh O Neal, Miles Reilie* and *Gerrald Fennell* Esquires,
15 or any seven or more of them shall name the said persons so to
be authorized, and doe all other things incident unto, and
necessarie for the setling of the said intended Judicatures.

34. Item at the instance, humble suit and earnest desire of
the General Assembly of the confederate Roman Catholikes;
20 It is concluded, accorded, and agreed upon, that the Roman
Catholike regular Clergie of this Kingdom, behaving themselves conformable to these Articles of Peace, shall not be
molested in the possessions, which at present they have of and
in the bodies scites and precincts of such Abbies and Monas-
25 teries belonging to any Roman Catholike within the said
Kingdom, until settlement by Parliament; and that the said
Clergie shall not be molested in the enjoying of such pensions
as hitherto since the Warres they enjoyed for their respective

livelihoods from the said Roman Catholikes, and the scites and precincts hereby intended are declared to be the bodie of the Abbie, one garden and Orchard to each Abbie, if any there be, and what else is contained within the walls, meares or ancient
5 fences or ditch that doth supply the wall thereof, and no more.

35. Item, it is concluded, accorded, and agreed, by and between the said parties, that as to all other demands of the said Roman Catholikes, for or concerning all or any the matters proposed by them, not granted or assented unto, in and
10 by the foresaid Articles, the said Roman Catholikes be referred to his Majesties gracious favour and further concessions. In witnesse whereof, the said Lord Lieutenant, for and on the behalfe of his most Excellent Majestie, to the one part of these Articles remaining with the said Roman Catholiques
15 hath put his hand and Seal; And Sir *Richard Blake* Knight in the Chaire of the Generall Assembly of the said Roman Catholikes, by order, command, and unanimous consent of the said Catholikes in full Assembly to the other part thereof remaining with the said Lord Lieutenant, hath put his hand and the
20 publique Seal hitherto used by the said Roman Catholiques the 17. of January 1648. And in the 24. year of the Reign of our Soveraign Lord CHARLES by the Grace of God, King of *Great Britain, France* and *Ireland,* &c.

SIR,
25 I HAVE not thus long forborn to invite you with these under your command to a submission to his Majesties authoritie in me, and a conjunction with me in the waies of his

service out of any the least aversion I had to you or any of them,
or out of any dis-esteem I had to your power to advance or
impede the same, but out of my fear, whiles those that have of
late usurped power over the Subjects of *England* held forth
5 the least colourable shadow of moderation in their intentions
towards the settlement of Church or State, and that in some
tollerable way with relation to Religion, the interest of the
King and Crown, the freedom of Parliament, the Liberties
of the subject, any addresses from mee proposing the with-
10 drawing of that party from those thus professing, from whom
they have received some, and expected further support, would
have been but coldly received, and any determination thereupon deferred in hope and expectation of the forementioned
settlement, or that you your selfe, who certainly have not
15 wanted aforesight of the sad confusion now covering the face
of *England,* would have declared with me, the Lord *Inche-*
queen, and the Protestant Army in *Munster* in prevention
thereof, yet my fear was it would have been as difficult for
you to have carried with you the main body of the Armie
20 under your command (not so clear sighted as your self) as it
would have been dangerous to you, and those with you well
inclined, to have attempted it without them, but now that the
mask of hypocrisie, by which the Independent Armie hath
ensnared and enslaved all estates and degrees of men is laid
25 aside, now that barefaced, they evidently appear to bee the
subverters of true religion, and to be the protectors and inviters, not only of all false ones, but of irreligion and Athe-
isme, now that they have barbarously and inhumanely laid

violent, sacrilegious hands upon, and murthered Gods an-
nointed, and our King, not as heretofore some Patricides have
done to make room for some usurper, but in a way plainly
manifesting their intentions to change the Monarchy of *Eng-*
5 *land* into Anarchy, unlesse their aime bee first to constitute
an elective Kingdome, and *Crumwell* or some such *John* of
Leiden being elected, then by the same force, by which they
have thus far compassed their ends to establish a perfect Turkish tyranny; now that of the three estates of King, Lords &
10 Commons, whereof in all ages, Parliaments have consisted,
there remains only a small number, and they the dregs and
scum of the House of Commons, pickt and awed by the
Armie, a wicked remnant left for no other end; then yet further, if it be possible to delude the people with the name of a
15 Parliament: The King being murthered, the Lords and the
rest of the Commons, being by unheard of violence, at severall
times forced from the Houses and some imprisoned. And
now that there remaines no other libertie in the subject but to
professe blasphemous opinions, to revile and tread underfoot
20 Magistracie, to murther Magistrates, and oppresse and undoe
all that are not like minded with them. Now I say, that I
cannot doubt but that you, and all with you under your command will take this opportunitie to act and declare against so
monstrous and unparaleld a rebellion, and that you and they
25 will cheerfully acknowledge, and faithfully serve and obey
our gracious King *Charles* the second undoubted heir of his
Father Crown and Vertues; under whose right and conduct
we may by Gods assistance restore Protestant Religion to puri-

tie, and therein settle it, Parliaments to their freedome, good
laws to their force, and our fellow-subjects to their just liberties, wherein how glorious and blessed a thing it will bee, to
be so considerablie instrumentall, as you may now make your
5 self, I leave to you now to consider. And though I conceive
there are not any motives relating to some particular interest
to be mentioned after these so weightie considerations, which
are such as the world hath not been at any time furnished with,
yet I hold it my part to assure you, that as there is nothing you
10 can reasonably propose for the safety, satisfaction or advantage
of your self, or of any that shall adhear to you in what I desire,
that I shall not to the uttermost of my power provide for, so
there is nothing I would, nor shall more industriously avoid,
then those necessities arising from my duty to God and man,
15 that may by your rejecting this offer force me to be a sad instrument of shedding English blood, which in such case must
on both sides happen. If thir overture finde place with you, as
I earnestly wish it may, let me know with what possible speed
you can, and if you please by the bearer in what way you
20 desire, it should bee drawne on to a conclusion. For in that,
as well as in the substance you shall find all ready complyance
from me that desire to bee

Your affectionate friend to serve you,

Carrick March 9.   O R M O N D.
25   1 6 4 8.

For Colonel *Michael Jones*
Governour of *Dublin.*

My Lord,

YOUR Lordships of the ninth, I received the twelfth instant, and therein have I your Lordships invitation to a conjunction with your self (I suppose) as Lord lieutenant of
5 *Ireland,* and with others now united with the Irish, and with the Irish themselves also.

As I understand not how your Lordship should be invested with that power pretended, so am I very well assured, That it is not in the power of any without the Parliament of *Eng-*
10 *land* to give and assure pardon to those bloodie Rebels, as by the Act to that end passed may appear more fully. I am also well assured that the Parliament of *England* would never assent to such a Peace (such as is that your Lordships with the Rebels wherin is little or no provision made either for the
15 Protestants or the Protestant Religion. Nor can I understand how the Protestant Religion should bee setled and restored to its puritie by an Armie of Papists, or the Protestant interests maintained by those very enemies by whom they have been spoiled and there slaughtered: And very evident it is that
20 both the Protestants and Protestant Religion are in that your Lordships Treaty, left as in the power of the Rebels to be by them born down, and rooted out at pleasure.

As for that consideration by your Lordship offered of the present and late proceedings in *England,* I see not how it may
25 be a sufficient motive to mee (or any other in like trust for the Parliament of *England* in the service of this Kingdome) to joyn with those Rebels upon any the pretences in that your Lordships letter mentioned, for therein were there a manifest

betraying that trust reposed in me in disserting the service and
work committed to me in joyning with those I should oppose,
and in opposing whom I am obliged to serve.

Neither conceive I it any part of my work and care to take
5 notice of any whatsoever proceedings of State forreign to my
charge and trust here, especially, they being found hereunto
apparently destructive.

Most certain it is, and former ages have approved it, that
the intermedling of Governors and parties in this Kingdom,
10 with sidings and parties in *England,* have been the very betraying of this kingdom to the Irish, whiles the Brittish forces
here had bin thereupon called off, and the place therin laid
open, and as it were given up to the common enemie.

It is what your Lordship might have observed in your for-
15 mer Treatie with the Rebels, that upon your Lordships thereupon withdrawing, and sending hence into *England* the most
considerable part of the English army then commanded by
you; thereby was the remaining Brittish party, not long after
over-poured, and your quarters by the Irish over-run to the
20 gates of *Dublin,* your self also reduced to that low condition,
as to be besieged in this very Citie (the Metropolis and prin-
cipall cittadell of the Kingdom) and that by those very Rebels,
who till then could never stand before you; and what the end
hath bin of that party, also, so sent by your Lordship into
25 *England,* (although the flower & strength of the English army
here both officers and souldiers) hath bin very observable.

And how much the dangers are at present (more then in
former ages) of hazarding the English interest in this King-

dom, by sending any parties hence into any other Kingdom upon any pretences whatsoever is very apparent, as in the generalitie of the Rebellion, now more then formerly; So considering your Lordships present conclusions with, and
5 concessions to the Rebels, wherein they are allowed the continued possession of all the cities, forts, and places of strength, whereof they stood possessed at the time of their Treatie with your Lordship, and that they are to have a standing force (if I well remember of 15000 foot, and 2500 horse (all of their
10 own party officers and souldiers) and they (with the whole kingdom) to be regulated by a Major party of Irish Trustees chosen by the Rebels themselves, as persons for their interests and ends to be by them confided in, without whom nothing is to be acted. Therein I cannot but mind your Lordship of
15 what hath been sometimes by your self delivered, as your sence in this particular; that the English interest in *Ireland* must be preserved by the English, and not by Irish, and upon that ground (if I be not deceived) did your Lordship then capitulate with the Parliament of *England,* from which cleer
20 principle I am sorrie to see your Lordship now receding.

As to that by your Lordship menaced us here, of blood and force, if dissenting from your Lordships waies and designes, for my particular I shall (my Lord) much rather chuse to suffer in so doing (for therein shall I doe what is becomming
25 and answerable to my trust) then to purchase my self on the contrary the ignominious brand of perfidie, by any allurements of whatsoever advantages offered me.

But very confident I am, of the same divine power which

hath still followed me in this work, and will still follow me;
and in that trust doubt I nothing of thus giving your Lordship plainly this my resolution in that particular, So I remain,
Dublin March 14. 1648.   *Your Lordships humble servant,*

5   Signed *Mic: Jones.*
For the Lord of *Ormond* these.

By the Lord Lieutenant Generall of Ireland.

Ormond,

WHEREAS our late Soveraign King *Charles* of happie
10   memory hath bin lately by a party of his rebellious
Subjects of *England* most traiterously, maliciously, and inhumanely put to death and murthered; and forasmuch as his
Majestie that now is, *Charles* by the grace of God King of
England, Scotland, France and *Ireland,* is son and heir of his
15 said late Majestie, and therefore by the Laws of the Land, of
force, and practised in all ages, is to inherit. We therefore in
discharge of the dutie we owe unto God, our allegiance and
loyaltie to our Soveraign, holding it fit him so to proclaim in
and through this his Majesties Kingdome, doe by this our
20 present proclamation declare and manifest to the world, that
Charles the second, son and heir of our late Soveraign King
Charles the first of happy memory, is, by the grace of God
the undoubted King of *England, Scotland, France,* and *Ireland,* Defender of the Faith, *&c.*

25   *Given at* Carrick *Febr.* 26. 1648.
God save the King.

A NECESSARY REPRESENTATION

of the present evills, and eminent dangers to Religion,
Lawes, and Liberties, arising from the late, and present
practises of the Sectarian party in *England:* together
with an Exhortation to duties relating to the Covenant,
unto all within our Charge; and to all the well-affected
within this Kingdome, by the Presbytery at Belfast,
February 15th 1649.

WHEN we doe seriously consider the great, and
many duties which we owe unto God, and his
people, over whom he hath made us Overseers;
and for whom we must give an accompt; and when wee be-
5 hold the laudable Examples of the worthy Ministers of the
Province of *London,* and of the Commissioners of the Generall Assembly of the Church of *Scotland,* in their free and
faithfull testimonies against the insolencies of the Sectarian
party in *England.* Considering also the dependency of this
10 Kingdome upon the Kingdome of *England,* and remembring
how against strong oppositions we were assisted by the Lord
the last yeare in discharge of the like dutie, and how he punished the Contempt of our warning upon the despisers thereof:
We finde our selves as necessitated; so the more encouraged to
15 cast in our Mite in the treasury, least our silence should involve
us in the guilt of unfaithfulnesse, and our People in security,
and neglect of duties.

In this discharge of the trust put upon us by God, we would
not be looked upon as sowers of sedition, or broachers of Na-

tionall and divisive motions, our record is in heaven, that
nothing is more hatefull unto us, nor lesse intended by us, and
therefore we shall not feare the malicious, and wicked aspersions, which we know Satan by his Instruments is ready to
5 cast, not onely upon us, but on all who sincerely endeavour
the advancement of Reformation.

What of late have been, and now are the insolent, and presumptuous practises of the Sectaries in *England,* is not un-
knowne to the world: For, first, notwithstanding their spe-
10 cious pretences for Religion, and Liberties, yet their late, and
present actings, being therewith compared, doe clearly evidence that they love a rough garment to deceive; since they
have with a high hand despised the Oath in breaking the
Covenant, which is so strong a foundation to both, whilest
15 they loaden it with slighting reproaches, calling it a Bundle
of particular and contrary Interests, and a Snare to the people;
and likewise labour to establish by Lawes an Universall Toleration of all Religions, which is in Innovation over-turning
of Unity in Religion, and so directly repugnant to the word
20 of God, the two first Articles of our Solemne Covenant, which
is the greatest wickednesse in them to violate, since many of
the chiefest of themselves, have with their hands testified to
the most high God, sworne, and sealed it.

Moreover; their great dis-affection to the Settlement of
25 Religion, and so their future breach of Covenant doth more
fully appeare by their strong oppositions to Presbyteriall Government (the hedge, and Bulwarke of Religion) whilest they
express their hatred to it, more then to the worst of errours,

by excluding it under the name of Compulsion; when they imbrace, even Paganisme, and Judaisme in the Armes of Toleration. Not to speake of their Aspersions upon it, and the Assertors thereof, as Antichristian, and Popish, though they
5 have deeply sworn to maintaine the same Government in the first Article of the Covenant, as it is established in the Church of *Scotland,* which they now so despite, and fully blaspheme.

Againe, It is more then manifest that they seek not the vindication, but the extirpation of Lawes, and Liberties, as ap-
10 peares by their seizing on the person of the King, and at their pleasures removing him from place to place, not onely without the consent, but (if we mis-take not) against a direct Ordinance of Parliament: their violent surprizing, imprisoning, and secluding many of the most worthy Members of the Hon-
15 ourable House of Commons, directly against a declared Priviledge of Parliament (an Action certainly without parallell in any age) and their purposes of abolishing Parliamentary power for the future, and establishing of a Representative (as they call it) in stead thereof. Neither hath their fury stayed
20 here, but without all rule, or example, being but private men, they have proceeded to the tryall of the King, against both the Interest, and Protestation of the Kingdome of *Scotland,* and the former publique Declarations of both Kingdomes (besides the violent hast, rejecting the hearing of any defences)
25 with cruell hands have put him to death; an act so horrible, as no history, divine or humane, hath laid a President of the like.

These, and many other their detestable insolencies, may abundantly convince every unbyassed Judgement, that the

present practise of the Sectaries, and their Abettors, doe directly over-turne the Lawes and Liberties of the Kingdomes, roote out lawfull, and supreme Magistracy (the just priviledges whereof we have sworne to maintaine) and introduce
5 a fearfull confusion, and lawlesse Anarchie.

The Spirit of God by *Solomon* tells us, *Pro.* 30. 21. *That a servant to reigne is one of the foure things for which the earth is disquieted, and which it cannot beare:* We wonder nothing that the earth is disquieted for these things; but we wonder
10 greatly, if the earth can beare them, and albeit the Lord so permit, that folly be set in great dignity, and they which sit in low place; *That servants ride upon horses, and Princes walke as servants upon the Earth,* Eccles. 10. *ver.* 6, 7. Yet the same Wise man saith, *Pro.* 19. 10. *Delight is not seemely*
15 *for a foole, much lesse for a servant to have rule over Princes.*

When we consider these things, we cannot but declare and manifest our utter dislike and detestation of such unwarrantable practises, directly subverting our Covenant, Religion, Lawes, and Liberties. And as Watchmen in *Sion* warne all
20 the Lovers of truth, and well-affected to the Covenant, carefully to avoyde compliance with, or not bearing witnesse against horrid Insolencies, least partaking with them in their sinnes, they also be partakers of their plagues. Therefore in the Spirit of meeknesse, wee earnestly intreate, and in the
25 authority of Jesus Christ, (whose servants wee are) Charge, and obtest all who resolve to adhere unto truth, and the Covenant, diligently to observe, and conscientiously to performe these following duties.

1. First, That according to our solemne Covenant, every one study more to the power of godlinesse, and personall reformation of themselves, and families, because for the great breach of this part of the Covenant, God is highly offended with these Lands, and justly provoked to permit men to be the Instruments of our misery and afflictions.

2. Secondly, That every one in their station and calling earnestly contend for the faith which was once delivered to the Saints, *Jude* 3. And seeke to have their hearts established with grace, that they be not unstable, and wavering, carried about with every winde of doctrine; but that they receive the truth in love, avoyding the company of such, as withdraw from, and vilifie the publique Ordinances; speake evill of Church-Government; invent damnable errors, under the specious pretence of a Gospel-way, and new Light; and highly extoll the persons and courses of notorious Sectaries, least God give them over to strong delusions (the plague of these times) that they may beleeve lies, and be damned.

3. Thirdly, That they would not be drawne by Councell, Command, or Example, to shake off the ancient, and fundamentall Government of these Kingdomes by King and Parliament, which we are so deeply ingaged to preserve by our solemne Covenant, as they would not be found guilty of the great evill of these times (condemned by the Holy Ghost) the despising of Dominion, and speaking evill of Dignities.

4. Fourthly, That they doe cordially endeavour the preservation of the Union amongst the well-affected in the Kingdomes, not being swayed by any Nationall respect: remem-

bring that part of the Covenant; *That wee shall not suffer our
selves directly, nor indirectly, by whatsoever Combination,
perswasion, or terrour, to be divided, or withdrawne from this
blessed Union; and Conjunction.*

5   And finally, albeit there be more present hazard from the
power of Sectaries, (as were from Malignants the last yeare)
yet wee are not ignorant of the evill purposes of Malignants,
even at this time in all the Kingdomes; and particularly in
this; and for this cause we exhort every one with equall watch-
10 fulnesse to keep themselves free from associating with such,
or from swerving in their judgements to Malignant principles;
and to avoyd all such persons as have been from the beginning
knowne opposers of Reformation, refusers of the Covenant,
combining themselves with Papists, and other notorious Ma-
15 lignants, especially such who have been chiefe Promotors of
the late Ingagement against *England,* Calumniators of the
worke of Reformation, in reputing the miseries of the present
times unto the advancers thereof, and that their just hatred to
Sectaries, incline not their mindes to favour Malignants, or
20 to thinke that because of the power of Sectaries, the cause of
God needs the more to feare the Enmity, or to stand in need
of the helpe of Malignants.

OBSERVATIONS UPON

the Articles of Peace with the *Irish* Rebels, on the Letter of *Ormond* to Col. *Jones*, and the Representation *of the* Presbytery *at* Belfast.

ALTHOUGH it be a Maxim much agreeable to wisdom, that just deeds are the best answer to injurious words, and actions of what ever sort, their own plainest Interpreters; yet since our enemies can finde the
5   leisure both wayes to offend us, it will be requisite we should be found in neither of those wayes neglectfull of our just defence. To let them know, that sincere and upright intentions can certainly with as much ease deliver themselvs into words as into deeds.
10   Having therefore seen of late those Articles of Peace granted to the Papist Rebels of *Ireland,* as speciall graces and favours from the late King, in reward, most likely, of their work don, and in his name and authority confirm'd and ratifi'd by *James* Earle of *Ormond;* together with his Letter to Col. *Jones,*
15   Governour of *Dublin,* full of contumely and dishonour, both to the Parliament and Army. And on the other side, an Insolent and seditious Representation from the *Scotch* Presbytery at *Belfast* in the North of *Ireland;* no lesse dishonourable to the State; and much about the same time brought hither;
20   there will be needfull as to the same slanderous aspersions but one and the same Vindication against them both. Nor can we sever them in our notice and resentment, though one part

intitl'd a *Presbytery,* and would be thought a Protestant Assembly, since their own unexampl'd virulence hath wrapt
them into the same guilt, made them accomplices and assistants to the abhorred *Irish* Rebels, and with them at present to
5 advance the same interest: if wee consider both their calum-
nies, their hatred, and the pretended Reasons of their hatred
to be the same; the time also, and the place concurring, as that
there lacks nothing but a few formall words, which may be
easily dissembl'd, to make the perfetest conjunction; and be-
10 tween them to divide that Iland.

As for these Articles of Peace made with those inhumane
Rebels and Papists of *Ireland* by the late King, as one of his
last Master-pieces, We may be confidently perswaded, that no
true borne *English-man,* can so much as barely reade them
15 without indignation and disdaine, that those bloudy Rebels,
and so proclaim'd and judg'd of by the King himself, after
the mercilesse and barbarous Massacre of so many thousand
English, (who had us'd their right and title to that Countrey
with such tendernesse and moderation, and might otherwise
20 have secur'd themselvs with ease against their Treachery)
should be now grac'd and rewarded with such freedomes and
enlargements, as none of their Ancestors could ever merit by
their best obedience, which at best was alwaies treacherous, to
be infranchiz'd with full liberty equall to their Conquerours,
25 whom the just revenge of ancient Pyracies, cruell Captivities,
and the causlesse infestation of our Coast, had warrantably
call'd over, and the long prescription of many hundred yeares;
besides what other titles are acknowledg'd by their own *Irish*

Parlaments, had fixt and seated in that soile with as good a
right as the meerest Natives.

These therefore by their own foregoing demerits and provo-
cations justly made our vassalls, are by the first Article of this
5 peace advanc'd to a Condition of freedome superior to what
any *English* Protestants durst have demanded. For what else
can be the meaning to discharge them the Common Oath of
Supremacy, especially being Papists (for whom principally
that oath was intended) but either to resigne them the more
10 into their own power, or to set a mark of dishonour upon the
Brittish Loyalty; by trusting *Irish* Rebels for one single Oath
of Alleageance, as much as all his Subjects of *Brittaine* for the
double swearing both of Alleageance and Supremacy.

The second Article puts it into the hands of an *Irish* Par-
15 lament to repeale, or to suspend, if they thinke convenient,
that act usually call'd *Poynings Act,* which was the maine,
and yet the civillest and most moderate acknowledgement impos'd of their dependance on the Crown of *England;* whereby
no Parlament could be summond there, no Bill be past, but
20 what was first to be transmitted and allowd under the great
seale of *England.* The recalling of which Act, tends openly to
invest them with a law-giving power of their own, enables
them by degrees to throw off all subjection to this Realme, and
renders them who by their endlesse treasons and revolts have
25 deserv'd to hold no Parlament at all, but to be govern'd by
Edicts and Garrisons, as absolute and supream in that Assembly as the People of *England* in their own Land. And the 12th
Article grants them in expresse words, that the *Irish* Parla-

ment shall be no more dependent on the Parlament of *England,* then the *Irish* themselves shall declare agreeable to the Lawes of *Ireland.*

The two and twentieth Article more ridiculous then dan-
5 gerous, coming especially from such a serious knot of Lords and Politicians, obtaines that those Acts prohibiting to plow with horses by the Tayle, and burne oates in the Straw, be repeald; anough if nothing else, to declare in them a dispo-sition not onely sottish but indocible and averse from all Civil-
10 ity and amendment, and what hopes they give for the future, who rejecting the ingenuity of all other Nations to improve and waxe more civill by a civilizing Conquest, though all these many yeares better shown and taught, preferre their own absurd and savage Customes before the most convincing evi-
15 dence of reason and demonstration: a testimony of their true Barbarisme and obdurate wilfulnesse to be expected no lesse in other matters of greatest moment.

Yet such as these and thus affected, the ninth Article en trusts with the Militia; a Trust which the King swore by God
20 at *New-Market,* he would not commit to his Parliament of *England,* no not for an houre. And well declares the confi-dence he had in *Irish* Rebels, more then in his Loyallest Sub-jects. He grants them moreover till the performance of all these Articles, that 15000 foote and 2500 horse, shall remaine
25 a standing Army of Papists at the beck and Command of *Dillon, Muskery,* and other arch Rebels, with power also of adding to that number as they shall see cause. And by other Articles allows them the constituting of Magistrates and

Judges in all Causes, whom they think fit: and till a settlement
to their own minds, the possession of all those Townes and
Countreys within their now Quarters being little lesse then
all the Iland, besides what their Cruelty hath dispeopl'd and
5 lay'd wast. And lastly, the whole managing both of peace
and warre is committed to Papists, and the chiefe Leaders of
that Rebellion.

Now let all men judge what this wants of utter alienating
and acquitting the whole Province of *Ireland* from all true
10 fealty and obedience to the Common-wealth of *England*.
Which act of any King against the Consent of his Parliament,
though no other Crime were layd against him, might of it
selfe strongly conduce to the dis-inthrowning him of all. In
France *Henry* the third demanding leave in greatest exigen-
15 cies to make Sale of some Crown Lands onely, and that to his
Subjects, was answerd by the Parlament then at *Blois,* that a
King in no case, though of extreamest necessity, might alien-
ate the Patrimony of his Crown, whereof he is but onely *Usu-*
fructuary, as Civilians terme it, the propriety remaining ever
20 to the Kingdome, not to the King. And in our own Nation,
King *John,* for resigning though unwillingly his Crown to
the Popes Legate, with little more hazard to his Kingdome
then the payment of 1000 Marks, and the unsightlinesse of
such a Ceremony, was depos'd by his Barons, and *Lewis* the
25 French Kings Sonne elected in his roome. And to have carried onely the Jewells, Plate, and Treasure into *Ireland* without consent of the Nobility, was one of those impeachments
that condemn'd *Richard* the second to lose his Crown.

But how petty a Crime this will seem to the alienating of a whole Kingdome, which in these Articles of Peace we see as good as done by the late King, not to friends, but to mortall Enemies, to the accomplishment of his own interests and ends, wholly separate from the Peoples good, may without aggravation be easily conceiv'd. Nay by the Covenant it self, since that so cavillously is urg'd against us, wee are enjoyn'd in the fourth Article, with all faithfulnesse to endeavour the bringing all such to public Triall and condigne Punishment, as shall divide one Kingdome from another. And what greater dividing then by a pernicious and hostile Peace, to disalliege a whole Feudary Kingdome from the ancient Dominion of *England*? Exception we finde there of no person whatsoever; and if the King who hath actually done this, or any for him claime a Priviledge above Justice, it is againe demanded by what expresse Law, either of God or man, and why he whose office is to execute Law and Justice upon all others, should sit himselfe like a demigod in lawlesse and unbounded *anarchy;* refusing to be accountable for that autority over men naturally his equals, which God himself without a reason givn is not wont to exercise over his creatures? And if God the neerer to be acquainted with mankind and his frailties, and to become our Priest, made himself a man, and subject to the Law, we gladly would be instructed why any mortal man for the good and wellfare of his brethren beeing made a King, should by a clean contrary motion make himself a God, exalted above Law; the readiest way to become utterly unsensible, both of his human condition, and his own duty.

And how securely, how smoothly, with how little touch or sense of any commiseration, either Princely or so much as human, he hath sold away that justice so oft demanded, and so oft by himself acknowledg'd to be due for the bloud of more
5 then 200000. of his Subjects, that never hurt him, never disobeyd him, assassinated and cut in pieces by those *Irish* Barbarians, to give the first promoting, as is more then thought, to his own tyrannicall designes in *England,* will appeare by the 18th Article of his peace; wherein without the least regard
10 of Justice to avenge the dead, while he thirsts to be aveng'd upon the living, to all the Murders, Massacres, Treasons, Pyracies, from the very fatall day wherein that Rebellion first broke out, he grants an act of Oblivion. If this can be justified, or not punisht in whomsoever, while there is any faith, any
15 Religion, any Justice upon Earth, there can no reason be alleg'd why all things are not left to confusion. And thus much be observd in brief concerning these Articles of peace made by the late King with his *Irish* Rebells.

The Letter of *Ormond* sent to Col. *Jones* Governour of
20 *Dublin,* attempting his fidelity, which the discretion and true worth of that Gentleman hath so well answerd and repulst, had pass'd heer with out mention, but that the other part of it not content to doe the errand of Treason, roves into a long digression of evill and reproachfull language to the
25 Parlament and Army of *England.* Which though not worth their notice, as from a Crew of Rebells whose inhumanities are long since become the horrour and execration of all that heare them, yet in the pursuance of a good endeavour, to give

the world all due satisfaction of the present doings, no fit opportunity shall be omitted.

He accuses first *that we are the Subverters of true Religion, the protectors & inviters not onely of all false ones, but of* 5 *irreligion & atheism.* An accusation that no man living could more unjustly use then our accuser himself; & which without a strange besottednesse, he could not expect but to be retorted upon his own head. All men who are true Protestants, of which number he gives out to be one, know not a 10 more immediate and killing Subverter of all true Religion then Antichrist, whom they generally believe to be the Pope and Church of *Rome,* he therefore who makes peace with this grand Enemy and persecutor of the true Church, he who joynes with him, strengthens him, gives him root to grow up 15 and spread his poyson, removing all opposition against him, granting him Schools, Abbeyes, and Revenues, Garrisons, Fortresses, Townes, as in so many of those Articles may be seen, he of all Protestants may be calld most justly the Subverter of true Religion, the Protector and inviter of irreligion 20 and atheism, whether it be *Ormond* or his Maister. And if it can be no way prov'd, that the Parlament hath countenanc'd Popery or Papists, but have every where brok'n their Temporall power, thrown down their public Superstitions, and confin'd them to the bare enjoyment of that which is not in 25 our reach, their Consciences, if they have encouragd all true Ministers of the Gospel, that is to say, afforded them favour and protection in all places where they preacht, and although they think not money or Stipend to be the best encouragement

of a true Pastor, yet therein also have not been wanting nor intend to be, they doubt not then to affirm themselves, not the Subverters, but the maintainers and defenders of true Religion; which of it self and by Consequence is the surest and
5 the strongest Subversion, not onely of all false ones, but of irreligion and atheism. For *the Weapons of that Warfare,* as the Apostle testifies who best knew, *are not carnall, but mighty through God to the pulling down of Strong Holds, and all reasonings, and every high thing exalted against the knowl-*
10 *edge of God, surprising every thought unto the obedience of Christ, and easily revenging all disobedience,* 2 Cor. 10. What Minister or Clergyman that either understood his high calling, or sought not to erect a secular and carnall Tyranny over spirituall things, would neglect this ample and sublime power
15 conferrd upon him, and come a begging to the weak hand of Magistracy for that kind of ayd which both the Magistrate hath no Commission to afford him, and in the way he seeks it hath been always found helplesse and unprofitable. Neither is it unknown, or by wisest men unobserv'd, that the Church
20 began then most apparently to degenerate, and goe to ruine, when shee borrow'd of the Civill power more then fair encouragement and protection; more then which Christ himself and his Apostles never requir'd. To say therefore that We protect and invite all false Religions, with irreligion also and
25 atheism, because wee lend not or rather missapply not the temporall power to help out, though in vaine, the sloth, the spleen, the insufficiency of Church-men, in the execution of spirituall discipline, over those within their Charge, or those without,

is an imputation that may be layd as well upon the best regulated States and Governments through the World. Who have
been so prudent as never to imploy the Civill sword further
then the edge of it could reach; that is, to Civill offences onely;
5 proving alwayes against objects that were spirituall a ridiculous weapon. Our protection therefore to men in Civill matters unoffensive we cannot deny; their Consciences we leave,
as not within our Cognisance, to the proper cure of instruction, praying for them. Neverthelesse, if any be found among
10 us declar'd atheists, malicious enemies of God, and of Christ;
The Parlament, I think, professes not to tolerate such, but
with all befitting endeavours to suppresse them. Otherwaies
to protect none that in a larger sense may be tax'd of irreligion
or atheism, may perhaps be the ready way to exclude none
15 sooner out of protection, then those themselves that most
accuse it to be so generall to others. Lastly, that we invite
such as these, or incourage them, is a meer slander without
proof.

He tells us next that they have murderd the King. And they
20 deny not to have justly and undauntedly, as became the Parlament of *England,* for more bloudshed and other hainous
Crimes then ever King of this Land was guilty of, after op'n
tryall, punisht him with death. A matter which to men whose
serious consideration thereof hath left no certain precept, or
25 example undebated, is so farr from giving offence, that wee
implore and beseech the Divine Majesty so to uphold and support thir spirits with like fortitude and Magnanimity, that all
thir ensuing actions may correspond and prove worthy that

impartiall and noble peece of Justice, wherein the hand of
God appear'd so evidently on our side. Wee shall not then
need to feare what all the rout and faction of men basely principl'd can doe against us.

5   The end of our proceedings, which he takes upon him to
have discover'd; *The changing* forsooth *of Monarchy into
Anarchy,* sounds so like the smattering of some raw Polititian,
and the overworne objection of every triviall talker, that wee
leave him in the number. But seing in that which followes he
10 containes not himself, but contrary to what a Gentleman
should know of Civility, proceeds to the contemptuous nam-
ing of a person, whose valour and high merit many enemies
more noble then himself have both honour'd and feard, to
assert his good name and reputation, of whose service the
15 Common-wealth receaves so ample satisfaction, tis answerd
in his behalf, that *Cromwell* whom he couples with a name
of scorne, hath done in few yeares more eminent and remarkable Deeds whereon to *found* Nobility in his house, though it
were wanting, and perpetuall Renown to posterity, then *Or-
20 mond* and all his Auncestors put together can shew from any
record of thir *Irish* exploits, the widest scene of thir glory.

He passes on in his groundless conjectures, that the aime
of this Parlament may be perhaps to set up first an elective
Kingdome, and after that a perfet Turkish tyranny. Of the
25 former wee suppose the late act against Monarchy will suffice
to acquitt them. Of the latter certainly there needed no other
patterne then that Tyranny which was so long modelling by
the late King himself, with *Strafford,* and that arch Prelat of

Canterbury, his chief Instruments; whose designes God hath dissipated. Neither is it any new project of the Monarchs, and their Courtiers in these dayes, though Christians they would be thought, to endeavour the introducing of a plain Turkish

5 Tyranny. Witnesse that Consultation had in the Court of *France* under *Charles* the ninth at *Blois,* wherein *Poncet,* a certain Court projector, brought in secretly by the Chancellor *Biragha,* after many praises of the *Ottoman* Government; proposes means and wayes at large in presence of the King,

10 the Queen Regent, and *Anjou* the Kings Brother, how with best expedition, and least noyse the Turkish Tyranny might be set up in *France.* It appeares therefore that the designe of bringing in that Tyranny, is a Monarchicall designe, and not of those who have dissolvd Monarchy.

15 As for Parlaments by three Estates, wee know that a Parlament signifies no more then the Supream and generall Councell of a Nation, consisting of whomsoever chos'n and assembld for the public good; which was ever practis'd, and in all sorts of Government, before the word *Parlament,* or the for-

20 mality, or the possibility of those three Estates, or such a thing as a Titular Marquess had either name or being in the World. The Originall of all which we could produce to be farr newer then those *all Ages* which he vaunts of, and by such first invented and contriv'd, whose authority, though it were *Charles*

25 *Martell,* stands not so high in our repute, either for himself, or the age he liv'd in, but that with as good warrant we may recede from what he ordain'd, as he ordaine what before was not.

But whereas besides he is bold to allege that of the three Estates there remaines onely a small number, and they the *Dreggs and Scum of the House of Commons,* this reproach and in the mouth of an *Irish* Man concernes not them onely,
5 but redounds to apparent dishonour of the whole *English* Nation. Doubtless there must be thought a great scarcity in *England* of persons honourable and deserving, or else of Judgement, or so much as honesty in the People, if those whom they esteem worthy to sit in Parlament be no better
10 then Scum and Dreggs in the *Irish* Dialect. But of such like stuffe wee meet not any where with more excrescence then in his own lavish pen; which feeling it selfe loose without the reines of discretion, rambles for the most part beyond all Soberness and Civility. In which Torrent he goes on negoti-
15 ating and cheapning the Loyalty of our Faithfull Governour of *Dublin,* as if the known and Try'd Constancy of that valiant Gentleman were to be bought with Court fumes.

He layes before him that *there remaines now no other liberty in the Subject but to professe blasphemous opinions, to*
20 *revile and tread underfoot Magistracy, to murther Magistrates, to oppresse and undoe all that are not like minded with us.* Forgetting in the mean while himself to be in the head of a mixt Rabble, part Papists, part Fugitives, and part Savages, guilty in the highest degree of all these Crimes.
25 What more blasphemous not opinion but whole Religion then Popery, plung'd into Idolatrous and Ceremoniall Superstition, the very death of all true Religion; figur'd to us by the Scripture it selfe in the shape of that Beast, *full of the names of*

Blasphemy, which wee mention to him as to one that would be counted Protestant, and had his breeding in the house of a Bishop. And who are those that have trod under foot Magistracy, murder'd Magistrates, oppress'd & undone all that

5 syded not with them, but the Irish Rebels, in that horrible Conspiracy, for which *Ormond* himselfe hath either been or seem'd to be their enemy; though now their Ringleader. And let him aske the Jesuites about him whether it be not their known Doctrine and also practise, not by faire and due proc-

10 esse of Justice to punish Kings and Magistrates, which we disavow not, but to murder them in the basest and most assassinous manner, if thir Church-Interest so require. There will not need more words to this Windy Railer, convicted openly of all those Crimes which he so confidently and yet

15 falsely charges upon others.

We have now to deale, though in the same Country, with another sort of Adversaries, in show farr different, in substance much what the same. These write themselves the Presbytery of *Belfast,* a place better known by the name of a late

20 Barony, then by the fame of these mens Doctrine or Ecclesiasticall Deeds; whose obscurity till now never came to our hearing. And surely wee should think this their Representment farr beneath considerable, who have neglected and past over the like unadvizednesse of their fellowes in other places

25 more neer us, were it not to observe in some particulars the Sympathy, good Intelligence, and joynt pace which they goe in the North of *Ireland,* with their Copartning Rebels in the South, driving on the same Interest to loose us that King-

dome, that they may gaine it themselves, or at least share in the spoile: though the other be op'n enemies, these pretended Brethren.

The Introduction of their Manifest out of doubt must be Zealous; *Their Duty,* they say, *to God and his people, over whom he hath made them Overseers, and for whom they must give accompt.* What meane these men? is the Presbytery of *Belfast,* a small Town in *Ulster,* of so large extent that their voyces cannot serve to teach duties in the Congregation which they oversee, without spreading and divulging to all parts farr beyond the Diocesse of *Patrick,* or *Columba,* their writt'n Representation, under the suttle pretence of Feeding their owne Flock? Or doe they think to oversee or undertake to give an accompt for all to whom their paper sends greeting? St. *Paul* to the Elders of *Ephesus* thinks it sufficient to give charge *that they take heed to themselves and to the Flocke,* over which they were made overseers; beyond those bounds hee inlarges not their Commission. And surely when we put down Bishops, and put up Presbyters, which the most of them have made use of to enrich and exalt themselves, and turn the first heele against their Benefactors, we did not think that one Classick Fraternity so obscure and so remote, should involve us and all State affairs within the Censure and Jurisdiction of *Belfast,* upon pretence of overseeing their own charge.

Wee very well know that Church Censures are limited to Church matters, and these within the compasse of their own Province, or to say more truly of their own Congregation: that affaires of State are not for their Medling, as we could

urge ev'n from their own Invectives and Protestations against
the Bishops, wherein they tell them with much fervency, that
Ministers of the Gospell, neither by that function nor by any
other which they ought accept, have the least Warrant to be
5 Pragmaticall in the State.

And surely in vain were Bishops for these and other Causes
forbid to sit and vote in the Hous, if these men out of the
house, and without vote shall claim and be permitted more
license on their Presbyteriall stooles, to breed continuall dis-
10 turbance by interposing in the Common Wealth. But seeing
that now, since their heaving out the Prelats to heave in themselves, they devise new wayes to bring both ends together
which will never meete, that is to say their former Doctrine
with their present doings, as *that they cannot else teach Mag-*
15 *istrates and Subjects their duty, and that they have besides a*
Right themselves to speake as Members of the Common
Wealth, Let them know that there is a wide difference between the generall exhortation to Justice and Obedience,
which in this point is the utmost of their Duty, and the State
20 disputes wherein they are now grown such busie Bodies, to
preach of Titles, Interests, and alterations in government:
more then our Saviour himselfe, or any of his Apostles ever
took upon them, though the Title both of *Cæsar* and of *Herod,*
and what they did in matters of State might have then ad-
25 mitted controversie anough.

Next for their Civill Capacities, we are sure that Pulpits
and Church-assemblies, whether Classicall or Provinciall,
never were intended or allowd by wise Magistrates, no nor

by him that sent them, to advance such purposes; but that as
Members of the Common Wealth they ought to mixe with
other Commoners, and in that temporall Body to assume
nothing above other Private persons, or otherwise then in a
5 usuall and legall manner: not by distinct Remonstrances and
representments, as if they were a Tribe and party by themselves, which is the next immediate way to make the Church
lift a Horne against the State, and claim an absolute and undepending Jurisdiction, as from like advantage and occasion
10 (to the trouble of all Christ'ndome) the Pope hath for many
Ages done; and not only our Bishops were climing after him,
but our Presbyters also, as by late experiment wee find. Of
this Representation therefore wee can esteem and judge no
other then of a slandrous and seditious libell, sent abroad by a
15 sort of Incendiaries, to delude and make the better way under
the cunning and plausible name of a Presbytery.

A second Reason of thir Representing is, *that they consider
the dependance of that Kingdome upon England,* which is
another shamelesse untruth that ever they consider'd; as their
20 own Actions will declare, by conniving, and in thir silence
partaking with those in *Ulster,* whose obedience by what we
have yet heard, stands dubious, and with an eye of Conformity rather to the North, then to that part where they owe thir
subjection; and this in all likelihood by the inducement and
25 instigation of these Representers: who are so farr from considering thir dependence on *England,* as to presume at every
word to terme proceedings of Parliament, *the Insolencies of
a Sectarian party, and of private men.* Despising Dominion,

and speaking evill of Dignities, which hypocritically they would seeme to disswade others from; and not fearing the due correction of their Superiors, that may in fit season overtake them. When as the least consideration of their Dependance on
5 *England* would have kept them better in their Duty.

The third Reason which they use, makes against them; The remembrance how God punisht the contempt of their warning last yeare upon the Breakers of Covnant, whenas the next year after they forget the warning of that punishment
10 hanging over their own heads for the very same transgression, their manifest breach of Covnant by this seditious Representation accompanied with the doubtfull obedience of that Province which represents it.

And thus we have their preface supported with three Rea-
15 sons; two of them notorious falsities, and the third against themselves; and two examples, *the Province of London, & the Commissioners of the Kirk Assembly.* But certain, if Canonicall examples bind not, much lesse doe Apocryphall.

Proceeding to avouch the Trust put upon them by God,
20 which is plainly prov'd to be none of this Nature, *They would not be lookd upon as sowers of Sedition, or authors of divisive motions, their Record,* they say, *is in heaven,* and their Truth and honesty no man knowes where. For is not this a shamelesse hypocrisie, and of meer wolves in sheeps cloathing,
25 to sow sedition in the Eares of all men, and to face us downe in the very Act, that they are Authors of no such matter. But let the sequell both of their paper, and the obedience of the place wherein they are, determine.

Nay while we are yet writing these things, and foretelling all men the rebellion which was eevn then design'd in the close purpose of these unhallow'd Priestlings, at the very time when with thir lips they disclaim'd all sowing of sedition, newes is
5 brought, and too true, that the *Scottish* Inhabitants of that Province are actually revolted, and have not only besieg'd in *London-Derry* those Forces which were to have fought against *Ormond,* and the Irish Rebels; but have in a manner declar'd with them, and begun op'n war against the Parlament; and
10 all this by the incitement and illusions of that unchristian Synagogue at *Belfast,* who yet dare charge the Parlament, *that notwithstanding specious pretences, yet thir actings doe evidence that they love a rough garment to deceive.* The Deceit we own not, but the Comparison, by what at first sight
15 may seem alluded, we accept: For that hairy roughnesse assum'd won *Jacob* the Birthright both Temporall and Eternall; and God wee trust hath so dispos'd the mouth of these *Balaams,* that comming to Curse, they have stumbled into a kind of Blessing, and compar'd our actings to the faithfull
20 Act of that Patriarch.

But if they mean, as more probably thir meaning was, that *rough garment* spok'n of *Zach.* 13. 4. We may then behold the pittiful store of learning, and theology, which these deceivers have thought sufficient to uphold their credit with the
25 people, who, though the rancour that levens them have somewhat quickn'd the common drawling of thir Pulpit elocution, yet for want of stock anough in Scripture-phrase to serve the necessary uses of thir malice, they are become so liberall,

as to part freely with their own budge gownes from off their backs, and bestow them on the Magistrate as *a rough garment* to deceive; rather then not be furnish'd with a reproach though never so improper, never so obvious to be turn'd upon
5 themselves. For but with half an eye cast upon that text, any man will soon discern that *rough garment* to be thir own coate, thir own livery, the very badge and cognisance of such false prophets as themselves. Who, when they understand, or ever seriously mind the beginning of that 4th. verse, may *be*
10 *asham'd every one of his lying vision,* and may justly fear that foregoing denouncement to such *as speak lies in the name of the Lord,* vers. 3. lurking under the *rough garment* of outward rigor and formality, whereby they cheat the simple. So that *this rough garment to deceiv* we bring ye once again,
15 Grave Sirs, into your own Vestry; or with *Zachary* shall not think much to fit it to your own shoulders. To bestow ought in good earnest on the Magistrate, we know your classic Priestship is too gripple, for yee are alwayes begging: and for this rough gown to deceav, we are confident yee cannot spare it;
20 it is your Sundays gown, your every day gown, your only gown, the gown of your faculty; your divining gowne; to take it from ye were sacrilege. Weare it therfore, & possesse it your selvs, most grave and reverend Carmelites, that all men both young and old, as we hope they will shortly, may yet
25 better know ye and distinguish ye by it; and give to your rough gown where ever they meete it, whether in Pulpit, Classis, or Provincial Synod, the precedency, and the preeminence of deceaving.

They charge us next that we have brokn the Cov'nant, &
load'n it with slighting Reproaches. For the reproaching, let
them answer that are guilty, wherof the State we are sure cannot be accus'd. For the breaking, let us hear wherin. *In*
5 *labouring* say they, *to establish by Law a universall tolleration
of all Religions*. This touches not the State; for certainly were
they so minded, they need not labour it, but do it, having
power in thir hands; and we know of no act as yet past to
that purpose. But suppose it done, wherin is the Covnant
10 broke? The Covnant enjoyns us to endeavor the extirpation
first of Popery and Prelacy, then of Heresy, Schism, and
prophaness, and whatsoever shall be found contrary to sound
Doctrin and the power of godliness. And this we ceas not to
do by all effectuall and proper means: But these Divines
15 might know, that to extirpat all these things can be no work
of the Civil sword, but of the spirituall which is the Word
of God.

No man well in his wits endeavoring to root up weeds out
of his ground, instead of using the spade will take a Mallet or
20 a Beetle. Nor doth the *Covnant* any way engage us to extir-
pate, or to prosecute the men, but the heresies and errors in
them, which we tell these Divines and the rest that understand
not, belongs chiefly to their own Function, in the diligent
preaching and insisting upon sound Doctrin, in the confuting
25 not the railing down errors, encountring both in public and
private Conference, and by the power of truth, not of perse-
cution, subduing those authors of hereticall opinions, & lastly
in the spirituall execution of Church discipline within thir

own congregations. In all these ways wee shall assist them,
favour them, and as far as appertains to us joyn with them,
and moreover not tolerate the free exercise of any Religion,
which shall be found absolutely contrary to sound Doctrin
5 or the power of godliness; for the conscience we must have
patience till it be within our verge. And thus doing we shall
believ to have kept exactly all that is requird from us by the
Covnant. Whilst they by thir seditious practises against us,
then which nothing for the present can adde more assistance
10 or advantage to those bloudy Rebels and Papists in the South,
will be found most pernicious Covnant-breakers themselves,
and as deep in that guilt as those of thir own Nation the last
year; the warning of whose ill successe like men hardn'd for
the same judgment, they miserably pervert to an incourage-
15 ment in the same offence, if not a far worse; For now they
have joyn'd interest with the *Irish Rebels,* who have ever
fought against the *Covnant,* wheras thir Country-men the
year before made the *Covnant* thir plea. But as it is a peculiar
mercy of God to his people, while they remain his, to preserve
20 them from wicked confederations: so it is a mark and punishment of hypocrites to be drivn at length to mix thir cause, and
the interest of thir *Covnant* with Gods enemies.

And wheras they affirm that the tolerating of all Religions
in the manner that we tolerat them, is an innovation, we must
25 acquaint them that we are able to make it good if need be,
both by Scripture and the Primitive Fathers, and the frequent
assertion of whole Churches and Protestant States in thir Remonstrances and expostulations against the Popish tyranny

over souls. And what force of argument do these Doctors
bring to the contrary? But we have long observ'd to what
passe the bold ignorance and sloth of our Clergy tends no
less now then in the Bishops days, to make thir bare sayings
5 and censures authentic with the People, though destitute of
any proofe or argument. But thanks be to God they are discern'd.

Thir next impeachment is, *that we oppose the Presbyteriall*
government, the hedg and bulwark of Religion. Which all
10 the Land knows to be a most impudent falshood, having establishd it with all freedom, wherever it hath been desir'd. Nevertheless as we perceave it aspiring to be a compulsive power
upon all without exception in Parochiall, Classicall, and Provinciall Hierarchies, or to require the fleshly arm of Magis-
15 tracy in the execution of a spirituall Discipline, to punish and
amerce by any corporall infliction those whose consciences
cannot be edifi'd by what authority they are compell'd, we
hold it no more to be *the hedg and bulwark of Religion,* then
the Popish and Prelaticall Courts, or the *Spanish Inquisition.*
20 But we are told, *We imbrace Paganism and Judaism in the*
arms of toleration. A most audacious calumny. And yet while
we detest *Judaism,* we know our selves commanded by St.
Paul, Rom. 11. to respect the *Jews,* and by all means to endeavor thir conversion.

25 Neither was it ever sworn in the *Covnant* to maintain a
universal Presbytery in *England,* as they falsly allege, but in
Scotland against the Common Enemy, if our aid were calld
for: being left free to reform our own Country according to the

Word of God, and the example of best reformed Churches; from which rule we are not yet departed.

But heer utterly forgetting to be Ministers of the Gospel, they presume to op'n their mouths not *in the spirit of meek-* 5 *nesse,* as like dissemblers they pretend, but with as much devillish malice, impudence and falshood as any Irish Rebell could have utter'd; and from a barbarous nook of *Ireland* brand us with the extirpation of laws and liberties; things which they seem as little to understand as ought that belongs 10 to good letters or humanity.

That wee seisd on the person of the King. Who was surrendred into our hands an Enemy and Captive by our own subordinate and paid Army of *Scots* in *England.* Next *our imprisoning many Members of the House.* As if it were im- 15 possible they should deserve it, conspiring and banding against the public good; which to the other part appearing, and, with the power they had, not resisting, had bin a manifest desertion of thir trust and duty. No question but it is as good and necessary to expell rott'n Members out of the House, 20 as to banish Delinquents out of the Land: and the reason holds as well in forty as in five. And if they be yet more, the more dangerous is thir number. They had no privilege to sit there and vote home the author, the impenitent author of all our miseries to freedom, honour, and royalty, for a few fraudulent 25 if not destructive concessions. Which that they went about to doe, how much more clear it was to all men, so much the more expedient, and important to the Common-Wealth was their speedy seisure and exclusion; and no breach of any just privilige, but a breach of their knotted faction. And heer they cry out, *An action without paralell in any age.* So heartily we wish all men were unprejudic'd in all our actions, as these illiterat denouncers never parallelld so much of any age as

5 would contribute to the tithe of a Century. *That wee abolish Parlamentary power, and establish a representative instead thereof.* Now we have the hight of them; these profound Instructors in the midst of thir Representation, would know the *English* of a Representative, and were perhaps of that

10 Classis, who heretofore were as much staggerd at *Trienniall.*

Thir grand accusation is our Justice don on the King, which that they may prove to be *without rule or example,* they venture all the credit they have in divine and human history; and by the same desperate boldness detect themselves

15 to be egregious liars and impostors, seeking to abuse the multitude with a show of that gravity and learning which never was their portion. Had thir knowledge bin equall to the knowledge of any stupid Monk, or Abbot, they would have known at least, though ignorant of all things else, the life and

20 acts of him, who first instituted thir order: but these blockish Presbyters of *Clandeboy* know not that *John Knox,* who was the first founder of Presbytery in *Scotland,* taught professedly the doctrine of deposing, and of killing Kings. And thus while they deny that any such rule can be found, the rule is found

25 in their own Country, givn them by thir own first presbyterian institutor; and they themselves like irregular Friers walking contrary to the rule of thir own foundation, deserv for so grosse an ignorance and transgression to be disciplin'd upon

thir own stools. Or had thir reading in history bin any, which
by this we may be confident is none at all, or thir malice not
highth'n'd to a blind rage, they never would so rashly have
thrown the dice to a palpable discovery of thir ignorance and
5 want of shame. But wherefore spend we two such precious
things as time & reason upon Priests, the most prodigal mis-
spenders of time, and the scarcest owners of reason? Tis sufficient we have publishd our defences, giv'n reasons, giv'n
examples of our Justice don; books also have bin writt'n to
10 the same purpose for men to look on that will; that no Nation
under heav'n but in one age or other hath don the like. The
difference onely is, which rather seemes to us matter of glory,
that they for the most part have without form of Law don
the deed by a kinde of martial Justice; wee by the deliberate
15 and well-weighd Sentence of legal Judicature.

But they tell us, *It was against the interest and protestation
of the Kingdom of Scotland.* And did exceeding well to joyn
those two together: heerby informing us what credit or regard
need be givn in *England* to a *Scotch* Protestation, usherd in by
20 a *Scotch* interest: certainly no more then we see is givn in
Scotland to an *English* Declaration, declaring the interest of
England. If then our interest move not them, why should
theirs move us? If they say, wee are not all *England;* we reply
they are not all *Scotland:* nay, were the last year so inconsider-
25 able a part of *Scotland* as were beholding to this which they
now term the Sectarian Army, to defend and rescue them at
the charges of *England* from a stronger party of thir own
Countrymen, in whose esteem they were no better then Sec-

tarians themselves. But they add, *It was against the former Declarations of both Kingdomes,* to seize, or proceed against the King. We are certain that no such Declarations of both Kingdomes as derive not thir full force from the sense and 5 meaning of the Covnant, can be produc'd.

And if they plead against us the Covenant, *To preserve and defend his person;* we aske them briefly whether they take the Covenant to be absolute or conditionall? If absolute, then suppose the King to have committed all prodigious crimes 10 and impieties against God, or nature, or whole Nations, he must neverthelesse be sacred from all violent touch. Which absurd opinion, how it can live in any mans reason, either naturall or rectifi'd, wee much marvell: Since God declard his anger as impetuous for the saving of King *Benhadad,* 15 though surrendring himselfe at mercy, as for the killing of *Naboth.* If it be conditionall, in the preservation and defence of Religion, and the peoples libertie, then certainly to take away his life beeing dangerous, and pernicious to both these, was no more a breach of the Covnant, then for the same 20 reason at *Edinburrow* to behead *Gordon* the Marquess *Huntley.* By the same Covnant we made vow to assist and to defend all those that should enter with us into this league: not absolutely but in the maintenance and pursuing thereof. If therefore no man else ever were so madd as to claime from 25 hence an impunitie from all Justice, why should any for the King? Whose life by other Articles of the same Covnant was forfet. Nay if common sense had not led us to such a cleer interpretation, the *Scotch* Commissioners themselves might

boast to have bin our first teachers: who when they drew to
the malignance which brought forth that perfidious last years
irruption against all the bands of Covnant or Christian neigh-
bourhood, making thir hollow plea the defence of his Maj-
5 esties person, they were constraind by thir own guiltinesse to
leave out that following morsell that would have choakd
them, the *preservation and defence of true Religion, and our
liberties*. And questionless in the preservation of these, wee
are bound as well, both by the Covnant, and before the Cov-
10 nant, to preserve and defend the person of any private man,
and the person and authoritie of any inferior Magistrate: So
that this Article objected with such vehemence against us,
containes not an exception of the Kings person, and autoritie
to doe by privilege what wickedness he list, and be defended,
15 as som fancy, but an express testification of our Loyaltie, and
the plaine words without wresting will beare as much, that
wee had no thoughts against his person, or just power, provided they might consist with the preservation and defence of
true Religion and our liberties. But to these how hazardous
20 his life was, will be needless to repeat so oftn. It may suffice
that while he was in custody, where wee expected his repentance, his remorse at last and compassion of all the innocent
bloud shed already and hereafter likely to be shed for his meer
wilfulness, he made no other use of our continuall forbear-
25 ance, our humblest Petitions and obtestations at his feet, but
to sit contriving and fomenting new plots against us, and as
his own phrase was, *playing his own game,* upon the miseries
of his people: Of which wee desire no other view at present

then these Articles of peace with the Rebells, and the rare game likely to ensue from such a cast of his Cards. And then let men reflect a little upon the slanders and reviles of these wretched Priests, and judge what modesty, what truth, what conscience, what anything fit for Ministers, or wee might say reasonable men can harbour in them. For what they began in shamelesness and malice, they conclude in frenzie: throwing out a sudden rapsody of Proverbs quite from the purpose; and with as much comliness as when *Saul* propheci'd. For casting off, as he did his garments, all modestie and meekness wherewith the language of Ministers ought to be cloath'd, speaking especially to thir supreme Magistrate, they talke at random of *servants raigning, servants riding, and wonder how the Earth can beare them.* Either these men imagin themselves to be marvellously high set and exalted in the chaire of *Belfast,* to voutsafe the Parlament of *England* no better stile then *servants,* or els thir high notion, which wee rather beleeve, falls as low as Court parasitism; supposing all men to be servants, but the King. And then all thir paines tak'n to seem so wise in proverbing, serves but to conclude them down right slaves: and the edge of thir own proverb falls reverse upon themselves. For as *Delight is not seemly for fooles,* much less high words to come from base minds. What they are for Ministers, or how they crept into the fould, whether at the window, or through the wall, or who set them there so haughtie in the Pontificall See of *Belfast,* wee know not. But this wee rather have cause to wonder if the Earth can beare this unsufferable insolency of upstarts; who from a

ground which is not thir own dare send such defiance to the
sovran Magistracy of *England,* by whose autoritie and in
whose right they inhabit there. By thir actions we might
rather judge them to be a generation of High-land theevs
5 and Red-shanks, who beeing neighbourly admitted, not as
the *Saxons* by merit of thir warfare against our enemies, but
by the courtesie of *England* to hold possessions in our Province, a Countrey better then thir own, have, with worse faith
then those Heathen, prov'd ingratefull and treacherous guests
10 to thir best friends and entertainers. And let them take heed,
lest while thir silence, as to those matters, might have kept
them blameless and secure under these proceedings which
they so feard to partake in, that these thir treasonous attempts
and practices, have not involv'd them in a farr worse guilt of
15 rebellion; and (notwithstanding that faire dehortatory from
joyning with Malignants) in the appearance of a co interest
and partaking with the *Irish* Rebells. Against whom, though
by themselves pronounced to be the enemies of God, they goe
not out to battell, as they ought, but rather by these thir doings
20 assist and become associats.

The End.

A DECLARATION OR LETTERS
PATENTS OF THE ELECTION OF THIS
PRESENT KING OF POLAND

Letters Patents of the Election of the most serene King of POLAND.

In the name of the most holy and Individual Trinity, the Father, Son, and Holy Spirit.

---

5 WE ANDREW TREZEBICKI, Bishop of *Cracovia*, Duke of *Severia*, JOHN GEMBICKI of *Uladislau* and *Pomerania,* &c. Bishops to the number of Ten.

10 STANISLAUS WARSZYCKI, Castellon of *Cracovia;* ALEXANDER MICHAEL LUBOMIRSKI of *Cracovia,* &c. Palatines to the number of Twenty Three.

CHRISTOPHERUS GRZYMALTOUSKI of *Posnania,* ALEXANDER GRATUS de *Tarnow* of *Sandimer:* Castellons to the number 15 of Twenty Four.

HILAREUS POLUBINSKI, High Marshal of the great Dukedom of *Lituania,* CHRISTOPHERUS PAC, High Chancelor of the great Dukedom of *Lituania,* Senators and Great Officers, to the number of Seventy five.

20 WE Declare by these our present Letters unto all and single Persons whom it may concern: Our Commonwealth being again left Widowed, by the unseasonable death of that famous MICHAEL late King of *Poland,* who having scarce reigned full five years, on the tenth

day of *November* of the year last past, at *Leopolis,* changed
his fading Crown for one Immortal; in the sence of so mourn-
ful a Funeral and fresh Calamity, yet with an undaunted
Courage, mindful of her self in the midst of Dangers, forbore
5 not to seek Remedies, that the World may understand she
grows in the midst of her losses; it pleased her to begin her
Counsels of preserving her Country, and delivering it from
the utmost chances of an Interreign, from the Divine Deity,
(as it were by the only motion of whose finger) it is easie that
10 Kingdoms be transferred from Nation to Nation, and Kings
from the lowest state to Thrones; And therefore the business
was begun according to our Countrey-Laws and Ancestors
Institutions. After the Convocation of all the States of the
Kingdom ended, in the month of *February* at *Warsaw,* by
15 the common consent of all those States on the day decreed for
the Election the 20th of *April;* At the report of this famous
Act, as though a Trumpet had been sounded, and a Trophy
of Vertue erected, the wishes and desires of Forreign Princes
came forth of their own accord into the Field of the *Polonian*
20 Liberty, in a famous strife of Merits and good-will towards
the Commonwealth, every one bringing their Ornaments,
advantages and Gifts to the Commonwealth: But the Commonwealth becoming more diligent by the prodigal ambition
used in the last Interreign, and Factions, and disagreeings of
25 minds, nor careless of the future, considered with her self
whether firm or doubtful things were promised, and whether
she should seem from the present state to transfer both the old
and new honours of *Poland* into the possession of strangers,

or the military glory, and their late unheard-of Victory over the *Turks,* and blood spilt in the war, upon the purple of some unwarlike Prince; as if any one could so soon put on the love of the Country, and that *Poland* was not so much an enemy
5 to her own Nation and Fame, as to favour strangers more than her own; and valour being found in her, should suffer a Guest of new Power to wax proud in her; therefore she thenceforth turned her thoughts upon some one in her own Nation, and at length abolished (as she began in the former Election) that
10 reproach cast upon her, under pretence of a secret Maxime, *That none can be elected King of* Poland *but such as are born out of Poland;* neither did she seek long among her Citizens whom she should prefer above the rest (for this was no uncertain or suspended Election, there was no place for delay; for
15 although in the equality of our Nobles many might be elected, yet the vertue of a Hero appeared above his equals, therefore the eyes and minds of all men were willingly and by a certain divine instinct turned upon the High Marshal of the Kingdom, Captain of the Army *John Sobietski.* The admirable
20 vertue of the Man, the High Power of Marshal in the Court, with his supreme command in Arms, Senatorial Honour, with his civil Modesty, the extraordinary Splendor of his Birth and Fortune, with open Courtesie, Piety towards God, love to his Fellow-Citizens in words and deeds; Constancy, Faith-
25 fulness, and Clemency towards his very enemies, and what noble things soever can be said of a Hero, did lay such Golden Chains on the Minds and Tongues of all, that the Senate and People of *Poland* and of the great Dukedome of

Lituania; with Suffrages and agreeing Voices named and chose him their KING; not with his seeking nor precipitate counsel, but with mature Deliberations continued and extended till the third day.

5   Certainly it conduced much for the honour of the most serene Elect, the Confirmation of a free Election, and the eternal praise of the People electing, that the great business of an Age was not transacted in one day, or in the Shadow of the night, or by one casual heat: for it was not right that a Hero
10 of the Age, should in a moment of time (and as it were by the cast of a Die) be made a King, when as Antiquity by an ancient Proverb has delivered, that *Hercules* was not begot in one night; and it hath taught that Election should shine openly under a clear Sky, in the open Light.

15   The most serene Elect took it modestly that his Nomination should be deferred till the third day, plainly shewing to endeavour, lest his sudden facility of assent being suspected, might detract from their Judgment, and the World might be enforced to believe by a more certain Argument, that he that
20 was so chosen was elected without his own Ambition, or the envy of corrupted Liberty: or was it by the appointed Counsel of God that this debate continued three whole days, from *Saturday* till *Munday,* as if the *Cotimian* Victory (begun on the Saturday, and at length on the third day after accom-
25 plished, after the taking of the *Cotimian* Castle) had been a lucky presage of his Royal Reward; or, as if with an auspicious *Omen,* the third day of Election had alluded to the Regal name of *JOHN* the Third.

The famous Glory of War paved his way to the Crown, and confirmed the favour of Suffrages to his most serene Elect. He the first of all the *Polonians* shewed that the *Scythian* swiftness (troublesome heretofore to all the Monarchies of the World) might be repressed by a standing Fight, and the terrible main Battalion of the *Turk*, might be broken and routed at one stroke. That we may pass by in silence the ancient Rudiments of Warfare which he stoutly and gloriously managed under the Conduct and Authority of another, against the *Swedes, Muscovites, Borussians, Transylvanians* and *Cossacks;* though about sixty Cities taken by him from the *Cossacks* be less noised in the mouth of fame; yet these often and prosperous Battels, were a *Prelude* to greatest Victories in the memory of man. Miriads of *Tartars* had overrun within this six years with their plundering Troops the coast of *Podolia;* when a small force and some shattered Legions were not sufficient against the hostile assault, yet our General knowing not to yeeld, shut himself up (by a new stratagem of War) in *Podhajecy*, a strait Castle, and fortified in haste, whereby he might exclude the cruel destruction which was hastening into the bowels of the Kingdom, by which means the Barbarian deluded and routed, took Conditions of Peace; as if he had made his inroad for this only purpose, that he might bring to the most serene Elect, matter of Glory, Victory.

For these Four last years the famous Victories of *Sobietski* have Signalized every year of his Warlike Command on the *Cossacks,* and *Tartarians,* both joyned together; the most strong Province of *Braclavia*, as far as it lyes between *Hypanis* and *Tyral,* with their Cities and Warlike people, were won from the *Cossack* enemy.

And those things are beyond belief which two years ago the most serene Elect, after the taking of *Camenick,* (being
5 undaunted by the Seige of *Laopolis,*) performed to a Miracle by the hardness and fortitude of the *Polonian* Army, scarce consisting of three thousand men, in the continual course of five days and nights, sustaining life without any food, except wild herbs; setting upon the *Tartarians,* he made famous the
10 names of *Narulum, Niemicrovia, Konarnum, Kalussia,* obscure Towns before, by a great overthrow of the Barbarians. He slew three Sultans of the *Crim-Tartars,* descended of the royal *Gietian* family, and so trampled on that great force of the *Scythians,* that in these latter years they could not re-
15 gain their Courage or recollect the Forces. But the felicity of this last Autumn exceeded all his Victories; when-as the fortifications at *Chocimum,* famous of old, were possessed and fortified by above forty thousand Turks, in which three and forty years ago the *Polonians* had sustained and repressed the
20 Forces of the *Ottoman* Family, drawn together out of *Asia, Africa,* and *Europe,* fell to the ground within a few hours; by the only (under God) Imperatorious Valour and Prudence, of *Sobietski;* for he counted it his chief part to go about the Watches, order the Stations, and personally to inspect the
25 preparations of Warlike Ordinance, to encourage the Soldiers with voice, hands, and countenance, wearied with hunger, badness of weather, and three days standing in arms; and he (which is most to be admired) on Foot at the head of the

foot-forces made thorough and forced his way to the Battery,
hazarding his life devoted to God and his Countrey; and
thereupon made a cruel slaughter within the Camp and Fortifications of the Enemy; while the desperation of the *Turks*
5 whetted their valour, and he performed the part of a most
provident and valiant Captain; at which time three *Bashaw's*
were slain, the fourth scarce passed with difficulty the swift
river of *Tyras;* eight thousand *Janizaries,* twenty thousand
chosen *Spachies,* besides the more Common Souldiers, were
10 cut off; the whole Camp with all their Ammunition, and great
Ordinance: besides the *Assyrian* and *Phrygian* wealth of luxurious *Asia,* were taken and pillaged, the famous Castle of
Cotimia, and the Bridg over *Tyras,* strong Fortresses, equal
to Castles on each side the River, were additions to the Victory.
15 Why therefore should not such renown'd Heroick Valour be
crowned with the legal reward of a Diadem? All *Christen-*
dom have gone before us in example, which being arrived
to the recovery of *Jerusalem* under the conduct of *Godfrey*
of Bullion, on their own accord gave him that Kingdom, for
20 that he first scaled the walls of that City. Our most serene
Elect is not inferior, for he first also Ascended two main Fortresses of the Enemy.

The moment of time adorns this Victory unheard-of in
many ages, the most serene King *Michael* dying the day be-
25 fore, as it were signifying thereby that he gave way to so
great valour, as if it were by his command and favour, that
this Conqueror might so much the more gloriously suceed
from the Helmet to the Crown, from the Commanders Staff

to the Scepter, from his lying in the Field to the Regal Throne.

The Commonwealth recalled the grateful, and never to be forgotten memory of his Renowned Father, the most Illustrious and Excellent *James Sobietski,* Castellion of *Cracovia,* a Man to be written of with sedulous care, who by his Golden Eloquence in the publick Counsels, and by his Hand in the Scene of War, had so often amplified the State of the Commonwealth, and defended it with the Arms of his Family. Neither can we believe it happened without Divine Providence, that in the same place wherein forty years ago his Renowned Father Embassador of the *Polonian*-Commonwealth, had made Peace and Covenants with *Cimanus* the Turkish General, his great Son should Revenge with his Sword the Peace broke, (Heaven it self upbraiding the perfidious Enemy). The rest of his Grandsires and Great-Grandsires, and innumerable Names of Famous Senators and great Officers have as it were brought forth light to the serene Elect by the emulous Greatness and Glory of his Mothers descent, especially *Stanislaus Zelkievius,* High Chancellor of the Kingdom, and General of the Army, at whose Grave in the Neighbouring fields, in which by the *Turkish* rage in the year 1620 he died, his victorious Nephew took full revenge by so remarkable an overthrow of the Enemy: The immortal valour and fatal fall of his most noble Uncle *Stanislaus Danilovitius* in the year 1635, Palatine of *Russia,* doubled the Glory of his Ancestors; whom desirous of honour and not induring that sluggish Peace wherein *Poland* then slept secure, valour and youthful heat accited at his own expence and

private forces, into the Taurick fields; that by his footing
and the ancient Warlike Polonian discipline, he might lead
and point the way to these merits of *Sobietski,* and being slain
by *Cantimiz* the Tartarian Cham, in revenge of his Son by
5 him slain, he might by his Noble blood give lustre to this
Regal Purple; neither hath the people of *Poland* forgot the
most illustrious *Marcus Sobietski* elder Brother of our most
serene Elect, who when the Polonian Army at *Batto* was
routed by the Barbarians, although occasion was offer'd him
10 of escape, yet chose rather to die in the overthrow of such
valiant men, a Sacrifice for his Countrey, than to buy his life
with a dishonourable retreat; perhaps the divine Judgment
so disposing, whose order is that persons pass away and fail,
and causes and events happen again the same; that by the re-
15 peated fate of the *Huniades,* the elder Brother of great hopes
removed by a lamented slaughter, might leave to his younger
Brother surviving the readier passage to the Throne. That
therefore which we pray may be happy, Auspicious and for-
tunate to our Orthodox Commonwealth, and to all Christen-
20 dome, with free and unanimous Votes, none opposing, all
consenting and applauding, by the right of our free Election,
notwithstanding the Absence of those which have been called
and not Appeared, We being led by no private respect, but
having only before our eyes the Glory of God, the increase of
25 the ancient Catholick Church, the safety of the Commonwealth, and the dignity of the *Polish* Nation and Name, have
thought fit to elect, create, and name, *JOHN in Zolkiew and*
Zloczew Sobietski, Supreme Marshal General of the King-

dom General of the Armies, Governour of *Neva, Bara, Strya, Loporovient,* and *Kalussien,* most eminently adorned with so high endowments, merits and splendor, to be *KING* of *Poland,* Grand-Duke of *Lituania, Russia, Prussia, Mazovia,*
5 *Samogitia, Kyovia, Volhinnia, Padlachia, Podolia, Livonia, Smolensko, Severia,* and *Czerniechovia,* as we have Elected Created Declared and Named Him; I the afore said Bishop of *Cracovia* (the Archiepiscopal See being vacant) exercising the Office and Authority of Primate and by consent of all the
10 States thrice demanded, opposed by none, by all and every one approved, conclude the Election: Promising faithfully that we will always perform to the same most serene and potent Elect Prince, Lord *John the third,* our King, the same Faith, Subjection, Obedience and Loyalty according to our
15 Rights and Liberties, as we have performed to his blessed Ancestor, as also that we will crown the same most serene Elect in the next Assembly at *Cracovia,* to that end ordained, as our true King and Lord, with the Regal Diadem, with which the Kings of *Poland* were wont to be crown'd, and
20 after the manner which the *Roman* Catholick Church before-time hath observed in Anointing and Inaugurating Kings, We will anoint and inaugurate him; Yet so as he shall hold fast and observe first of all the Rights, Immunities both Ecclesiastical and Secular, granted and given to us by his Ancestor
25 of Blessed memory; as also these Law's which we our Selves, in the time of this present and former Inter-reign, according to the Right of our Liberty, and better preservation of the Commonwealth have established. And if moreover the most

Serene Elect will bind himself by an Oath, to perform the
conditions concluded with those persons sent by his Majesty,
before the exhibition of this present Decree of Election, and
will provide in best manner for the performance of them by
5 his authenick Letters; which Decree of Election we by Divine
aid, desirous to put in execution, do send by common consent, to deliver it into the hands of the most Serene Elect, the
most illustrious and reverend Lord Bishop of *Cracovia*, together with some Senators and chief Officers, and the illus-
10 trious and magnificent *benedictus Sapieha,* Treasurer of the
Court of the Great Dukedom of *Lituania,* Marshal of the
Equestrian Order; commiting to them the same Decree of
intimating an Oath, upon the aforesaid premises, and receiving his Subscription; and at length to give and deliver the
15 same Decree into the hands of the said Elect, and to act and
perform all other things which this affair requires, in assurance whereof the Seals of the Lords Senators, and those of the
Equestrian Order deputed to sign, are here affixed.

Given by the hands of the most illustrious and reverend
20 Father in Christ, the Lord *Andrew Olssonski,* Bishop of
Culma and *Pomisania,* High Chancellor of the Kingdom, in
the general ordinary Assembly of the Kingdom, and great
Dukedom of *Lituania,* for the Election of the new King.
Warsaw the 22th day of May, in the year of our Lord 1674.
25 In the presence of *Franciscus Praszmouski,* provost of
Guesna, Abbot of *Sieciethovia,* chief Secretary of the
Kingdom; *Joannes Malachowski,* Abbot of *Mogila,*
Referendary of the Kingdom, &c. with other great Offi-

cers of the Kingdom and Clergy, to the number of foure-
score and two. And the rest, very many great Officers,
Captains, Secretaries, Courtiers, and Inhabitants of the
Kingdom, and great Dukedom of *Lituania,* gathered
together at *Warsaw,* to the present Assembly of the Elec-
tion of the Kingdom and great Dukedom of *Lituania.*
Assistants at the solemn Oath taken of his sacred Majesty
on the 5th day of the Month of *June,* in the Palace at
Warsaw, after the Letters Patents delivered upon the
Covenants, and Agreements, or Capitulations, the most
Reverend and Excellent Lord *Francisco Bonvisi,* Arch-
bishop of *Thessalonica,* Apostolick Nuntio; Count *Chris-
topherus a scaffgotsch, Cæcareus Tussanus de Forbin, de
Jason* Bishop of *Marseilles* in *France, Joannes* free-barron
Hoverbeck, from the Marquess of *Brandenburg,* Em-
bassadors; and other Envoyes and Ministers of State.

The End.

ACCEDENCE
COMMENC'T
GRAMMAR

TO THE

R E A D E R.

IT hath been long a general complaint, not without cause, in the bringing up of Youth, and still is, that the tenth part of mans life, ordinarily extended, is taken up in learning, and that very scarcely, the Latin Tongue. Which
5 tardy proficience may be attributed to several causes: In particular, the making two labours of one, by learning first the Accedence, then the Grammar in Latin, ere the Language of those Rules be understood. The only remedy of this, was to joyn both Books into one, and in the English
10 Tongue; whereby the long way is much abbreviated, and the labour of understanding much more easie: A work suppos'd not to have been done formerly; or if done, not without such difference here in brevity and alteration, as may be found of moment. That of Grammar, touching Letters and
15 Syllables, is omitted, as learnt before, and little different from the English Spelling-book; especially, since few will be perswaded to pronounce Latin otherwise then thir own English. What will not come under Rule, by reason of too much variety in Declension, Gender, or Construction, is
20 also here omitted, least the course and clearness of method be clog'd with Catalogues instead of Rules, or too much interruption between Rule and Rule: Which Linaker setting down the various Idiomes of many verbs, was forc't to do by Alphabet; and therefore, though very learned, not thought

fit to be read in Schools. But in such words, a Dictionary
stor'd with good Authorities *will be found the readiest guide.*
Of figurate Construction what is usefull is digested into
several Rules of Syntaxis: *and* Prosodie, *after this* Gram-
5 mar *well learnt, will not need to be English for him who*
hath a mind to read it. Account might be now givn what
addition or alteration from other Grammars hath been here
made, and for what reason. But he who would be short in
teaching, must not be long in Prefacing: The Book it self
10 *follows, and will declare sufficiently to them who can discern.*

J. M.

ACCEDENCE
COMMENC'T
GRAMMAR

LATIN *Grammar* is the Art of right understanding, speaking, or writing Latine, observd from them who
have spoken or written it best.

Grammar hath two Parts: Right-wording, usually call'd
5 *Etymologie;* and right-joyning of words, or *Syntaxis.*

Etymologie, or Right-wording, teacheth what belongs to
every single word or part of Speech.

Of Latin *SPEECH*

are Eight General Parts:

Noun		*Adverb*	
Pronoun		*Conjunction*	
10 *Verb*	Declin'd.	*Preposition*	Undeclin'd.
Participle		*Interjection*	

Declin'd are those Words which have divers endings; as
Homo a man, *hominis* of a man; *Amo* I love, *amas* thou lov-

est. *Undeclin'd* are those words which have but one ending, as *bene* well, *cum* when, *tum* then.

Nounes, Pronounes, and Participles, are declin'd with Gender, Number, and Case; Verbs, as hereafter in the Verb.

Of Genders.

5   Genders are three, the Masculin, Feminin, and Neuter. The Masculin may be declin'd with this Article *Hic,* as *hic Vir* a Man; The Feminin with this Article *Hæc,* as *hæc Mulier* a Woman; The Neuter with this Article *Hoc,* as *hoc Saxum* a Stone.

10   Of the Masculin are generally all Nounes belonging to the Male kind, as also the Names of Rivers, Months, and Winds.

Of the Feminin, all Nounes belonging to the Female kind, as also the names of Countries, Cities, Trees, some few of the

15 two latter excepted: Of Cities, as *Agragas* and *Sulmo,* Masculin; *Argos, Tibur, Præneste,* and such as end in *um,* Neuter; *Anxur* both. Of Trees, *Oleaster* and *Spinus,* Masculin; but *Oleaster* is read also Feminin, *Cic.* verr. 4. *Acer, siler, suber, thus, robur,* Neuter.

20   And of the Neuter are all Nouns, not being proper Names, ending in *um,* and many others.

Some Nouns are of two Genders, as *hic* or *hæc dies* a Day; and all such as may be spoken both of Male and Female, as *hic* or *hæc Parens* a Father or Mother; some be of three, as

25 *hic hæc* and *hoc Felix* Happy.

Of Numbers.

Words Declin'd have two Numbers, the Singular, and the Plural. The Singular speaketh but of one, as *Lapis* a Stone. The Plural of more then one, as *Lapides* Stones; yet sometimes but of one, as *Athenæ* the City *Athens, Literæ* an Epistle, *ædes ædium* a House.

Note that some Nounes have no Singular, and some no Plural, as the nature of thir signification requires. Some are of one Gender in the Singular; of another, or of two Genders in the Plural, as reading will best teach.

Of Cases.

Nounes, Pronounes, and Participles are declin'd with six Endings, which are called Cases, both in the Singular and Plural Number. The Nominative, Genitive, Dative, Accusative, Vocative, and Ablative.

The *Nominative* is the first Case, and properly nameth the thing, as *Liber* a Book.

The *Genitive* is Englisht with this Sign *of*, as *Libri* of a Book.

The *Dative* with this Sign *to*, or *for*, as *Libro* to or for a Book.

The *Accusative* hath no sign.

The *Vocative* calleth or speaketh to, as *O Liber* O Book, and is commonly like the Nominative.

But in the Neuter Gender the Nominative, Accusative, and Vocative, are like in both Numbers, and in the *Plural* end always in *a*.

The *Ablative* is Englisht with these Signs, *in, with, of, for, from, by,* and such like, as *de Libro* of or from the Book, *pro Libro* for the Book. And the Ablative Plural is alwayes like the Dative.

5 Note, that some Nouns have but one ending throughout all Cases, as *Frugi, nequam, nihil;* and all words of number from three to a hundred, as *quatuor* four, *quinque* five, *&c.*

Some have but one, some two, some three Cases only, in the Singular or Plural, as use will best teach.

Of a Noune.

10 A Noune is the Name of a thing, as *Manus* a Hand, *Domus* a House, *Bonus* Good, *Pulcher* Fair.

Nounes be Substantives or Adjectives.

A Noun Substantive is understood by it self, as *homo* a man, *domus* a house.

15 An Adjective, to be well understood, requireth a Substantive to be joyn'd with it, as *bonus* good, *parvus* little, which cannot be well understood unless somthing good or little be either nam'd, as *bonus vir* a good man, *parvus puer* a little boy; or by use understood, as *honestum* an honest thing, *boni* 20 good men.

The Declining of Substantives.

Nounes Substantive have five Declensions or forms of ending thir Cases, chiefly distinguisht by the different ending of thir Genitive Singular.

The first Declension.

The first is when the Genitive and Dative singular end in *æ, &c.* as in the Example following.

Singular.	Plural.
Nom. Voc. Abl. *musa*	Nom. Voc. *musæ*
Gen. Dat. *musæ*	Gen. *musarum*
Acc. *musam*	Dat. Abl. *musis*
	Acc. *Musas*

This one word *familia* joyn'd with *pater, mater, filius,* or *filia,* endeth the Genitive in *as,* as *pater familias,* but somtimes *familiæ. Dea, mula, equa, liberta,* make the Dative and Ablative plural in *abus; filia* and *nata* in *is* or *abus.*

The first Declension endeth alwayes in *a,* unless in some words deriv'd of the Greek: and is always of the Feminin Gender, except in names attributed to men, according to the general Rule, or to Stars, as *Cometa, Planeta.*

Nounes, and especially proper Names derived of the Greek, have here three endings, *as, es, e,* and are declin'd in some of their Cases after the Greek form. *Æneas,* acc. *Ænean,* voc. *Ænea. Anchises,* acc. *Anchisen,* voc. *Anchise* or *Anchisa,* abl. *Anchise. Penelope, Penelopes, Penelope, Penelopen,* voc. abl. *Penelope.* Somtimes following the Latin, as *Marsya, Philocteta,* for *as* and *es; Philoctetam, Eriphylam,* for *an* and *en.* Cic.

The second Declension.

The second is when the Genitive Singular endeth in *i,* the Dative in *o, &c.*

	Sing.			Plur.
Nom. Voc. *Liber*			Nom. Voc. *Libri*
Gen. *libri*			Gen. *librorum*
Dat. Abl. *libro*			Dat. Abl. *libris*
Acc. *librum*			Acc. *libros.*

5　　Note that when the Nominative endeth in *us*, the Vocative shall end in *e*, as *Dominus ô Domine*, except *Deus ô Deus.* And these following, *Agnus, lucus, vulgus, populus, chorus, fluvius, e* or *us.*

10　　When the Nominative endeth in *ius*, if it be the proper name of a man, the Vocative shall end in *i*, as *Georgius ô Georgi;* hereto add *filius ô fili*, and *genius ô geni.*

All Nounes of the Second Declension are of the Masculin or Neuter Gender; of the Masculin, such as end in *ir, or*, or 15 *us, except* some few, *humus, domus, alvus*, and others deriv'd of the Greek, as *methodus, antidotus*, and the like, which are of the Feminin, and some of them somtimes also Masculin, as *atomus, phaselus;* to which add *ficus* the name of a disease, *grossus, pampinus*, and *rubus.*

20　　Those of the Neuter, except *virus, pelagus*, and *vulgus* (which last is sometimes Masculin) end all in *um*, and are declin'd as followeth:

	Sing.			Plur.
Nom. Ac. Voc. *Studium*			Nom. Ac. Voc. *Studia*
25 Gen. *studii*			Gen. *Studiorum*
Dat. Abl. *studio*			Dat. Abl. *studiis.*

Some Nouns in this Declension are of the first Example Singular, of the second Plural, as *Pergamus* the City *Troy,*

Plur. *Hæc Pergama;* and some names of hills, as *Mænalus,*
Ismarus, hæc Ismara; So also *Tartarus,* and the Lake *Aver-*
nus; others are of both, as *sibilus, jocus, locus, hi loci,* or *hæc*
loca. Some are of the Second Example Singular, of the first
5 Plural, as *Argos, Cælum,* Plur. *hi Cæli;* others of both, as
Rastrum, Capistrum, Filum, Frænum; Plur. *fræni* or *fræna.*
Nundinum, & *Epulum,* are of the first Declension Plural,
Nundinæ, Epulæ; Balneum of both, *balneæ* or *balnea.*

Greek proper names have here three endings, *os, on,* and
10 *us* long from a Greek Diphthong. *Hæc Delos, hanc Delon.*
Hoc Ilion. The rest regular, *Hic panthus, ô panthu,* Virg.

The third Declension.

The third is when the Genitive singular endeth in *is,* the
Dative in *i,* the Accusative in *em* and somtimes in *im,* the
Ablative in *e,* and somtimes in *i,* the Nom. Acc. Voc. Plural
15 in *es,* the Genitive in *um* and somtimes in *ium,* &c.

Sing.	Plur.
Nom. Gen. Voc. *Panis*	Nom. Ac. Vo. *panes*
Dat. *pani*	Gen. *panum*
Acc. *panem*	Dat. Abl. *panibus.*
20 Abl. *pane*	

Sing.	Plur.
Nom. Voc. *Parens*	No. Ac. Voc. *parentes*
Gen. *parentis*	Gen. *parentum*
Dat. *parenti*	Dat. Abl. *parentibus.*
25 Acc. *parentem*	
Abl. *parente*	

This third Declension, with many endings, hath all Genders, best known by dividing all Nounes hereto belonging into such as either increase one syllable long or short in the Genitive, or increase not at all.

5 Such as increase not in the Genitive are generally Feminin, as *Nubes nubis, Caro carnis.*

Except such as end in *er,* as *hic venter ventris,* and these in *is* following, *natalis, aqualis, lienis, orbis, callis, caulis, collis, follis, mensis, ensis, fustis, funis, panis, penis, crinis, ignis,*
10 *cassis, fascis, torris, piscis, unguis, vermis, vectis, postis, acis,* and the Compounds of *assis, as centussis.*

But *Canalis, finis, clunis, restis, sentis, amnis, corbis, linter, torquis, anguis, hic* or *hæc;* To these add *vepres.*

Such as end in *e* are Neuters, as *mare, rete,* and two Greek
15 in *es,* as *hippomanes, cacoëthes.*

Nounes encreasing Long.

Nounes encreasing one syllable long in the Genitive are generally Feminin, as *hæc pietas pietatis, virtus virtutis.*

Except such as end in *ans* Masculin, as *dodrans, quadrans, sextans;* in *ens,* as *oriens, torrens, bidens* a pick-axe.

20 In *or,* most commonly deriv'd of Verbs, as *pallor, clamor;* in *o,* not thence deriv'd, as *ternio, senio, sermo, temo,* and the like.

And these of one syllable, *sal, sol, ren, splen, as, bes, pes, mos, flos, ros, dens, mons, pons, fons, greco.*

25 And words deriv'd from the Greek in *en,* as *lichen;* in *er,*

as *crater;* in *as,* as *adamas;* in *es,* as *lebes;* to these, *hydrops,*
thorax, phœnix.

But *scrobs, rudens, stirps* the body or root of a tree, and
calx a heel, *hic* or *hæc.*

5   Neuter, these of one syllable, *mel, fel, lac, far, ver, cor,*
æs, vas vasis, os ossis, os oris, rus, thus, jus, crus, pus. And of
more syllables in *al* and *ar,* as *capital, laquear,* but *halec hoc*
or *hæc.*

Nounes encreasing Short.

Nounes encreasing short in the Genitive are generally
10 Masculin, as *hic sanguis sanguinis, lapis lapidis.*

Except, Feminin all words of many syllables ending in *do*
or *go,* as *dulcedo, compago, arbor, hyems, cuspis, pecus,*
pecudis: These in *ex, forfex, carex, tomex, supellex:* In *ix,*
appendix, histrix, coxendix, filix. Greek Nounes in *as* and
15 *is,* as *lampas, iaspis:* To these add *chlamys, bacchar, syndon,*
icon.

But *margo, cinis, pulvis, adeps, forceps, pumex, ramex,*
imbrex, obex, silex, cortex, omix and *sardonix, hic* or *hæc.*

Neuters are all ending in *a* as *problema,* in *en,* except *hic*
20 *pecten,* in *ar* as *jubar,* in *er* these, *verber, iter, uber, cadaver,*
zinziber, laser, cicer, siser, piper, papaver; somtimes in *ur,*
except *hic furfur,* in *us* as *onus,* in *ut* as *caput;* to these, *mar-*
mor, æquor, ador.

Greek proper names here end in *as, an, is,* and *eus,* and
25 may be declin'd some wholly after the Greek form, as *Pallas*
pallados palladi pallada; others in some Cases, as *Atlas,* acc.

Atlanta, voc. *Atla. Garamas,* plur. *garamantes,* acc. *gara-*
mantas. Pan panos pana. Phyllis phyllidos, voc. *phylli,* plur.
Phyllides, acc. *phyllidas. Tethys, tethyos,* acc. *tethyn,* voc.
tethy. Neapolis, neapolios, acc. *neapolin. Paris, paridos* or
5 *parios,* acc. *parida* or *parin. Orpheus orpheos orphei orphea*
orpheu. But Names in *eus* borrow somtimes thir Genitive of
the Second Declension, as *Erechtheus, erechthei.* Cic. *Achil-*
les or *Achilleus, Achillei;* and somtimes their Accusative in
on or *um,* as *Orpheus Orpheon, Theseus Theseum, Perseus*
10 *Perseum,* which somtimes is formd after Greek words of the
First Declension Latin, *Perseus* or *Perses, Persæ Persæ Per-*
sen Persæ Persa.

The fourth Declension.

The fourth is when the Genitive Singular endeth in *us,*
the Dative Singular in *ui,* and somtimes in *u,* plural in *ibus,*
15 and sometimes in *ubus.*

Sing.		Plur.
Nom. Gen. Vo. *Sensus*		Nom. Ac. Voc. *Sensus*
Dat. *sensui*		Gen. *sensuum*
Acc. *sensum*		Dat. Abl. *sensibus.*
20 Abl. *sensu*		

The fourth Declension hath two endings, *us* and *u; us*
generally Masculin, except some few, as *hæc manus, ficus,*
the fruit of a tree, *acus, porticus, tribus:* but *penus* and *specus*
hic or *hæc. U* of the Neuter, as *gelu, genu, veru;* but in the
25 Singular most part defective.

Proper Names in *os* and *o* long pertaining to the Fourth

Declension Greek, may belong best to the fourth in Latin,
as *Androgeos,* Gen. *Androgeo,* Acc. *Androgeon.* Hic *Athos,*
hunc *Atho,* Virg. Hæc *Sappho,* Gen. *Sapphus,* Acc. *Sappho.*
Better Authors follow the Latin form, as *Dido didonis dido-*
5 *nem.* But *Iesus Iesu Iesu Iesum Iesu Iesu.*

The fifth Declension.

The fifth is when the Genitive and Dative Singular end
in *ei,* &c.

Sing.	Plur.
Nom. Voc. *Res*	Nom. Acc. Voc. *res*
Gen. Dat. *rei*	Gen. *rerum*
Acc. *rem*	Dat. Abl. *rebus.*
Abl. *re*	

All Nounes of the fifth Declension are of the Feminin
Gender, except *dies hic* or *hæc,* and his Compound *meridies*
15 *hic* only.

Some Nounes are of more Declensions then one, as *vas
vasis* of the third in the Singular, of the second in the Plural
vasa vasorum. *Colus, laurus,* and some others, of the second
and fourth. *Saturnalia, saturnalium* or *saturnaliorum, satur-*
20 *nalibus,* and such other names of feasts, *Poëmata poëmatum,
Poëmatis* or *poëmatibus,* of the second and third Plural. *Plebs*
of the third and fifth, *plebis* or *plebei.*

The declining of Adjectives.

A Noun Adjective is declin'd with three Terminations, or
with three Articles.

An Adjective of three terminations is declin'd like the first and second Declension of Substantives joyn'd together after this manner.

	Sing.		Plur.
5	Nom. *bonus bona bonum*		Nom. Vo. *boni bonæ bona*
	Gen. *boni bonæ boni*		Gen. *bonorum bonarum bonorum*
	Dat. *bono bonæ bono*		Dat. Abl. *bonis*
	Ac. *bonum bonam bonum*		Ac. *bonos bonas bona.*
	Voc. *bone bona bonum*		
10	Abl. *bono bona bono*		

In like manner those in *er* and *ur,* as *sacer sacra sacrum, satur satura saturum:* but *unus, totus, solus, alius, alter, ullus, uter,* with their compounds *Neuter, uterque,* and the like, make thir Genitive Singular in *ius,* the Dative in *i,* as *Unus* 15 *una unum,* Gen. *unius,* Dat. *uni,* in all the rest like *bonus,* save that *alius* maketh in the Neuter Gender *aliud,* and in the Dative *alii,* and somtimes in the Genitive.

Ambo and *duo* be thus declin'd in the plural only.

Nom. Voc. *Ambo ambæ ambo.*
20 Gen. *amborum ambarum amborum.*
Dat. Abl. *ambobus ambabus ambobus.*
Acc. *ambos* or *ambo, ambas ambo.*

Adjectives of three Articles have in the Nominative either one ending, as *hic, hæc, & hoc felix;* or two, as *hic & hæc* 25 *tristis, & hoc triste;* and are declin'd like the Third Declension of Substantives, as followeth.

Sing.

Nom. *hic hæc & hoc Felix*
Gen. *felicis*
Dat. *felici*
5 Acc. *hunc & hanc felicem,*
 & hoc felix
Voc. *ô felix*
Abl. *felice* or *felici*

Plur.

Nom. *hi & hæ felices, &*
 hæc felicia
Gen. *felicium*
Dat. Abl. *felicibus*
Acc. *hos & has felices, &*
 hæc felicia
Voc. *ô felices, & ô felicia.*

Sing.

10 No. *hic & hæc tristis, &*
 hoc triste
Gen. *tristis*
Dat. Abl. *tristi*
Acc. *hunc & hanc tristem,*
15 *& hoc triste*
Voc. *ô tristis, & ô triste*

Plur.

Nom. *hi & hæ tristes; &*
 hæc tristia
Gen. *tristium*
Dat. Abl. *tristibus*
Acc. *hos & has tristes, &*
 hæc tristia
Voc. *ô tristes, & ô tristia.*

There be also another sort which have in the Nominative
Case three Terminations and three Articles, as *hic acer, hic
& hæc acris, hoc acre.* In like manner be declined *equestor,*
20 *volucer,* and some few others, being in all other cases like the
Examples beforegoing.

Comparisons of Nounes.

Adjectives, whose signification may increase or be diminish't, may form Comparison, whereof there be two degrees
above the positive word it self, The Comparative, and Su-
25 perlative.

The Positive signifieth the thing it self without comparing, as *durus* hard.

The Comparative exceedeth his Positive in signification, compar'd with some other, as *durior* harder; and is formd of the first Case of his Positive that endeth in *i*, by putting thereto *or* and *us*, as of *duri, hic & hæc durior, & hoc durius;* of *dulci, dulcior dulcius.*

The Superlative exceedeth his Positive in the highest degree, as *durissimus* hardest; and it is formd of the first case of his Positive that endeth in *is*, by putting thereto *simus*, as of *duris durissimus, dulcis dulcissimus.*

If the Positive end in *er*, the Superlative is formd of the Nominative case by putting to *rimus*, as *pulcher pulcherrimus.* Like to these are *vetus veterrimus, maturus maturimus;* but *dexter dextimus*, and *sinister sinisterior sinistimus.*

All those Nouns ending in *lis* make the Superlative by changing *is* into *limus*, as *humilis, similis, facilis, gracilis, agilis, docilis docillimus.*

All other Nounes ending in *lis* do follow the general Rule, as *utilis utilissimus.*

Of these Positives following are formd a different sort of Superlatives; of *superus, supremus* and *summus; inferus, infimus* and *imus; exterus, extimus* and *extremus; posterus postremus.*

Some of these want the Positive, and are form'd from Adverbs; of *intra, interior intimus, ultra ulterior ultimus, citra citerior citimus, pridem prior primus, prope propior proximus.*

Others from Positives without Case, as *nequam nequior nequissimus.*

Some also from no Positive, as *ocior ocissimus.* Some want the Comparative, as *novus novissimus, sacer sacerrimus.*

Some the Superlative, as *senex senior, juvenis junior, adolescens adolescentior.*

5 Some ending in *us,* frame thir Comparative as if they ended in *ens, benevolus, maledicus, magnificus magnificentior magnificentissimus.*

These following are without Rule, *Bonus melior optimus, Malus pejor pessimus, Magnus major maximus, Parvus minor* 10 *minimus; Multus plurimus, multa plurima, multum plus plurimum.*

If a Vowel come before *us,* it is compared with *magis* and *maximè* as *pius, magis pius, maximè pius; idoneus, magis* and *maximè idoneus.* Yet some of these follow the general 15 Rule, as *Assiduus assiduissimus, strenuus strenuior, exiguus exiguissimus, tenuis tenuior tenuissimus.*

Of a Pronoun.

A Pronoun is a part of Speech that standeth for a Noun Substantive, either at present or before spoken of, as *ille* he or that, *hic* this, *qui* who.

20 There be Ten Pronounes, *Ego, tu, sui, ille, ipse, iste, hic, is, qui* and *quis,* besides their Compounds, *egomet, tute, hicce, idem, quisnam, aliquis,* and such others. The rest so call'd, as *meus, tuus, suus, noster, vester, nostras, vestras, cujus* and *cujas,* are not Pronouns, but Adjectives thence deriv'd.

25 Of *Pronounes* such as shew the thing present are called *Demonstratives,* as *ego, tu, hic;* and such as refer to a thing

antecedent or spoken of before are called Relatives, as *qui* who or which.

Quis, and often *qui,* because they ask a question, are called Interrogatives, with their Compounds *ecquis, num-*
5 *quis.*

Declensions of Pronouns are three.

Ego, tu, sui, be of the First Declension, and be thus declin'd.

Sing.		Plur.
Nom. *Ego*		Nom. Acc. *Nos*
Gen. *mei*		Gen. *nostrum* or *nostri*
10　Dat. *mihi*		Dat. Abl. *nobis*
Acc. Abl. *me*		Voc. *Caret.*
Voc. *Caret*		

Sing.		Plur.
Nom. Voc. *Tu*		Nom. Acc. Voc. *vos*
15　Gen. *tui*		Gen. *vestrum* or *vestri*
Dat. *tibi*		Dat. Abl. *vobis.*
Acc. Abl. *te*		

Sing. } { Nom. Voc. *Caret* } { Dat. *sibi*
Plur. } { Gen. *sui* } { Acc. Abl. *se.*

20　From these three be deriv'd *meus, tuus, suus, noster, vester, nostras, vestras,* (which are called Possessives) whereof the former five be declin'd like Adjectives of three Terminations, except that *meus* in the Vocative Case maketh *mi, mea, meum; Nostras, Vestras,* with three Articles, as *hic &*
25　*hæc nostras & hoc nostras* or *nostrate, vestrate.* In other Cases according to Rule.

These three, *ille, iste, ipse,* be of the Second Declension, making thir Genitive singular in *ius,* their Dative in *i;* and the former two be declin'd like the Adjective *alius,* and the Third like *unus* before spoken of.

5 Sing. {
Nom. *ille illa illud,* Gen. *illius,* Dat. *illi.*
Nom. *iste ista istud,* Gen. *istius,* Dat. *isti.*
Nom. *ipse ipsa ipsum,* Gen. *ipsius,* Dat. *ipsi.*

These four, *hic, is, qui* and *quis,* be of the third Declension, making thir Genitive singular in *jus* with j consonant, 10 and be declin'd after this manner.

Sing.	Plur.
Nom. *hic hæc hoc*	Nom. *hi hæ hæc*
Gen. *hujus*	Gen. *horum harum horum*
Dat. *huic*	Dat. Abl. *his*
15 Acc. *hunc hanc hoc*	Acc. *hos has hæc*
Voc. *Caret*	Voc. *Caret*
Abl. *hoc hac hoc*	

Of *iste* and *hic* is compounded *istic istæc, istoc* or *istuc.* Acc. *istunc istanc, istoc* or *istuc.* Abl. *istoc istac istoc.* Plur. 20 *istæc* only.

Sing.	Plur.
Nom. *is ea id*	Nom. *ii eæ ea*
Gen. *ejus*	Gen. *eorum earũ eorum*
Dat. *ei*	*Dat. Abl. iis* or *eis*
25 Acc. *eum eam id*	Acc. *eos eas ea*
Voc. *Caret*	Voc. *Caret*
Abl. *eo ea eo*	

	Sing.			Plur.
Nom.	*qui quæ quod*		Nom.	*qui quæ quæ*
Gen.	*cujus*		Gen.	*quorum quarum*
Dat.	*cui*			*quorum*
Acc.	*quem quam quod*		Dat. Abl.	*quibus* or *queis*
Voc.	*Caret*		Acc.	*quos quas quæ*
Abl.	*quo qua, quo* or *qui*		Voc.	*Caret*

In like manner *quivis, quilibet,* and *quicunque* the Compounds.

Sing. Nom. *Quis, qua* or *quæ, quid.* Gen. &c. like *qui.* So *quisquam, quisnam,* Compounds.

Of *Quis* are made these Pronoun Adjectives, *cujus cuja cujum,* whose; and *hic & hæc cujas* and *hoc cujate,* of what Nation.

Quisquis is defective, and thus declin'd.

No. { *Quisquis* *Quicquid* }   Ac. { *Quicquid* }   Ab. { *Quoquo* *Quaqua* *Quoquo* }

Of a Verb.

A Verb is a part of Speech, that betokeneth *being,* as *Sum* I am, or *doing,* as *Laudo* I praise; and is declin'd with Mood, Tense, Number and Person.

Moods.

There be four Moods, which express the *manner of doing;* the Indicative, the Imperative, the Potential or Subjunctive, and the Infinitive.

The Indicative Mood *sheweth* or *declareth*, as *Laudo* I praise.

The Imperative *biddeth* or *exhorteth*, as *Lauda* praise thou.

The Potential or Subjunctive is Englisht with these Signs, *may, can, might, would could, should,* Or without them as
5 the Indicative, if a Conjunction go before or follow. As *Laudem,* I may or can praise. *Cum Laudarem* when I praised. *Cavissem, si prævidissem,* I had bewar'd if I had foreseen.

The Infinitive is englisht with this sign *To,* as *Laudare* to praise.

Tenses.

10 There be three Tenses which express the *time of doing:* The Present, the Preterit or past, and the Future.

The Present Tense speaketh of the time that *now is,* as *Laudo* I praise.

The Preterit speaketh of the time *past,* and is distinguisht
15 by three degrees: the Preterimperfect, the Preterperfect, and the Preterpluperfect.

The Preterimperfect speaketh of the time *not perfectly past,* as *Laudabam* I praised or did praise.

The Preterperfect speaketh of the time *perfectly past,* as
20 *Laudavi* I have praised.

The Preterpluperfect speaketh of the time *more then perfectly past,* as *Laudaveram* I had praised.

The Future Tense speaketh of the time *to come,* as *Laudabo* I shall or will praise.

Persons.

25 Through all Moods, except the Infinitive, there be three Persons in both Numbers, as, Sing. *Laudo* I praise, *laudas* thou

praisest, *laudat* he praiseth; Plur. *Laudamus* we praise, *lau-
datis* ye praise, *laudant* they praise. Except some Verbs which
are declin'd or form'd in the Third Person only, and have
before them this sign, *It;* as *Tædet* it irketh, *oportet* it behov-
5 eth, and are called Impersonals.

The Verb which betokeneth *being,* is properly this Verb
Sum only, which is therefore call'd a Verb Substantive, and
formd after this manner.

Indicative.

Pres.
10 *sing.*
> I am.
> Sum, es, est, *Plur.* sumus, estis, sunt.

Pret.
imp.
> I was.
> Eram, eras, erat, *Pl.* eramus, eratis, erant.

Pret.
perfect
15
> I have been.
> Fui, fuisti, fuit, *Plur.* fuimus, fuistis, fuerunt *or*
> fuere.

Pret.
plup.
> I had been.
> Fueram, fueras, fuerat, *Pl.* fueramus, fueratis,
> fuerant.

Future.
20
> I shall or will be.
> Ero, eris, erit, *Pl.* erimus, eritis, erunt.

Imperative.

Be thou.

| *Sing.* | Sis, es, esto. | Sit, esto. | *Plur.* | Si-mus, | Sitis, este, estote. | Sint, sunto |

Potential.

Pres.
sing. {
I *may* or *can be.*
Sim, sis, sit, *Pl.* simus, sitis, sint.
}

Preter
imperf. {
I *might* or *could be.*
Essem *or* forem, es, et, *Plur.* essemus, essetis, es-
sent *or* forent.
}

Preter-
perfect {
I *might* or *could have been.*
Fuerim, ris, rit, *Pl.* rimus, ritis, rint.
}

Preterplup.
with a con-
junction. Si {
If I had been.
Fuissem, es, et, *Pl.* emus, etis, ent.
}

Future
Si {
If I shall be or *shall have been.*
Fuero, ris, rit, *Pl.* rimus, ritis, rint.
}

Infinitive.

Pres.
and
preter-
imperf. {
Esse, *to be.*
} {
Preter-
perfect,
& *pret.*
pluper.
} Fuisse, *to have*
or had been.

Future { Fore, *to be hereafter.*

In like manner are form'd the Compounds; *Absum, ad-sum, desum, obsum, præsum, prosum, possum;* but *possum* somthing varies after this manner.

Indicat. Pres. Sing. *Possum, potes, potest,* Plur. *possumus, potestis, possunt.* The other are regular, *poteram, potui, po-tueram, potero.*

Imperative *it wants*.

Potent. Pres. *Possim,* &c. *Preterimperfect, Possem*

Infin. *Pres. Posse.* Preterit. *Potuisse.*

Voices.

In Verbs that betoken *doing* are two Voices, the *Active*
5 and the *Passive*.

The Active signifieth *to do,* and always endeth in *o,* as
Doceo, I teach.

The Passive signifieth *what is done to one by another,* and
always endeth in *or,* as *Doceor* I am taught.

10　　From these are to be excepted two sorts of Verbs. The first
are called *Neuters,* and cannot take *or* in the Passive, as *Curro*
I run, *Sedeo* I sit; yet signifie sometimes passively, as *Vapulo*
I am beaten.

The second are call'd *Deponents,* and signifie actively, as
15 *Loquor* I speak; or Neuters, as *Glorior* I boast: but are form'd
like Passives.

Conjugations.

Verbs both Active and Passive have four Conjugations, or
forms of declining, known and distinguisht by thir Infinitive
Mood Active, which alwayes endeth in *re.*

20　　In the first Conjugation, after *a* long, as *Laudare* to praise.

In the second, after *e* long, as *habere* to have.

In the third, after *e* short, as *legere* to read.

In the fourth, after *i* long, as *audire* to hear.

In these four Conjugations, Verbs are declin'd or formd by
25 Mood, Tense, Number, and Person, after these Examples.

Indicative Mood,

Present Tense

Singular.			Plural.		
I	*Thou*	*He*	*We*	*Ye*	*They*
praise.	*praisest.*	*praiseth*	*praise.*	*praise.*	*praise.*
Laudo,	laudas,	laudat,	laudamus,	laudatis,	laudant.
Habeo,	habes,	habet,	habemus,	habetis,	habent.
Lego,	legis,	legit,	legimus,	legitis,	legunt.
Audio,	audis,	audit,	audimus,	auditis,	audiunt.

5 (Habeo line)

Preter-imperfect tens. sing.

Laudabam,
Habebam,
Legebam,
Audiebam,

I praisd or *did praise.*

bas, bat, *Plur.* bamus, batis, bant.

10

Preter perfect tens. sing.

Laudavi
Habui
Legi
Audivi

I have praisd.

isti, it, *Plur.* imus, istis, erunt *or* ere.

15

Preter-pluperfect tense sing.

Laudaveram
Habueram
Legeram
Audiveram

I had praisd.

ras, rat, *Plur.* ramus, ratis, rant.

20

Future tense sing.

Laudabo
Habebo
Legam
Audiam

I shall or will praise.

bis, bit, *Plur.* bimus, bitis, bunt.
es, et, *Plur.* emus, etis, ent.

Imperative Mood.

Praise thou.	*Let him praise.*	*Let us praise.*	*Praise ye.*	*Let them praise.*
Lauda, laudato.	Laudet laudato.	*Pl.* laudemus.	Laudate, laudatote.	Laudent, laudanto.
Habe, habeto.	Habeat habeto.	*Pl.* habeamus,	Habete, habetote.	Habeant, habento.
Lege, legito.	Legat legito.	*Pl.* legamus.	Legite, legitote.	Legant, legunto.
Audi, audito.	Audiat audito.	*Pl.* audiamus.	Audite, auditote.	Audiant, audiunto.

Pres. Sing. (bracket grouping the four conjugations)

5

10

Potential Mood.

I may or *can praise.*

Present tense sing.
Laudem, laudes, laudet, *Pl.* laudemus, laudetis, laudent.
Habeam,
Legam,   as, at, *Pl.* amus, atis, ant.
Audiam,

15

Preterim-perfect tense sing.
Laudarem,
Haberem,   *I might* or *could praise.*
Legerem,   res, ret, *Plur.* remus, retis, rent.
Audirem,

20 *Preter-perfect tense sing.*
Laudaverim,   *I might* or *should have praisd.*
Habuerim,
Legerim,   ris, rit, *Pl.* rimus, ritis, rint.
Audiverim,

| *Preterplu. sing. with a Conjunction.* Si. | Laudavissem, Habuissem, Legissem, Audivissem, | *If I had praisd.* ses, set, *Pl.* semus, setis, sent. |

5

If I shall praise or *shall have praisd.*

| *Future tense sing.* Si | Laudavero, Habuero, Legero, Audivero, | ris, rit, *Plur.* rimus, ritis, rint. |

Infinitive Mood.

| *Present and Preterimperfect tense* | Laudare, Habere Legere, Audire, | *To* | Praise. Have. Read. Hear. |

| *Preterperfect & Preterpluperfect tense.* | Laudavisse, Habuisse, Legisse, Audivisse, | *To have or had* | Praised. Read. Heard. |

Verbs of the third Conjugation irregular in some Tenses of the Active Voice.

Indicative Mood
Present Tense singular.

20

Volo, vis, vult,		Volumus, vultis, volunt.
Nolo, ———	*Plur.*	Nolumus, ——— nolunt.
The rest is want		*ing in this Tense.*
Malo, mavis, mavult		Malumus, mavultis, malunt.

Preterit. } Volui.
Nolui.
Malui.

Volo and *Malo* want the Imperative Mood.

Imperative.

5   *Sing.* { Noli,
Nolito. }   *Plur.* { Nolite,
Nolitote.

Potential.

*Present
tens. sing.* { Velim,
Nolim,
Malim, } is, it, *Plur.* imus, itis, int.

10 *Preterim-
perfect
tens. sing.* { Vellem,
Nollem,
Mallem, } es, et, *Pl.* emus, etis, ent.

Infinitive.

Present. { Velle,
Nolle,
15   Malle.

Indicat. Pres. *Edo, edis* or *es, edit* or *est;* Plur. *Editis,* or *estis.*

Imper. *Ede* or *es, edito* or *esto. Edat, edito* or *esto.* Plur. *Edite este editote estote.*

20   Poten. Preterimperfect Tense, *Ederem* or *essem.*

Infinit. *Edere* or *esse.*

Verbs of the fourth Conjugation irregular
in some Tenses Active.

Eo and *queo,* with his Compound *Nequeo,* make *eunt* and *queunt* in the Plural Indicative present, and in thir Preterimperfect *ibam* and *quibam,* thir Future *ibo* and *quibo.*

Imperat. *I, ito. Eat, ito.* Plur. *Eamus. Ite itote. Eant,* 5 *eunto.*

Potent. *Eam. Irem.* &c.

The forming of the Passive Voice.

Indicative.

I am praised.

Pres. Sing.		Plur.	
	Laudor, aris *or* are, atur,		amur, amini, antur.
	Habeor, eris *or* ere, etur,		emur, emini, entur.
10	Legor, eris *or* ere, itur,		imur, imini, untur.
	Audior, iris *or* ire, itur,		imur, imini, iuntur.

Preterim- perfect tens. sing.			
	Laudabar,	*I was praisd.*	
	Habebar,	baris *or* bare, batur, *Plur.* bamur,	
	Legebar,	bamini, bantur.	
15	Audiebar,		

Note that the *Passive Voice* hath no Preterperfect, nor the Tenses deriv'd from thence in any Mood.

I shall or *will be praisd.*

20 Future tense sing.			
	Laudabor,	beris *or* bere, bitur, *Plur.* bimur,	
	Habebor,	bimini, buntur.	
	Legar,	eris *or* ere, etur, *Plu.* emur,	
	Audiar,	emini, entur.	

Imperative.

Be thou praisd.	*Let him be praisd.*	*Let us be praisd.*	*Be ye praisd.*	*Let them be praisd.*
Laudare, laudator.	laudetur, laudator.	*Pl.* lau- demur.	laudamini, laudaminor.	laudentur, laudantor
Habere, habetor.	habeatur, habetor.	*P.* habe- amur.	habemini, habeminor.	habeantur, habentor.
Legere, legitor.	legatur, legitor.	*Pl.* lega- mur.	legimini, legiminor.	legantur, leguntor.
Audire, auditor.	audiatur, auditor.	*P.* audi- amur.	audimini, audiminor.	audiantur, audiuntor.

Present Singular. (bracket, lines 5, 10)

Potential.

I may or *can be praisd.*

Present sing.
{
Lauder, eris *or* ere, etur, *Plur.* emur, emini, entur.

Habear,
Legar,
Audiar,
} aris *or* are, atur, *Plu.* amur, amini, antur.

Preterimperfect sing.
{
Laudarer,
Haberer,
Legerer,
Audirer,
}
I might or *should be praisd.*
reris *or* rere, retur, *Pl.* remur, remini, rentur.

Infinitive.

| *Present* & *Preterim-* *perfect* | { Laudari
Haberi
Legi
Audiri } | *To be* | { Praisd.
Had.
Read.
Heard. } |

Verbs irregular in some Tenses
Passive.

5 *Edor, editur* or *estur:* The rest is Regular.

The Verb *Fio,* is partly of the Third, and partly of the Fourth Conjugation, and hath only the Infinitive of the Passive Form.

Indicat. Pres. Sing. *Fio, fis, fit,* Plur. *fimus, fitis, fiunt.*
10 Preterimperfect, *Fiebam.* Preterperfect *it wants.* Future *Fiam,* &c.

Imperat. *Fi, fito.* Plur. *fite, fitote. Fiant. fiunto.*

Potent. Pres. *Fiam,* &c. Preterimperfect. *Fierem.*

Infinit. *Fieri.*

15 Also this Verb *Fero,* is contracted or short'n'd in some Tenses, both Active and Passive, as *Fers, fert,* for *feris, ferit,* &c.

Indicat. Pres. Sing. *Fero, fers, fert,* Plur. —— *fertis,* ——
Preterperfect, *Tuli.*
20 Imperat. *Fer ferto,* &c. Plur. *Ferte, fertote.*

Potent. Preterimperfect, *Ferrem,* &c.

Infinit. *Ferre.*

Passive.

Indicat. Pres. Sing. *Feror, ferris* or *ferre, fertur,* &c.

Imperat. Sing. *Ferre, fertor,* &c.

Potent. Preterimperfect, *Ferrer.*

Infinit. *Ferri.*

Of Gerunds and Supines.

5   There be also belonging to the Infinitive Mood of all Verbs certain Voices called Gerunds and Supines, both of the Active and Passive signification.

The first Gerund endeth in *di,* as *Laudandi* of praising or of being praisd. The second in *do,* as *Laudando* in prais-

10 ing or in being praisd. The third in *dum,* as *Laudandum* to praise or to be praisd.

Note that in the two latter Conjugations, the Gerunds end somtimes in *undi, do, dum,* as *dicendi* or *dicundi:* But from *Eo* alwayes *eundi,* except in the Compound *Ambiendi.*

15 Supines are two. The first signifieth Actively, as *laudatum* to praise; the latter Passively, as *laudatu* to be praised. Note that most Neuters of the second Conjugation, and *volo, nolo, malo,* with many other Verbs, have no Supine.

Verbs of the four Conjugations irregular in the Preterperfect Tense or Supines.

Verbs of the first Conjugation form thir Preterperfect Tense

20 in *avi,* Supine in *atum,* as *Laudo laudavi laudatum.*

Except,

Poto potavi potatum or *potum; neco necavi necatum* or *nectum.*

Domo, tono, sono, crepo, veto, cubo, form *ui, itum,* as *cubui cubitum;* but *secui sectum, fricui frictum, mico micui:* yet some of these are found Regular in the Preterperfect Tense or Supine, especially compounded, as *increpavit, discrepavit,* 5 *dimicavit, sonatum, dimicatum, intonatum, infricatum,* and the like.

Plico and his Compounds form *ui* or *avi,* as *explicui explicavi explicitum* or *explicatum;* except *supplico,* and such as are compounded with a Noun, as *Duplico Multiplico* in *avi* 10 only.

But *Lavo lavi lautum lotum* or *lavatum, juvo juvi, adjuvo adjuvi adjutum.*

Do dedi datum, Sto steti statum, in the Compounds, *stiti, stitum* and somtimes *statum,* as *Presto prestiti prestitum* and 15 *prestatum.*

Verbs of the second Conjugation form thir Preterperfect Tense in *ui,* thir Supine in *itum,* as *habeo habui habitum.*

Some are Regular in thir Preterperfect Tense, but not in thir Supines, as *doceo docui doctum, misceo miscui mistum,* 20 *teneo tenui tentum, torreo torrui tostum, censeo censui censum, pateo patui passum, careo carui cassum* and *caritum.*

Others are Irregular both in Preterperfect Tense and Supines, as *Jubeo jussi jussum, sorbeo sorbui sorpsi sorptum, mulceo mulsi mulsum, luceo luxi.*

25 *Deo* in *di,* as *sedeo sedi sessum, video vidi visum, prandeo prandi pransum.* And some in *si,* as *suadeo suasi suasum, rideo risi risum, ardeo arsi arsum.* Four double thir first Letters, as *Pendeo pependi pensum, mordeo momordi morsum,*

spondeo spopondi sponsum, tondeo totondi tonsum, but not in thir Compounds, as *dependi depensum.*

Geo in *si,* and some in *xi,* as *urgeo ursi, mulgeo mulsi mulxi mulctum, augeo auxi auctum, indulgeo indulsi indul-*
5 *tum, frigeo frixi, lugeo luxi.*

ieo leo and *neo nevi, vieo vievi vietum,* But *Cieo cievi citum, deleo delevi deletum, fleo, flevi fletum, compleo com-plevi completum;* as also the Compounds of *Oleo,* except *redoleo* and *suboleo;* but *adolevi adultum, neo nevi netum,*
10 but *maneo mansi, torqueo torsi tortum, hæreo hæsi.*

Veo in *vi,* as *ferveo fervi,* but *deferveo deferbui, conniveo connivi* and *connixi, movi motum, vovi votum, cavi cautum, favi fautum.*

The third Conjugation formeth the Preterperfect Tense,
15 by changing *O* of the Present Tense into *I;* the Supine with-out certain Rule, as *lego legi lectum, bibo bibi bibitum, lambo lambi, scabo scabi, ico ici ictum, mando mandi mansum, pando pandi passum, edo edi esum* or *estum,* in like manner *comedo,* the other compounds *esum* only; *rudo rudi, sallo*
20 *salli salsum, psallo psalli, emo emi emptum, viso visi visum, verto verti versum, solvo solvi solutum, volvo volvi volutum, exuo exui exutum,* but *ruo rui ruitum,* in compound *rutum,* as *derui derutum; ingruo, metuo metui.*

Others are irregular both in Preterperfect Tense and Supine.
25 In *bo, scribo scripsi scriptum, nubo nupsi nuptum, cumbo cubui cubitum.*

In *co, vinco vici victum, dico dixi dictum,* in like manner *duco, parco peperci* and *parsi parsum* and *parcitum.*

In *do*, these three loos *n*, *findo fidi fissum*, *scindo scidi scissum*, *fundo fudi fusum*. These following, *vado*, *rado*, *lædo*, *ludo*, *divido*, *trudo*, *claudo*, *plaudo*, *rodo*, *si* and *sum*, as *rosi rosum*, but *cedo cessi cessum*. The rest double thir first Letter in the Preterperfect Tense, but not compounded, as *tundo tutudi tunsum*, *contundo contudi contusum*, and so in the other Compounds. *Pendo pependi pensum*, *dependo dependi*, *tendo tetendi tensum* and *tentum*, *contendo contendi*, *pedo pepedi peditum*, *cado cecidi casum*, *occido*, *recido recidi recasum*. The other Compounds have no Supine. *Cædo cecidi cæsum*, *occido occidi occisum*. To these add all the compounds of *do* in this Conjugation, *addo*, *credo*, *edo*, *dedo*, *reddo*, *perdo*, *abdo*, *obdo*, *condo*, *indo*, *trado*, *prodo*, *vendo vendidi venditum*, except the double Compound, *abscondo abscondi*.

In *go*, *ago egi actum*, *dego degi*, *satago sategi*, *frango fregi fractum*, *pango* to joyn *pegi pactum*, *pango* to sing *panxi*, *ango anxi*, *jungo junxi junctum;* but these five, *fingo*, *mingo*, *pingo*, *stringo*, *ringo*, loos *n* in their Supines, as *finxi fictum*, *ningo ninxi*, *figo fixi fixum*, *rego rexi rectum;* *diligo*, *negligo*, *intelligo*, *lexi lectum*, *spargo sparsi sparsum*. These double thir first Letter, *tango tetigi tactum*, but not in his Compounds, as *contingo contigi*, *pango* to bargain *pepigi pactum*, *pungo* and *repungo pupugi* and *punxi punctum*, the other Compounds *punxi* only.

Ho in *xi*, *traho traxi tractum*, *veho vexi vectum*.

In *lo*, *vello velli* and *vulsi vulsum*, *colo colui cultum;* *excello*, *precello*, *cellui celsum;* *alo alui alitum altum*. The rest, not compounded, double thir first Letter, *Fallo fefelli falsum, refello refelli, pello pepuli pulsum, compello compuli, cello ceculi, percello perculi perculsi perculsum.*

In *mo, vomo vomui vomitum, tremo tremui, premo pressi pressum, como, premo, demo, sumo,* after the same manner, as *sumpsi, sumptum.*

In *No, sino sivi situm, sterno stravi stratum, sperno sprevi spretum, lino levi lini* and *livi litum, cerno crevi cretum, temno tempsi, contemno contempsi contemptum, gigno genui genitum, pono posui positum, cano cecini cantum, concino concinui concentum.*

In *Po, rumpo rupi ruptum, scalpo scalpsi scalptum,* the rest in *ui,* as *strepo strepui strepitum.*

In *quo, linquo liqui, relinquo reliqui relictum, coquo coxi coctum.*

In *Ro, verro verri* and *versi versum, sero* to sow *sevi satum,* in compound *situm,* as *insero insitum; sero* of another signification most us'd in his compounds, *Assero, consero, desero, exero, serui, sertum, uro ussi ustum, gero gessi gestum, quæro quæsivi quæsitum, tero trivi tritum, curro, excurro, præcurro, cucurri cursum,* the other compounds double not, as *concurro concurri.*

In *So, accerso, arcesso, incesso, lacesso, ivi itum, capesso* both *i* and *ivi, pinso pinsui pistum* and *pinsitum.*

In *sco, pasco pavi pastum; compesco, dispesco,* but; *posco poposci, disco didici, quinisco quexi, nosco novi notum,* but *agnosco agnitum, cognosco cognitum.*

In *to, sisto stiti statum, flecto flexi flexum, pecto pexui pexi pexum* and *pectitum, necto nexui nexi nexum, plecto plexi plexum, sterto stertui, meto messui messum, mitto misi missum, peto petivi petitum.*

In *vo, vivo vixi victum.*

In *xo, texo texui textum, nexo nexui nexum.*

5 *In cio, facio feci factum, jacio jeci jactum, lacio lexi lectum, specio spexi spectum,* with thir Compounds, but *elicio elicui elicitum.*

In *dio, fodio fodi fossum.*

In *gio, fugio fugi fugitum.*

10 In *pio, capio cepi captum, rapio rapui raptum, cupio cupivi cupitum, sapio sapui sapivi sapitum.*

In *rio, pario peperi partum.*

In *tio, quatio quassi quassum, concutio concussi concussum.*

In *uo, pluo plui pluvi plutum, struo struxi structum, fluo* 15 *fluxi fluxum.*

The fourth Conjugation formeth the Preterperfect Tense in *ivi*, the Supine in *itum*.

Except, *Venio veni ventum, comperio, reperio reperi re-pertum, cambio campsi campsum, sepio sepsi septum, sarcio* 20 *sarsi sartum, fulceo fulsi fultum, sentio sensi sensum, haurio hausi haustum, sancio sanxi sanctum sancitum, vincio vinxi vinctum salio salui saltum,* in Compound *sultum,* as *desilio desilui desultum, amicio amicui amictum, aperio, operio perui pertum, veneo venivi venum, singultivi singultum, sepelivi* 25 *sepultum.*

Of Verbs Compounded.

These Verbs Compounded change *a* into *e* throughout, *Damno, lacto, sacro, fallo, arceo, tracto, partio, sarcio, carpo, patro, scando, spargo,* as *conspergo conspersi conspersum.*

These following change thir first vowel into *i,* and some of them thir Supines into *e, habeo, lateo, salio, statuo, cado, lædo, cano, quæro, cædo, tango, egeo, teneo, taceo, sapio, rapio, placeo, displiceo, displicui displicitum;* Except *com-*
5 *placeo, perplaceo, posthabeo.*

Scalpo, calco salto, change *a* into *u,* as *exculpo.*

Claudo, quatio, lavo loos *a,* as *excludo, excutio, eluo.*

These following change thir first Vowel into *i,* but not in the Preterperfect Tense, and somtimes *a* into *e* in the Supine,
10 *emo, sedeo, rego, frango, capio, jacio, lacio, specio, premo,* as *comprimo compressi compressum, conjicio conjeci conjectum, pango* in two only, *compingo, impingo: Ago,* in all but *perago, satago, circumago, dego* and *cogo coegi: Facio* with a Preposition only, not in other Compounds, as *inficio, olfacio:*
15 *Lego* in these only, *diligo, eligo, intelligo, negligo, seligo,* in the rest not, as *prælego,* add to these *supersedeo.*

Of Verbs Defective.

Verbs called Inceptives ending in *sco,* borrow thir Preterperfect Tense from the Verb whereof they are deriv'd, as *tepesco tepui* from *tepeo, ingemisco ingemui* from *ingemo;*
20 as also these Verbs, *cerno* to see, *vidi* from *video, sido sedi* from *sedeo, fero tuli* from *tulo* out of use, in the Supine *latum, tollo sustuli sublatum* from *suffero.*

These want the Preterperfect Tense.

Verbs ending in *asco,* as *puerasco;* in *isco,* as *fatisco;* in
25 *urio,* except *parturio, esurio:* these also, *vergo, ambigo, ferio, furo, polleo, nideo,* have no Preterperfect Tense.

Contrary, these four, *Odi, cœpi, novi, memini,* are found in the Preterperfect Tense only, and the Tenses thence deriv'd, as *odi, oderam, oderim, odissem, odero, odisse,* except *memini,* which hath *memento mementote* in the Imperative.

Others are defective both in Tense and Person, as *Aio, ais, ait,* Plur. *aiunt.* The Preterimperfect *aiebam* is intire. Imperative, *ai.* Potential, *aias, aiat,* Plur. *aiamus, aiant.*

Ausim for *ausus sim, ausis, ausit,* Plur. *ausint.*

Salveo, salvebis, salve salveto, salvete salvetote, salvere.

Ave aveto, avete avetote.

Faxo, faxis, faxit, faxint.

Quæso, Plur. *quæsumus.*

Infit, infiunt.

Inquio or *inquam, inquis inquit,* Plur. *inquiunt. Inquibut,* Cic. Topic. *inquisti, inquit.* Future, *inquies, inquiet* Imperat. *Inque inquito.* Potent. *Inquiat.*

Dor the first person Passive of *do,* and *for* before *faris* or *fare* in the Indicative, are not read, nor *der* or *fer* in the Potential.

Of a Participle.

A Participle is a part of Speech, partaking with the Verb from whence it is deriv'd in Voice, Tense, and signification, and with a Noun Adjective in manner of Declining.

Participles are either of the Active or Passive Voice.

Of the *Active* Two. One of the Present Tense ending in *ans,* or *ens,* as *laudans* praising, *habens, legens, audiens,* and is declin'd like *fælix,* as *hic hæc* and *hoc habens,* Gen. *habentis,* Dat. *habenti,* &c. *Docens docentis,* &c. But from *eo, euns,* and in the compounds *iens euntis,* except *ambiens ambientis.* Note that some Verbs otherwise defective, have this Participle, as *aiens, inquiens.*

The other of the future Tense is most commonly formd of 5 the first Supine, by changing *m* into *rus,* as of *laudatum laudaturus* to praise or about to praise, *habiturus, lecturus, auditurus;* but some are not regularly formd, as of *sectum secaturus,* of *jutum juvaturus, sonitum sonaturus, partum pariturus, argutum arguiturus,* and such like; of *sum, futu-* 10 *rus:* This, as also the other two Participles following are declin'd like *bonus.*

This Participle, with the Verb *Sum,* affordeth a second Future in the Active Voice, as *laudaturus sum, es, est,* &c. as also the Future of the Infinitive, as *laudaturum esse* to praise 15 hereafter, *futurum esse,* &c.

Participles of the Passive Voice are also two, one of the Preterperfect tense, another of the Future.

A Participle of the Preterperfect Tense, is formd of the latter Supine, by putting thereto *s,* as of *laulatu laudatus* 20 praisd, of *habitu habitus, lectu lectus, auditu auditus.*

This Participle joyn'd with the Verb *Sum,* supplyeth the want of a Preterperfect and Preterpluperfect Tense in the Indicative Mood passive, and both them and the Future of the Potential; as also the Preterperfect and Preterpluperfect 25 of the Infinitive, and with *ire* or *fore* the Future; as *laudatus sum* or *fui* I have been praisd, *Plur. laudati sumus* or *fuimus* we have been praisd, *laudatus eram* or *fueram,* &c. Potential, *laudatus sim* or *fuerim, laudatus essem* or *fuissem, laudatus ero* or *fuero*, Infinit. *laudatum esse* or *fuisse* to have or had been praisd; *laudatum ire* or *fore* to be praisd hereafter.

Nor only Passives, but some Actives also or Neuters, besides thir own Preterperfect Tense, borrow another from this
5 Participle; *Cæno Cænavi* and *Cænatus sum, Juravi* and *juratus, Potavi* and *potus sum, Titubavi* and *titubatus, Careo carui cassus sum, Prandeo prandi* and *pransus, Pateo patui* and *passus sum, Placeo placui placitus, Suesco suevi suetus sum, Liget libuit* and *libitum est, Licet licuit licitum, Pudet puduit*
10 *puditum, Piget piguit pigitum, Tædet teduit pertæsum est,* and this Deponent *Mereor merui* and *meritus sum.*

These Neuters following, like Passives, have no other Preterperfect Tense, but by this Participle, *Gaudeo gavisus sum, fido fisus, audeo ausus, fio factus, soleo solitus sum.*

15 These Deponents also form this Participle from Supines irregular; *Labor lapsus, patior passus, perpetior perpessus, fateor fassus, confiteor, diffiteor diffessus, gradior gressus, ingredior ingressus, fatiscor fessus, metior mensus, utor usus, ordior* to spin *orditus,* to begin *orsus, nitor nisus* and *nixus,*
20 *ulciscor ultus, irascor iratus, reor ratus, obliviscor oblitus, fruor fructus* or *fruitus, miserior misertus, tuor* and *tueor tuitus, loquor locutus, sequor secutus, experior expertus, paciscor pactus, nanciscor nactus, apiscor aptus, adipiscor adeptus, queror questus, proficiscor profectus, expergiscor experrectus,*
25 *comminiscor commentus, nascor natus, morior mortuus, orior ortus sum.*

A Participle of the Future Passive is formd of the Gerund in *dum,* by changing *m* into *s,* as of *laudandum laudandus* to be praisd, of *habendum habendus,* &c. And likewise of this Participle with the Verb *Sum,* may be formd the same Tenses in the Passive, which were form'd with the Participle of the Preterperfect Tense, as *laudandus sum* or *fui,* &c.

5 Infinit. *Laudandum esse,* or *fore.*

Of Verbs Deponent come Participles, both of the Active and Passive form, as *loquor loquens locutus locuturus loquendus;* whereof the Participle of the Preter Tense signifieth somtimes both Actively and Passively, as *dignatus, testatus,*
10 *meditatus,* and the like.

Of an Adverb.

An Adverb is a part of Speech joynd with some other to explain its signification, as *valdè probus* very honest, *benè est* it is well, *valdè doctus* very learned, *benè mane* early in the morning.

15 Of Adverbs, some be of *Time,* as *hodiè* to day, *Cras* to morrow, &c.

Some be of *Place,* as *Ubi* where, *ibi* there, &c. And of many other sorts needless to be here set down.

Certain Adverbs also are compar'd, as *Doctè* learnedly,
20 *doctiùs doctissimè, fortiter fortiùs fortissimè, sæpe sæpius sæpissime,* and the like.

Of a Conjunction.

A Conjunction is a part of Speech, that joyneth Words and Sentences together.

Of conjunctions some be Copulative, as *et* and, *quoque*
25 also, *nec* neither.

Some be Disjunctive, as *aut* or.

Some be Causal, as *nam* for, *quia* because, and many such like.

Adverbs when they Govern Mood and Tense, and joyn Sentences together, as *cum, ubi, postquam,* and the like, are rather to be call'd Conjunctions.

Of a Preposition.

A Preposition is a part of Speech most commonly, either set before Nouns in Apposition, as *ad patrem,* or joyn'd with any other words in Composition, as *indoctus.*

These six, *di, dis, re, se, am, con,* are not read but in Composition.

As Adverbs having Cases after them, may be call'd Prepositions, so Prepositions having none, may be counted Adverbs.

Of an Interjection.

An Interjection is a part of Speech, expressing some passion of the mind.

Some be of sorrow, as *heu, hei.*

Some be of marvelling, as *papæ.*

Some of disdaining, as *vah.*

Some of praising, as *euge.*

Some of exclaiming, as *ô, proh,* and such like.

Figures of Speech.

Words are somtimes encreast or diminisht by a Letter or Syllable in the beginning, middle or ending, which are call'd *Figures of Speech:*

Encreast

In the beginning, as *Gnatus* for *Natus, Tetuli* for *tuli*. *Prothesis*.

In the middle, as *Rettulit* for *Retulit, Cinctutus* for *Cinctus*. *Epenthesis*.

5   In the end, as *Dicier,* for *dici*. *Paragoge*.

Diminisht

In the beginning, as *Ruit* for *Eruit*. *Apherisis*.

In the middle, as *Audiit* for *Audivit, Dixti* for *dixisti, Lamna* for *lamina*. *Syncope*.

In the end, as *Consili* for *consilii; scin* for *scisne*. *Apocope*.

The second part of Grammar,
commonly called *Syntaxis*,
or *Construction*.

10   HITHERTO the Eight Parts of speech Declin'd and Undeclin'd have been spoken of single, and each one by it self: Now followeth *Snytaxis* or *Construction,* which is the right joyning of these parts together in a Sentence.

15   Construction consisteth either in the agreement of words together in Number, Gender, Case, and Person, which is call'd Concord; or the governing of one the other in such Case or Mood as is to follow.

Of the Concords.

There be *Three* Concords or Agreements.

The *First* is of the Adjective with his Substantive.

The *Second* is of the Verb with his Nominative Case.

The *Third* is of the Relative with his Antecedent.

5   An Adjective (under which is comprehended both Pronoun and Participle) with his Substantive or Substantives, a Verb with his Nominative Case or Cases, and a Relative with his Antecedent or Antecedents, agree all in number, and the two latter in person also: as *Amicus certus. Viri docti. Præ-*

10 *ceptor prælegit, vos vero negligitis.* Xenophon & Plato *fuere æquales. Vir sapit, qui pauca loquitur. Pater & Præceptor veniunt.* Yea though the Conjunction be disjunctive, as *Quos neque desidia neque luxuria vitiarant.* Celsus. *Pater & Præceptor, quos quæritis.* But if a Verb singular follow many

15 Nominatives, it must be applyed to each of them apart, as *Nisi foro & curiæ officium ac verecundia sua constiterit.* Val. max.

    An Adjective with his Substantive, and a Relative with his Antecedent agree in Gender and Case; but the Relative not

20 in case alwayes, being oft-times govern'd by other constructions: as *Amicus certus in re incerta cernitur. Liber quem dedisti mihi.*

    And if it be a Participle serving the Infinitive Mood future, it oft-times agrees not with the Substantive neither in Gender

25 nor in Number, as *Hanc sibi rem præsidio sperat futurum.* Cic. *Audierat non datum ire filio Uxorem.* Terent. *Omnia potius actum iri puto quam de provinciis.* Cic.

But when a Verb cometh between two Nominative cases not of the same number, or a Relative between two Substantives not of the same Gender, the Verb in Number, and the Relative in Gender may agree with either of them; as

5 *Amantium iræ amoris integratio est. Quid enim nisi vota supersunt. Tuentur illum globum qui terra dicitur. Animal plenum rationis, quem vocamus hominem. Lutetia est quam nos Parisios dicimus.*

And if the Nominative cases be of several persons, or the

10 Substantives and Antecedents of several Genders, the Verb shall agree with the second person before the third, and with the first before either; And so shall the Adjective or Relative in thir Gender; as *Ego & tu sumus in tuto. Tu & Pater periclitamini. Pater & Mater mortui sunt. Frater & Soror quos*

15 *vidisti.*

But in things that have not life, an Adjective or Relative of the Neuter Gender, may agree with Substantives or Antecedents, Masculin or Feminin, or both together; as *Arcus & calami sunt bona. Arcus & calami quæ fregisti. Pulcritudi-*

20 *nem, constantiam, ordinem in Consiliis factisque conservanda putat.* Cic. Off. 1. *Ira & ægritudo permista sunt.* Sal.

Note that the Infinitive Mood, or any part of a Sentence may be instead of a Nominative Case to the Verb, or of a Substantive to the Adjective, or of an Antecedent to the Relative,

25 and then the Adjective or Relative shall be of the Neuter Gender; And if there be more parts of a Sentence then one, the Verb shall be in the plural number; *Diluculo surgere saluberrimum est. Virtutem sequi, vita est honestissima.*

Audito proconsulem in Ciliciam tendere. In tempore veni,
quod omnium rerum est primum. Tu multum dormis & sæpe
potas, quæ duo sunt corpori inimica.

    Somtimes also an Adverb is put for the Nominative Case
5 to a Verb, and for a Substantive to an Adjective; as *Partim*
signorum sunt combusta. Propè centies & vicies erogatum
est. Cic. verr. 4.

    Somtimes also agreement, whether it be in Gender or
Number, is grounded on the sense, not on the words; as *Illum*
10 *senium* for *illum senem. Iste scelus* for *iste scelestus.* Ter.
Transtulit in Eunuchum suam, meaning *Comædiam.* Ter.
Pars magna obligati, meaning *Homines.* Liv. *Impliciti la-*
queis nudus uterq; for *Ambo.* Ov. *Alter in alterius jactantes*
lumina vultus. Ovid, that is, *Alter & alter. Insperanti ipsa*
15 *refers te nobis,* for *mihi.* Catul. *Disce omnes.* Virg. Æn. 2.
for *tu quisquis es. Duo importuna prodigia, quos egestas tri-*
buno plebis constrictos addixerat. Cic. pro Sest. *Pars mersi*
tenuere ratem. Rhemus cum fratre Quirino jura dabant. Virg.
that is, *Rhemus & frater Quirinus. Divellimur inde Iphitus*
20 *& Pelias mecum.* Virg.

Construction of Substantives.

    Hitherto of Concord or agreement; the other part follow-
eth, which is *Governing,* whereby one part of Speech is govern'd by another, that is to say, is put in such Case or Mood
as the word that governeth or goeth before in construction
25 requireth.

    When two Substantives come together, betokening divers

things, whereof the former may be an Adjective in the Neuter Gender taken for a Substantive; the latter (which also may be a Pronoun) shall be in the Genitive Case; as *Facundia Ciceronis. Amator studiorum. Ferimur per opaca locorum. Corruptus vanis rerum.* Hor. *Desiderium tui. Pater ejus.*

Somtimes the former Substantive, as this word *Officium* or *Mos,* is understood; as *Oratoris est,* It is the part of an Oratour. *Extremæ est dementiæ,* It is the manner of extream madness. *Ignavi est,* It is the quality of a sloathful man. *Ubi ad Dianæ veneris; Templum* is understood. *Justitiæne prius mirer belline laborum.* Virg. Understand *Causâ. Neque illi seposui Ciceris, neque longæ invidit avenæ.* Hor. Supply *partem.*

But if both the Substantives be spoken of one thing, which is call'd apposition, they shall be both of the same case; as *Pater meus vir, amat me puerum.*

Words that signifie Quality, following the Substantive whereof they are spoken, may be put in the Genitive or Ablative Case; as *Puer bonæ indolis,* or *bona indole.* Some have a Genitive only; as *Ingentis Rex nominis.* Liv. *Decem annorum puer. Hujusmodi pax. Hujus generis animal.* But *genus* is sometimes in the Accusative: as *Si hoc genus rebus non proficitur.* Varr. *de re rust.* And the cause or manner of a thing in the Ablative only; as *Sum tibi natura parens, preceptor consiliis.*

Opus and *Usus* when they signifie Need, require an Ablative; as *Opus est mihi tuo judicio. Viginti minis usus est filio.* But *Opus* is somtimes taken for an Adjective undeclin'd, and signifieth Needful; as *Dux nobis & Author opus est. Alia quæ opus sunt para.*

Construction of Adjectives, Governing a Genitive.

Adjectives that signifie Desire, Knowledge, Ignorance, Remembrance, Forgetfulness, and such like; as also certain
5 others deriv'd from Verbs, and ending in *ax,* require a Genitive; as *Cupidus auri. Peritus belli. Ignarus omnium. Memor præteriti. Reus furti. Tenax propositi. Tempus edax rerum.*

Adjectives call'd Nouns Partitive, because they signifie part
10 of some whole quantity or number, govern the word that signifieth the thing parted or divided, in the Genitive; as *Aliquis nostrum. Primus omnium. Aurium mollior est sinistra. Oratorum eloquentissimus.* And oft in the Neuter Gender; as *Multum lucri. Id negotii. Hoc noctis.* Sometimes,
15 though seldom, a word signifying the whole is read in the same Case with the Partitive, as *Habet duos gladios quibus altero te occisurum minatur, altero villicum,* Plaut. For *Quorum altero. Magnum opus habeo in manibus; quod jampridem ad hunc ipsum (me autem dicebat) quædam institui.*
20 Cic. Acad. 1. *Quod quædam* for *cujus quædam.*

A Dative.

Adjectives that betoken Profit or Disprofit, Likeness or Unlikeness, Fitness, Pleasure, Submitting, or Belonging to any thing, require a Dative; as *Labor est utilis corpori. Æqualis Hectori. Idoneus bello. Jucundus omnibus. Parenti sup-*
25 *plex. Mihi proprium.*

But such as betoken Profit or Disprofit have somtimes an Accusative with a Preposition; as *Homo ad nullam partem utilis.* Cic. *Inter se æquales.*

And some Adjectives signifying Likeness, Unlikeness, or
5 Relation, may have a Genitive. *Par hujus. Ejus culpæ affines. Domini similis es. Commune animantium est conjunctionis appetitus. Alienum dignitatis ejus.* Cic. Fin. 1. *Fuit hoc quondam proprium populi Romani longè a domo bellare.* But *propior* and *proximus* admit somtimes an Accusative;
10 as *proximus Pompeium sedebam.* Cic.

An Accusative.

Nouns of Measure are put after Adjectives of like signification in the Accusative, and somtimes in the Ablative; as *Turris alta centum pedes. Arbor lata tres digitos. Liber crassus tres pollices,* or *tribus pollicibus.* Somtimes in the
15 Genitive; as *Areas latas pedum denûm facito.*

All words expressing part or Parts of a thing, may be put in the Accusative, or somtimes in the Ablative; as *Saucius frontem* or *fronte. Excepto quòd non simul esses cætera lætus.* Hor. *Nuda pedem.* Ov. *Os humerosque deo similis.* Virg.
20 Somtimes in the Genitive, as *Dubius mentis.*

An Ablative.

Adjectives of the Comparative degree, englisht with this sign *then* or *by,* as also *Dignus, Indignus, Præditus, Contentus,* and these words of Price, *Carus, vilis,* require an Ablative; as *Frigidior glacie. Multo doctior. Uno pede altior.*

Dignus honore. Virtute præditus. Sorte sua contentus. Asse charum.

But of Comparatives, *plus, amplius,* and *minus,* many govern a Genitive, also a Nominative, or an Accusative; as *Plus*
5 *quinquaginta hominum. Amplius duorum millium. Ne plus tertia pars eximatur mellis.* Varro. *Paulo plus quingentos passus. Ut ex sua cujusque parte ne minus dimidium ad fratrem perveniret.* Cic. Verr. 4. And *Dignus, Indignus,* have somtimes a Genitive after them; as *Militia est operis altera*
10 *digna tui. Indignus avorum.* Virg.

Adjectives betokening Plenty or Want, will have an Ablative, and somtimes a Genitive; as *Vacuus ira,* or *iræ. Nulla Epistola inanis re aliqua. Ditissimus agri. Stultorum plena sunt omnia. Integer vitæ, scelerisque purus. Expers omnium.*
15 *Vobis immunibus hujus esse mali dabitur.*

Words also betokening the cause, or form, or manner of a thing, are put after Adjectives in the Ablative Case; as *Pallidus ira. Trepidus morte futura. Nomine Grammaticus, re Barbarus.*

Of Pronouns.

20 Pronouns differ not in Construction from Nouns, except that Possessives, *Meus, tuus, suus, noster, vester,* by a certain manner of speech, are sometimes joyn'd to a Substantive, which governs thir Primitive understood with a Noun or Participle in a Genitive Case; as *Dico mea unius opera rempublicam esse liberatam.* Cic. For *Mei unius opera.* In like
25 manner *Nostra, duorum, trium, paucorum, omnium virtute,* for *nostrum duorum, &c. Meum solius peccatum,* Cic. *Ex*

tuo ipsius animo, For *Tui ipsius. Ex sua cujusque parte,* Id. Verr. 2. *Ne tua quidem recentia proximi Prætoris vestigia persequi poterat.* Cic. verr. 4. *Si meas presentis preces non putas profuisse,* id. *Pro* Planc. *Nostros vidisti flentis ocellos.*
5 Ovid.

Also a Relative, as *qui* or *is,* somtimes answers to an Antecedent Noun or Pronoun Primitive understood in the Possessive; as *Omnes laudare fortunas meas qui filium haberem tali ingenio præditum.* Terent.

Construction of Verbs.

10   Verbs for the most part govern either one case after them, or more then one in a different manner of Construction.

Of the Verb Substantive Sum, and such like, with a Nominative, and other oblique Cases.

Verbs that signifie Being, as *Sum, existo, fio;* and certain Passives, as *dicor, vocor, salutor, appellor, habeor, existimor, videor;* also Verbs of motion or rest, as *incedo, discedo, sedeo,*
15 with such like, will have a Nominative Case after them as they have before them, because both Cases belong to the same person or thing, and the latter is rather in apposition with the former, then govern'd by the Verb; as *Temperantia est virtus. Horatius salutatur Poeta. Ast ego quæ divum incedo regina.*
20   And if *est* be an impersonal, it may sometimes govern a Genitive, as *Usus Poetæ, ut moris est, licentia,* Phædrus l. 4. *Negavit moris esse Græcorum, ut &c.* Cic. verr. 2.

But if the following Noun be of another person, or not directly spoken of the former, both after *Sum* and all his

Compounds, except *possum,* it shall be put in the Dative; as *Est mihi domi pater. Multa petentibus desunt multa.*

And if a thing be spoken of, relating to the person, it may be also in the Dative; as *Sum tibi præsidio. Hæc res est mihi* 5 *voluptati. Quorum alteri Capitoni cognomen fuit.* Cic. *Pastori nomen Faustulo fuisse ferunt.* Liv.

Of Verbs Transitives with an Accusative, and the Exceptions thereto belonging.

Verbs Active or Deponent, call'd Transitive, because thir action passeth forth on some person or thing, will have an Accusative after them of the person or thing to whom the 10 action is done; as *Amo te. Vitium fuge. Deum venerare. Usus promptos facit. Juvat me. Oportet te.*

Also Verbs call'd Neuters, may have an Accusative of thir own signification; as *Duram servit servitutem. Longam ire viam. Endimionis somnum dormis. Pastillos Rufillus olet.* 15 *Nec vox hominem sonat. Cum Glaucum saltasset.* Pater. *Agit lætum convivam.* Horat. *Hoc me latet.*

But these Verbs, though Transitive, *Misereor* and *Miseresco,* pass into a Genitive; as *Miserere mei.* Somtimes into a Dative: *Huic misereor.* Sen. *Dilige bonos, miseresce malis.* 20 Boet.

Reminiscor, Obliviscor, Recordor, and *Memini,* somtimes also require a Genitive; as *Datæ fidei reminiscitur. Memini tui. Obliviscor carminis.* Somtime retain the Accusative; as *Recordor pueritiam. Omnia quæ curant senes meminerunt.* 25 Plaut.

These Impersonals also, *interest* and *refert*, signifying to concern, require a Genitive, except in these Ablatives Feminine, *Mea, tua, sua, nostra, vestra, cuja.* And the measure of concernment is often added in these Genitives, *magni, parvi,*
5 *tanti, quanti,* with thir Compounds; as *Interest omnium rectè agere. Tua refert teipsum nosse. Vestra parvi interest.*

But Verbs of Profiting or Disprofiting, Believing, Pleasing, Obeying, Opposing, or being angry with, pass into a Dative; as *non potes mihi commodare nec incommodare. Placeo om-*
10 *nibus. Crede mihi. Nimium ne crede colori. Pareo paren-tibus. Tibi repugno. Adolescenti nihil est quod succenseat.* But of the first and third sort, *Juvo, adjuvo, lædo, offendo,* retain an Accusative.

Lastly, these Transitives, *fungor, fruor, utor, potior,* and
15 Verbs betokening want, pass direct into an Ablative. *Fungi-tur officio. Aliena frui insania, Utere sorte tua.* But *fungor, fruor, utor,* had antiently an Accusative. Verbs of want, and *potior,* may have also a Genitive. *Pecuniæ indiget. Quasi tu hujus indigeas patris. Potior Urbe,* or *Urbis.*
20 Somtimes a phrase of the same signification with a single Verb, may have the Case of the Verb after it; as *Id operam do,* that is to say, *id ago. Idne estis authores mihi?* for *id suadetis. Quid me vobis tactio est?* for *tangitis.* Plaut. *Quid tibi hanc curatio est rem?* Id.

The Accusative with a Genitive.

25 Hitherto of Transitives governing thir Accusative, or other Case, in single and direct Construction: Now of such

as may have after them more Cases then one in Construction direct and oblique, that is to say, with an Accusative, a Genitive, Dative, other Accusative, or Ablative.

Verbs of Esteeming, Buying or Selling, besides thir Accusative, will have a Genitive betokening the value of price, *flocci, nihili, pili, hujus,* and the like after Verbs of Esteeming: *Tanti, quanti, pluris, minoris,* and such like, put without a Substantive, after Verbs of Buying or Selling; as *Non hujus te æstimo. Ego illum flocci pendo. Æqui boni hoc facio* or *consulo. Quanti mercatus es hunc equum? Pluris quam vellem.*

But the word of Value is somtimes in the Ablative; as *Parvi* or *parvo æstimas probitatem.* And the word of Price most usually; As *Teruncio eum non emerim.* And particularly in these Adjectives, *Vili, paulo, minimo, magno, nimio, plurimo, dimidio, duplo,* put without a Substantive, as *Vili vendo triticum. Redimete captum quàm queas minimo.* And somtimes *minore* for *minoris. Nam a Cælio propinqui minore centessimis nummum movere non possunt.* Cic. Att. l. 1. But Verbs Neuter or Passive have only the oblique Cases after them; as *Tanti eris aliis, quanti tibi fueris. Pudor parvi penditur.* Which is also to be observ'd in the following Rules.

And this Neuter *Valeo* governeth the word of value in the Accusative; as *Denarii dicti quod denos æris valebant.* Varr.

Verbs of admonishing, accusing, condemning, acquitting, will have, besides thir Accusative, a Genitive of the Crime, or Penaltie, or Thing; as *Admonuit me errati. Accusas me furti? Vatem sceleris damnat. Furem dupli condemnavit.* And somtimes an Ablative with a preposition, or without; as *Condemnabo eodem ego te crimine. Accusas furti, an stupri, an utroque? De repetundis accusavit,* or *damnavit.* Cic.

Also these impersonals, *pœnitet, tædet, miseret, miserescit,* 5 *pudet, piget,* to thir Accusative will have a Genitive, either of the person, or of the thing; as *Nostri nosmet pœnitet. Urbis me tædet. Miseret me tui. Pudet me negligentiæ.*

An Accusative with a Dative.

Verbs of Giving or Restoring, Promising or Paying, Commanding or Shewing, Trusting or Threatning, add to thir 10 Accusative a Dative of the person; as *Fortuna multis nimium dedit. Hæc tibi promitto. Æs alienum mihi numeravit. Frumentum imperat civitatibus. Quid & cui dicas, videto. Hoc tibi suadeo. Tibi* or *ad te scribo. Pecuniam omnem tibi credo. Utrique mortem minatus est.*

15 To these add Verbs Active compounded with these prepositions, *præ, ad, ab, con, de, ex, ante, sub, post, ob, in* and *inter;* as *Præcipio hoc tibi. Admovit urbi exercitum. Collegæ suo imperium abrogavit. Sic parvis componere magna solebam.*

20 Neuters have a dative only; as *Meis majoribus virtute præluxi.* But some compounded with *præ* and *ante* may have an accusative; as *Præstat ingenio alius alium. Multos anteit sapientia.* Others with a Preposition; as *Quæ ad ventris victum conducunt. In hæc studia incumbite.* Cic.

25 Also all Verbs Active, betokening acquisition, likening, or relation, commonly english with *to* or *for,* have to thir ac-

cusative a dative of the person; as *Magnam laudem sibi pe-*
perit. Huic habeo non tibi. Se illis æquarunt. Expedi mihi
hoc negotium: but *mihi, tibi, sibi,* somtimes are added for
Elegance, the sense not requiring; as *Suo hunc sibi jugulat*
5 *gladio.* Terent. Neuters a dative only; as *Non omnibus*
dormio. Libet mihi. Tibi licet.

Somtimes a Verb Transitive will have to his accusative a
double dative, one of the person, another of the thing; as *Do*
tibi vestem pignori. Verto hoc tibi vitio. Hoc tu tibi laudi
10 *ducis.*

A double Accusative.

Verbs of asking, teaching, arraying, and concealing, will
have two accusatives, one of the person, another of the thing;
as *Rogo te pecuniam. Doceo te literas. Quod te jamdudum*
hortor. Induit se calceos. Hoc me celabas.
15 And being Passives, they retain one accusative of the thing,
as *Sumptumque recingitur anguem* Ovid. Met. 4. *Induitur*
togam. Mart.

But Verbs of arraying somtimes change the one accusative
into an ablative or dative; as *Induo te tunica,* or *tibi tunicam.*
20 *Instravit equum penula,* or *equo penulam.*

An Accusative with an Ablative.

Verbs Transitive may have to thir accusative an ablative of
the instrument or cause, matter, or manner of doing; and
Neuters the ablative only; As *Ferit eum gladio. Taceo metu.*
Malis gaudet alienis. Summa eloquentia causam egit. Capi-

tolium saxo quadrato substructum est. Tuo consilio nitor.
Vescor pane. Affluis opibus. Amore abundas. Somtimes with
a Preposition of the manner; as *Summa cum humanitate me*
tractavit.

5   Verbs of endowing, imparting, depriving, discharging, filling, emptying, and the like, will have an ablative, and somtimes a genitive; as *Dono te hoc annulo. Plurima salute te*
impertit. Aliquem familiarem suo sermone participavit. Pa-
ternum servum sui participavit consilii. Interdico tibi aqua
10 *& igni. Libero te hoc metu. Implentur veteris Bacchi.*

    Also Verbs of comparing, or exceeding, will have an ab-
lative of the excess; as *Præfero hunc multis gradibus. Magno*
intervallo eum superat.

    After all manner of Verbs, the word signifying any part of
15 a thing, may be put in the genitive, accusative, or ablative; as
Absurdè facis qui angas te animi. Pendet animi. Discrucior
animi. Desipit mentis. Candet dentes. Rubet capillos. Ægro-
tat animo, magis quàm corpore.

Nouns of Time and Place after Verbs.

    Nouns betokening part of time, be put after Verbs in the
20 ablative, and somtimes in the accusative; as *Nocte vigilas, luce*
dormis. Nullam partem noctis requiescit. Cic. *Abhinc trien-*
nium ex Andro comigravit. Ter. *Respondit triduo illum, ad*
summum quatriduo periturum, Cic. Or if continuance of
time, in the accusative, somtimes in the Ablative; as *Sexaginta*
25 *annos natus. Hyemem totam stertis. Imperium deponere*
maluerunt, quam id tenere punctum temporis contra Reli-

gionem. Cic. *Imperavit triennio, & decem mensibus.* Suet.
Somtimes with a Preposition; as *Ferè in diebus paucis, quibus
hæc acta sunt.* Ter. Rarely with a genitive; as *Temporis an-
gusti mansit concordia discors.* Lucan.

5   Also Nouns betokening Space between places are put in
the accusative, and somtimes in the ablative; as *Pedem hinc
ne discesseris. Abest ab Urbe quingentis milibus passuum.
Terra marique gentibus imperavit.*

   Nouns that signifie Place, and also proper Names of greater
10 places, as Countries, be put after Verbs of moving or remaining, with a Preposition, signifying *to, from, in* or *by,* in such
case as the Preposition requireth; as *Proficiscor ab Urbe.
Vivit in Anglia. Veni per Galliam in Italiam.*

   But if it be the Proper Name of a Lesser Place, as of a City,
15 Town, or Lesser Island, or any of these four, *Humus, Domus,
Militia, Bellum,* with these signs, *on, in,* or *at* before them,
being of the first or second Declension, and singular number,
they shall be put in the genitive; if of the third Declension, or
Plural Number, or this word *rus,* in the dative or ablative; as
20 *Vixit Romæ, Londini. Ea habitabat Rhodi. Conon plurimum
Cypri vixit.* Cor. Nep. *Procumbit humi bos. Domi bellique
simul viximus. Militavit Carthagini* or *Carthagine. Studuit
Athenis. Ruri* or *rure educatus est.*

   If the Verb of moving be to a Place, it shall be put in the
25 accusative; as *Eo Romam, Domum, Rus.* If from a Place, in
the ablative; as *Discessit Londino. Abiit Domo. Rure est
reversus.*

   Somtimes with a Preposition; as *A Brundisio profectus est.*

Cic. Manil. *Ut ab Athenis in Bœotiam irem*. Sulpit. apud.
Cic. Fam. l. 4. *Cum te profectum ab domo scirem*. Liv. l. 8.

Construction of Passives.

A Verb Passive will have after it an ablative of the doer,
with the Preposition *a* or *ab* before it, somtimes without, and
5 more often a dative: as *Virgilius legitur a me*. *Fortes creantur
fortibus*. Hor. *Tibi fama petatur*. And Neutropassives, as
Vapulo, veneo, liceo, exulo, fio, may have the same Construction; as *Ab hoste venire*.

Somtimes an accusative of the thing is found after a Pas-
10 sive; as *Coronari Olympia*. Hor. Epist. 1. *Cyclopa movetur*.
Hor. for *saltat* or *agit*. *Purgor bilem*. Id.

Construction of Gerunds and Supines.

Gerunds and Supines will have such cases as the Verb from
whence they come; as *Otium scribendi literas*. *Eo auditum
Poetas*. *Ad consulendum tibi*.

15 A Gerund in *di* is commonly govern'd both of Substantives
and Adjectives in manner of a genitive; as *Causa videndi*.
Amor habendi. *Cupidus visendi*. *Certus eundi*. And sometimes governeth a genitive Plural; as *illorum videndi gratia*.
Ter.

20 Gerunds in *do* are us'd after Verbs in manner of an ablative,
according to former Rules, with or without a preposition; as
Defessus sum ambulando. *A discendo facile deterretur*. *Cæsar
dando, sublevando, ignoscendo, gloriam adeptus est*. *In ap-
parando consumunt diem*.

A Gerund in *dum* is us'd in manner of an accusative after prepositions governing that case; as *Ad capiendum hostes. Ante domandum ingentes tollent animos.* Virg. *Ob redimendum captivos. Inter cœnandum.*

5 Gerunds in signification are oft-times us'd as Participles in *dus; Tuorum consiliorum reprimendorum causa.* Cic. *Orationem Latinam legendis nostris efficies pleniorem.* Cic. *Ad accusandos homines præmio ducitur.*

A Gerund in *dum* joyn'd with the Impersonal *est,* and im-
10 plying some necessity or duty to do a thing, may have both the Active and Passive construction of the Verb from whence it is deriv'd; as *Utendum est ætate.* Ov. *Pacem Trojano a rege petendum.* Virg. *Iterandum eadem ista mihi.* Cic. *Serviendum est mihi amicis. Plura dixi quam dicendum fuit.* Cic.
15 pro Sest.

Construction of Verb with Verb.

When two Verbs come together without a nominative case between them, the latter shall be in the Infinitive Mood; as *Cupio discere.* Or in the first Supine after Verbs of moving; as *Eo cubitum, spectatum.* Or in the latter with an adjective;
20 as *Turpe est dictu. Facile factu opus scitu.*

But if a Case come between, not govern'd of the former Verb, it shall alwayes be an accusative before the Infinitive Mood; as *Te rediisse incolumem gaudeo. Malo me divitem esse, quam haberi.*

25 And this Infinitive *esse,* will have alwayes after it an accusative, or the same case which the former Verb governs; as *Expedit bonos esse vobis. Quo mihi commisso, non licet esse*

piam. But this accusative agreeth with another understood before the Infinitive; as *Expedit vobis vos esse bonos. Natura beatis omnibus esse dedit. Nobis non licet esse tam disertis.* The same Construction may be us'd after other Infinitives 5 Neuter or Passive like to *esse* in signification; as *Maximo tibi postea & civi, & duci evadere contigit.* Val. Max. L. 6.

Somtimes a Noun Adjective or Substantive governs an Infinitive; as *Audax omnia perpeti. Dignus amari. Consilium ceperunt ex oppido profugere.* Cæs. *Minari divisoribus ratio* 10 *non erat.* Cic. verr. 1.

Somtimes the Infinitive is put absolute for the preterimperfect or preterperfect Tense; as *Ego illud sedulo negare factum.* Ter. *Galba autem multas similitudines afferre.* Cic. *Ille contra hæc omnia ruere, agere vitam.* Ter.

Construction of Participles.

15 Participles govern such cases as the Verb from whence they come, according to their Active or Passive signification; as *Fruiturus amicis. Nunquam audita mihi. Diligendus ab omnibus. Sate sanguine divûm. Telamone creatus. Corpore mortali cretus.* Lucret. *Nate deâ. Edite regibus. Lævo sus-* 20 *pensi loculos tabulasque lacerto.* Hor. *Census equestrem summam.* Id. *Abeundum est mihi. Venus orta mari. Exosus Bella.* Virg. *Exosus diis.* Gell. *Arma Perosus.* Ovid. But *Pertæsus* hath an accusative otherwise then the Verb; as *Pertæsus Ignaviam. Semet ipse pertæsus.* Suet. To these add 25 participial adjectives ending in *bilis* of the Passive significa-

tion, and requiring like case after them; as *Nulli penetrabilis astro lucus erat.*

Participles chang'd into Adjectives have thir Construction by the Rules of Adjectives; as *Appetens vini. Fugitans litium.* 5 *Fidens animi.*

An Ablative put absolute.

Two Nouns together, or a Noun and Pronoun with a Participle exprest or understood, put absolutely, that is to say, neither governing nor govern'd of a Verb, shall be put in the ablative; as *Authore Senatu bellum geritur. Me duce vinces.* 10 *Cæsare veniente hostes fugerunt. Sublato clamore prælium committitur.*

Construction of Adverbs.

En and *ecce* will have a Nominative, or an accusative, and somtimes with a dative; as *En Priamus. Ecce tibi status noster. En habitum. Ecce autem alterum.*

15 Adverbs of quantity, time, and place require a genitive; as *Satis loquentiæ, sapientiæ parum Satis* also compounded with a Verb; as *Is rerum suarum satagit. Tunc temporis. Ubique gentium. Eò impudentiæ processit. Quoad ejus fieri poterit.*

To these add *Ergo* signifying the cause; as *Illius ergo.* Virg. 20 *Virtutis ergo. Fugæ atque formidinis ergo non abiturus.* Liv.

Others will have such case as the Nouns from whence they come; as *Minime gentium. Optime omnium. Venit obviam illi. Canit similiter huic. Albanum, sive Falernum te magis appositis delectat.* Hor.

25 Adverbs are joyn'd in a Sentence to several Moods of Verbs.

Of Time, *Ubi, postquam, cum* or *quum*, to an Indicative or Subjunctive; as *Hæc ubi dicta dedit. Ubi nos laverimus. Postquam excessit ex Ephebis. Cum faciam vitula.* Virg. *Cum canerem reges.* Id.

5 *Donec* while, to an Indicative. *Donec eris felix. Donec* untill, to an Indicative or Subjunctive; *Cogere donec oves jussit.* Virg. *Donec ea aqua decocta sit.* Colum.

Dum while, to an Indicative. *Dum apparatur Virgo. Dum* untill, to an Indicative or Subjunctive; as *Dum redeo. Tertia* 10 *dum Latio regnantem viderit æstas. Dum* for *dummodo* so as, or, so that, to a Subjunctive. *Dum prosim tibi.*

Quoad while, to an Indicative. *Quoad expectas contubernalem. Quoad* untill, to a Subjunctive. *Omnia integra servabo, quoad exercitus huc mittatur.*

15 *Simulac, simulatque* to an Indicative or Subjunctive; as *Simulac belli patiens erat simulatque adoleverit ætas.*

Ut as, to the same Moods. *Ut salutabis, ita resalutaberis. Ut sementem feceris, ita & metes.* Hor. *Ut* so soon as, to an Indicative only: as *Ut ventum est in Urbem.*

20 *Quasi, tanquam, perinde, ac si,* to a Subjunctive only; as *Quasi non norimus nos inter nos. Tanquam feceris ipse aliquid.*

Ne of forbidding, to an Imperative or Subjunctive; as *Ne sævi. Ne metuas.*

25 Certain Adverbs of quantity, quality, or cause; as *Quam, quoties, cur, quare,* &c. Thence also *qui, quis, quantus, qualis,* and the like, coming in a sentence after the principal Verb, govern the Verb following in a Subjunctive; as *videte*

quàm valdè malitiæ suæ confidat. Cic. *Quid est cur tu in isto loco sedeas?* Cic. pro Cluent. *Subsideo mihi diligentiam comparavi quæ quanta sit intelligi non potest, nisi* &c. Cic. pro Quint. *Nam quid hoc iniquius dici potest, Quam me qui*
5 *caput alterius fortunasq; defendam, Priore loco dicere.* Ibid. *Nullum est Officium tam sanctum atq; solenne, quod non avaritia violare soleat.* Ibid. *Non me fallit, si consulamini quid sitis responsuri.* Ibid. *Dici vix potest quam multa sint quæ respondeatis ante fieri oportere.* Ibid. *Docui quo die hunc*
10 *sibi promisisse dicat, eo die ne Romæ quidem eum fuisse.* Ibid. *Conturbatus discedit neq; mirum, cui hæc optio tam misera daretur.* Ibid. *Narrat quo in loco viderit Quintium.* Ibid. *Recte majores eum qui socium fefellisset in virorum bonorum numero non putarunt haberi oportere.* Cic. pro Rosc. Am.
15 *Quæ concursatio percontantium quid Prætor edixisset, ubi cænaret, quid enuntiasset.* Cic. Agrar. 1.

Of Conjunctions.

Conjunctions Copulative and Disjunctive, and these four, *Quam, nisi, præterquam, an,* couple like cases; as *Socrates docuit Xenophontem & Platonem. Aut dies est, aut nox.*
20 *Nescio albus an ater sit. Est minor natu quàm tu. Nemini placet præterquam sibi.*

Except when some particular construction requireth otherwise; as *Studui Romæ & Athenis. Emi fundum centum nummis & pluris. Accusas furti, an stupri, an utroque?*
25 They also couple for the most part like Moods and Tenses; as *Recto stat corpore, despicitque terras.* But not always like

Tenses; as *Nisi me lactasses, & vana spe produceres. Et habetur, & referetur tibi a me gratia.*

Of other Conjunctions, some govern an Indicative, some a Subjunctive, according to thir several significations.

5 *Etsi, tametsi, etiamsi, quanquam* an Indicative; *quamvis* and *licet* most commonly a Subjunctive; as *Etsi nihil novi afferrebatur. Quanquam animus meminisse horret. Quamvis Elysios miretur Græcia campos. Ipse licet venias.*

Ni, nisi, si, siquidem, quod, quia, postquam, posteaquam, 10 *antequam, priusquam* an Indicative or Subjunctive; as *Nisi vi mavis eripi. Ni faciat. Castigo te, non quòd odeo habeam, sed quòd amem. Antequam dicam. Si* for *quamvis* a Subjunctive onely. *Redeam? Non si me obsecret.*

Si also conditional may somtimes govern both Verbs of the 15 sentence in a Subjunctive; as *Respiraro, si te videro.* Cic. ad Attic.

Quando, quandoquidem, quoniam, an Indicative; as *Dicite quandoquidem in molli consedimus herba. Quoniam convenimus ambo.*

20 *Cum* seeing that, a Subjunctive; as *Cum sis officiis Gradive virilibus aptus.*

Ne, an, num, of doubting, a Subjunctive; as *Nihil refert, fecerisne, an persuaseris. Vise num redierit.*

Interrogatives also of disdain or reproach understood gov-
25 ern a Subjunctive; as *tantum dem, quantum ille poposcerit?* Cic. verr. 4. *Sylvam tu Scantiam vendas?* Cic. Agrar. *Hunc tu non ames?* Cic. ad Attic. *Furem aliquem aut rapacem accusaris? Vitanda semper erit omnis avaritiæ suspicio.* Cic.

verr. 4. Sometimes an Infinitive; as *Méne incœpto desistere victam?* Virg.

Ut that, lest not, or although, a Subjunctive; as *Te oro, ut redeat jam in viam. Metuo ut substet hospes. Ut omnia contingant quæ volo.*

Of Prepositions.

Of Prepositions, some will have an accusative after them, some an ablative, some both, according to thir different signification.

An accusative these following, *Ad, apud, ante, adversus adversum, cis citra, circum circa, circiter, contra, erga, extra, inter, intra, infra, juxta, ob, ponè, per, propè, propter, post, penes, præter, secundùm, supra, secùs, trans, ultra, usque, versus;* But *versus* is most commonly set after the case it governs, as *Londinum versus.*

And for an accusative after *ad*, a dative somtimes is us'd in Poets; as *It clamor cœlo.* Virg. *Cœlo si gloria tollit Æneadum.* Sil. for *ad cœlum.*

An ablative these, *A, ab, abs, absque, cum, coram, de, e, ex, pro, præ, palàm, sine, tenus,* which last is also put after his case, being most usually a genitive, if it be Plural; as *Capulo tenus. Aurium tenus.*

These, both cases, *In, sub, super, subter, clam, procul.*

In, signifying *to, towards, into,* or *against,* requires an accusative; as *Pisces emptos obolo in cœnam seni. Animus in Teucros benignus. Versa est in cineres Troja. In te committere tantum quid Troes potuere?* lastly, when it signifies *future time* or *for;* as *Bellum in trigesimum diem indixerunt.*

Designati consules in annum sequentem. Alii pretia faciunt in singula capita canum. Var. Otherwise *in* will have an ablative; as *In Urbe. In Terris.*

Sub, when it signifies *to,* or *in time, about,* or *a little before,* 5 requires an accusative; as *sub umbram properemus. Sub id tempus. Sub noctem.* Otherwise an Ablative. *Sub pedibus. Sub umbra.*

Super signifying *beyond,* or *present time,* an accusative; as *Super Garamantas & Indos. Super cœnam.* Suet. at supper 10 time. *Of* or *concerning,* an ablative; as *Multa super Priamo rogitans. Super hac re.*

Super, over or *upon,* may have either case; as *Super ripas Tiberis effusus. Sæva sedens super arma. Fronde super viridi.*

So also may *subter;* as *pugnatum est super subterque terras.* 15 *Subter densa testudine.* Virg. *Clam patrem* or *patre. Procul muros.* Liv. *Patria procul.*

Prepositions in composition govern the same cases as before in apposition. *Adibo hominem. Detrudunt naves scopulo.* And the Preposition is somtimes repeated; as *Detrahere* 20 *de tua fama nunquam cogitavi.* And somtimes understood, governeth his usuall case; as *Habeo te loco parentis. Apparuit humana specie. Cumis erant oriundi.* Liv. *Liberis parentibus oriundus.* Colum. *Mutat quadrata rotundis.* Hor. *Pridie Compitalia. Pridie nonas* or *calendas. Postridie Idus. Postri-* 25 *die ludos.* Before which accusatives *ante* or *post* is to be understood, *Filii id ætatis.* Cic. *Hoc noctis.* Liv. Understand *Secundum.* Or refer to part of time. *Omnia Mercurio similis.* Verg. Understand *per.*

Of Interjections.

Certain Interjections have several cases after them. *O,* a Nominative, Accusative or Vocative; as *O festus dies hominis. O ego lævus.* Hor. *O fortunatos. O formose puer.*

Others a Nominative, or an Accusative; as *Heu prisca fides!*
5 *Heu stirpem invisam! Proh sancte Jupiter! Proh deum atque hominum fidem! Hem tibi davum!*

Yea, though the Interjection be understood; as *Me miserum! Me cæcum, qui hæc ante non viderim!*

Others will have a Dative; as *Hei mihi. Væ misero mihi.*
10 Terent.

F I N I S.

NOTES

TREATISE OF CIVIL POWER

A TREATISE of *Civil Power in Ecclesiastical Causes* was published in London in 1659, "*The author J. M. . . . Printed by Tho. Newcomb.*" The work was registered with the Stationers' Company on February 16 of the same year (Masson *Life,* V, 581–87). Milton's name was affixed in full to the preface. Richard Cromwell had succeeded to the protectorate upon the death of his father, September 3, 1658, and Parliament assembled on January 27. Agitation for the complete disestablishment of ecclesiastical authority was immediately renewed, and Milton endeavored to assist the movement by addressing the present pamphlet to Parliament. The text of the present edition has been set up from a photostat of an original copy in the library of Yale University compared with a copy in the New York Public Library. The New York copy, referred to as B, shows a few slight differences from the Yale copy. These, together with certain unimportant corrections made in the text, are recorded in the notes which follow. Unless otherwise indicated, the notes refer to the Yale copy of the original.

PAGE 7
—2 visible] visibie
PAGE 9
—21 powr] B power   —22 *Feed*] B *feed*
PAGE 10
—5 spiritual] spiri ual
PAGE 12
—5 it] t   BUT THE CATCHWORD IS it
PAGE 16
—24 Scripture] Scipture   —26 a] a a

PAGE 17
—3 cause;] cause.
PAGE 31
—14 men,] men.
PAGE 34
—13 that] That
PAGE 37
—6 then] them
PAGE 38
—16 God,] God
PAGE 39
—3 pretend] ptetend

MEANS TO REMOVE HIRELINGS

Considerations touching the likeliest means to remove Hirelings out of the Church was published in London in 1659, "The author *J. M.* . . . Printed by *T. N.* [probably Thomas Newcome] for *L. Chapman* at the Crown in Popeshead Alley." The copy in the Thomason Collection has on the title-page in Thomason's hand the word "Aug" but without indication of the day. Milton's name was affixed in full to the preface. As he himself indicates in the opening sentence, this work was intended as a companion to *A Treatise of Civil Power in Ecclesiastical Causes.* Richard Cromwell's parliament having been dissolved on April 22, the old "Rump" Parliament had been restored on May 7, and Richard abdicated on May 25. In June petitions were received by Parliament for disestablishment of the church and abolition of tithes, and the matter referred to a committee (Masson V, 603–4). Milton's pamphlet was apparently written to influence Parliament at this juncture. The text of the present edition has been set up from a photostat of an original copy in the Yale University Library compared with two original copies in the New York Public Library which seem to be identical. A few obvious misprints have been corrected and recorded in the notes.

PAGE 55
—19 declar'd] declar'd
PAGE 75
—7 particularly] paricularly
PAGE 83
—7 to] to to

A Letter to a Friend, Concerning the Ruptures of the Commonwealth first appeared in the *Works of John Milton* published by Toland in 1698 in London but with Amsterdam on the title-page. Toland states that the work was published from the manuscript. There is no other evidence of Milton's authorship except the style and tenor of the work itself. The name of the friend to whom it was addressed is not known. Toland gives at the end the date, October 20, 1659. Milton apparently took occasion to comment in this manner on the dissolution of the restored "Rump" Parliament by Lambert on October 13, 1659 (Masson V, 617). The text of the present edition reproduces that given by Toland in 1698.

The Present Means and brief Delineation of a Free Commonwealth first appeared in Toland's edition of Milton's *Works* in 1698 (See above, *A Letter to a Friend*). Toland states that it was published from the manuscript. No other direct evidence for Milton's authorship exists. The work is a brief summary of *The Readie and Easie Way to Establish a*

Free Commonwealth (see below), apparently sent with a copy of that work to General Monk. The present edition reproduces the text as given by Toland in 1698.

The Readie and Easie Way to Establish a Free Commonwealth was first published in London in 1660, *"The author J. M. . . . printed by T. N.* [probably Thomas Newcome] *and are to be sold by Livewell Chapman at the Crown in Popes-Head Alley."* Wood notes (*Fasti*) that the book was published in February. On the title-page of the copy in the Thomason Collection appears the date March 3 in Thomason's hand. The work appears to have been written after February 6 when Monk, having entered London three days before, addressed the "Rump" Parliament in terms which seemed to leave still open the question whether monarchy should be restored. The main body of the pamphlet was probably written before February 21 when Parliament voted to restore secluded members to their seats. The opening paragraph, probably added just before publication, refers to the resolution of February 22 for the recall of writs which had been issued for new elections. The pamphlet was doubtless published between that date and March 3, 1660.

The second edition appeared in the same year with the words, *"The second edition revis'd and augmented,"* added to the original title, and in place of the names of printer and bookseller, *"Printed for the Author."* In this edition the original text was extensively changed to accord with the rapid movement of events. Milton says that he thinks it useful to write "in the midst of our Elections to a free Parlia-

ment, or their sitting to consider freely of Government."
Writs for the elections referred to were approved on March
16. Sir Roger L'Estrange in *No Blinde Guides* (April 20)
quotes from the first edition of Milton's pamphlet. Few
copies of the second edition seem ever to have been in cir-
culation. Every indication points to its having been published only very shortly before the Restoration on May 1,
1660. (*Ready and Easy Way* ed. by Clark; Masson *Life* V,
645–655.)

The text of the present edition is that of the only extant
copy of the second edition, formerly in the possession of the
late Mr. W. A. White of New York. This has been collated
with a photostat of a copy of the first edition in the Yale
University Library. Variations and additions appearing in
the second edition together with the corrections of a few
obvious misprints have been recorded in the notes, in which
1 refers to the first edition and 2 to the second. No indication being given to the contrary, reference is always to 1.

READIE AND EASIE WAY

Page 111

—2 som] some   —4 exclusion,] exclusion, to sit again in
Parlament,   —5 declar'd] declar'd,   resolution] resolutions
those] all those   in] now in   —6 tending] jointly tending
—7 remove,] remove   noxious humor] unsound humour   —8
bondage] old bondage   som] some cunning   nourishd] nourished
—11–p. 112, l. 4 hoping . . . follows.] hoping it may perhaps (the Parlament now sitting more full and frequent) be now much more useful then
before: yet submitting what hath reference to the state of things as they
then stood, to present constitutions; and so the same end be persu'd, not
insisting on this or that means to obtain it. The treatise was thus written as
follows.

PAGE 112

—5 Parliament] Parlament   *England*,]   *England*   —6 ap-
peerd] appeard   —7 defence] the defence   —8–9 unnecessarie . . . dangerous,] burdensom, expensive, useless and dangerous,
—10 regal bondage] regal-bondage   —11 terrour] terror   emulous]
NOT IN 1   neighbours.] neighbours,   —11–p. 116, l. 10. They
. . . reinthron'd.] and the stirring up of *France* it self, especially in
Paris and *Bourdeaux*, to our imitation.

PAGE 113

—5 covnant] 2 covant

PAGE 116

—10 thir] our   —12 Commonwealth:] Commonwealth;   —13
armie] the Army   people] of the People   —14 writings]
writings,   —15 Commonwealth] Comonwealth   —16 *Greeks*]
Greeks   *Romans*] Romans   —16–24 Nor . . . abroad.] NOT IN 1
—25 and Religion] NOT IN 1   prosperously] successfully   —27
remov'd,] removed, and wonderfully now the third time brought together our old Patriots, the first Assertours of our religious and civil
rights,   remains,] remains   —28 speedie] speedy   immediat
settlement] immediate settlement to this nation

PAGE 117

—1–3 for . . . heaven,] NOT IN 1   —3 back] back,   —4
would] would,   —5 Kingship] kingship   —5–20 to . . . impious,]
NOT IN 1   —21 contagion] corruption   us] us,   —24 at best]
NOT IN 1   us] us,   and . . . name,] NOT IN 1   —25 builder,] builder
—26 tower] Tower   it. Where] it: where   —27 Commonwealth,]
Common-wealth   —28 English] *English*   build] build,   kings,]
kings

PAGE 118

—2 wors] worse   —7 inferior] inferiour   advantages;] advantages: —9 courageously] couragiously   —10 setl'd] settl'd
enjoiments] injoiments   —11 Republic] Republick   —12 re-
turne] return   Kingship] kingship   —14 encroachments]
incroachments   —19 advanc'd] advanc'd,   —20 never] never
likely   possession] possession,   —21 voutsaf't] voutsaf'd   —23–
24 fruitless; . . . answers] fruitless to ourselves, all his gratious condescensions and answers   —26 under:] under to become now of no
effect, by returning of our own foolish accord, nay running headlong
again with full stream wilfully and obstinately into the same bondage:
—27 *English*] English

PAGE 119

—2 wonn] wonne   —2–3 together ... conquer,] NOT IN 1
—6–7 treading ... reformation;] NOT IN 1   —12 human] humane
civil,] civil   —14 commended,] commended   —16 disallowance,] disallowance   —17 *gentilism*] *Gentilism*   —19 *Christ*]
Christ   —21 and they that] *and they that*   —22 *authoritie*]
autoritie benefactors: but] *benefactors. But*   —23 *so;*] *so:*   —25
words] words,   —26 sons,] sons   thir] their

PAGE 120

—2 coms] comes   —5 public] publick   —6 brethren;]
brethren,   —9 Wheras] Whereas   —12–p. 121, l. 6 not in
thir ... bestow] nor at his own cost, but on the publick revenue; and
all this to do nothing but to bestow

PAGE 121

—10–11 for ... it.] who for the most part deserves none of this by
any good done to the people   —11 For] (for   hee] he   —12
man?] man?)   who] but   court-poet] court-Poet   —15 King]
king   —17 wors] worse   —21 governor] governour   coun-
selor] counselour   —22 punishd] punishd,   —25 person:]
person;

PAGE 122

—1, 3 thir] their   —2 swaies] swayes   —6 performe]
perform   —10 felicity] felicitie   safetie] safety   —13 industrie;] industrie.   —14 *Solomon;*] *Solomon,*   —16 Which
evidently] 1 Which evidently   2 which evidenly   —18 look grave
or] swell and look   —19 pismire:] Pismire.   —20–26 neither
... Lord.] NOT IN 1   —26 Nation] nation,   —27 hereditarie]
NOT IN 1   —28 when as] whenas

PAGE 123

—3 and ... especially] NOT IN 1   who have] that hath   —4
liberty] libertie   —5 actions,] actions   majesty] majestie
—6 court flatteries] court-flatteries   —7 on. That] on; that
—8 winn] winne   —9 liberty] libertie   —10 heartless and]
NOT IN 1   —11 use it,] NOT IN 1   with it] with it,   —12 warr]
war   —13 their] thir   —15 naught] nothing   —16–17
and ... of,] NOT IN 1   —18 ignominie] 1 ignominie,   2 ignomine
—19 libertie;] libertie: whatsoever] whosoever   —20 slaves:]
slaves;   —23 bondage.] bondage, and reservd, I trust, by Divine
providence to a better end; since God hath yet his remnant, and hath not
yet quenchd the spirit of libertie among us.   things] things,   —24
furder] further   —27 know] know,   —28 superior] superiour

PAGE 124

—2 splendor] splendour   —3 or] or,   —5 Christ] Christ,
—6 *gentilish*] *Gentilish*   —7 disciples.] disciples?   Protestants]
Protestanus   hold] hold,   —8 church] Church   power] kingly
power   —9 deputie] deputy   therof] thereof   —10 Christian-
man] Christian man   —11 wors] worse   —12 church] Church
—13 shaddow] shadow   —15 declar'd,] declar'd   —17 therin.]
therein?   —20 government] goverment   —21 while] while,
they] they,   —22–p. 125, l. 2 Tis . . . Yet] I answer, that

PAGE 125

—2 therof] thereof   —5 som] some   —6 Armie] armie
beleeve] believe   mind] minde   —8 once] when they were once
Now] Neither ought the small number of those remaining in Parlament,
be made a by-word of reproach to them, as it is of late by the rable,
whenas rather they should be therefor honourd, as the remainder of those
faithfull worthies, who at first freed us from tyrannie, and have continu'd
ever since through all changes constant to thir trust; which they have
declar'd, as they may most justly and truly, that no other way they can
discharge, no other way secure and confirme the peoples libertie, but by
setling them in a free Commonwealth. And doubtless, no Parlament will
be ever able under royaltie to free the people from slavery: and when
they go about it, will finde it a laborious task; and when they have don
all, they can, be forc'd to leave the contest endless between prerogative
and petition of right, till only dooms-day end it: And now   —10
Commonwealth] Commonwealth,   —11–18 Writs . . . libertie:]
The Parlament have voted to fill up their number: —20 good]
good,   both . . . civil,] NOT IN 1   —21 thereof] therof   —23–
24 (which . . . formerly] NOT IN 1   —25 Parlament)] Parlament,
—27 firmly] is firmly

PAGE 126

—2 commiting] committing   councel] Councel   —3 public]
publick   —4–8 In . . . libertie;] This Grand Council must have the
forces by sea and land in thir power,   manage] mannage   —9
public] Publick   —9–11 at . . . laws;] make lawes, as need requires,   —12 warr] war   nations,] nations;   —13 affairs]
affairs of State   —14 alreadie] already   —16 And] NO PARA-
GRAPH   —17 prepossessd] 1 prepossessd] 2 prepossed   notion]
conceit   —18 affirme] affirm   —19 be] sit   thir] their
—20 is] is,   —20–25 or . . . abroad,] and they will become thereby
skillfullest,   —25 at home] NOT IN 1   —27 under sail] under-
sail

PAGE 127

—1 Add] Adde   —3 not] unless they be   —4 therefor,] therefore   —5 and transitorie] NOT IN 1   —6 government;] government,   —8–p. 128, l. 16 to . . . Yet] and serve only to satisfie the ambition of such men, as think themselves injur'd, and cannot stay till they be orderly chosen to have thir part in the government. If the ambition of such be at all to be regarded, the best expedient will be, and with least danger, that everie two or three years a hundred or some such number may go out by lot or suffrage of the rest, and the like number be chosen in thir places; (which hath bin already thought on heer, and done in other Commonwealths:) but in my opinion better nothing mov'd, unless by death or just accusation: and I shall make mention of another way to satisfie such as are reasonable, ere I end this discourse. And

PAGE 128

—16 which I affirme,] NOT IN 1   —17 add] adde   —18 therefor] therefore   —19 and,] and   councel] Councel chang'd] changd   —21 therin] therein   fortune:] fortune; for] for that   —22 ofttimes] oft-times   —23 Senator] Senatour bodie] body   —24 permanent] unchang'd   —25 Therefor] Therefore   —26 *Jews*] Jews   supreme councel] supream Councel —27 *Athens,*] *Athens*   of] the   *Sparta,*] *Lacedaemon*   —28 *Rome,*] *Rome*

PAGE 129

—1 as it were] NOT IN 1   —3 every] everie   —4 other] others   true Senat] full Senate   —5–6 is . . . immovable.] sits immovable   —7 councel] Councel   state] State   deputed] delegated   —9 States . . . citie] Provincial States   —10 sovrantie . . . minde,] true sovrantie is plac'd,   Senat] Senate   —12 liberty] libertie   —13 every] everie   orderd] ordered   —14 Senat] whole Senate   — 15 Senat] Senate   20 knowledge] knowledg   — 22 here] heer   —23 other] all other   fickl'ness] fick'lness   —24 Ilanders: but] Ilanders. But   —25 acquisit] acquisite   —26 watry] watrie   —26–p. 132, l. 22 It . . . The] I suppose therefor that the

PAGE 132

—23 and performing] NOT IN 1   I suppose] NOT IN 1   —24 fear] fear or murmur   —24 *Parlament*] Parlament   —25 Lords and] NOT IN 1   —27 should . . . perpetual,] should perpetuate themselves,

PAGE 133

—1 Councel. Till] Councel: nay till   don] done   —2 cer-

tainly] certainlie   —3 setl'd;] setl'd: and say again therefor, that if
the Parlament do this, these nations will have so little cause to fear or
suspect them, that they will have cause rather to gratulate and thank
them: nay more, if they understand thir own good rightly, will sollicit
and entreat them not to throw off the great burden from thir shoulders
which none are abler to bear, and to sit perpetual;   —3, 5 our] thir
—4 changes] changes,   —5 libertie.] libertie. And the government
being now in so many faithful and experienc'd hands, next under God,
so able, especially filling up their number, as they intend, and abundantly
sufficient so happily to govern us, why should the nation so little know
thir own interest as to seek change, and deliver themselves up to meer
titles and vanities, to persons untri'd, unknown, necessitous, implacable,
and every way to be suspected: to whose power when we are once made
subject, not all these our Patriots nor all the wisdom or force of the well
affected joind with them can deliver us again from most certain miserie
and thraldom. To return then to this most easie, most present and only
cure of our distempers, the   —9 plentifull] plentiful   thereupon]
therupon   —14 worthie] worthy   —16 ordaind] ordaind,
work] worke   redemption] redemtion   —17 Universal] universal   mankinde] mankind   —18 plane] plain   intricacies]
intricases   —18–p. 134, l. 9 without . . . And] without the mixture
of inconveniencies, or any considerable objection to be made, as by some
friviously, that it is not practicable: and   —10 Commonwealth]
Commonwealth,   —12 sutly] suttly   —13 notion] prettie
notion   lurch] NOT IN 1   —15 ingagement] ingag'ment   fami-
lie] family   Nassaw] Nassaw,   —19 mark] marke   —20
state] State   —21 immediatly] immediately   —22 shewd]
said   before,] before, is both the basis and main pillar in everie government, and   perpetually] perpetually,   —23 som] some
vacations,] vacations   —25 endeavor] endeavour   —26 seldom]
seldome   be.] be; and then for his own ends: for it will soon return
to that, let no man hope otherwise, whatever law or provision be made
to the contrarie.   —27 parlament] Parlament   —28 appear]
appeer
PAGE 135
    —3 petition of right] right of subject   —5 oft times] oft-times
—6 appeering] appearing   —7 people,] people;   and thir
libertie,] NOT IN 1   —8 which] which,   —9 faithfull] faithful
—10 to] do   troublesom] troublesome   —12–13 spiritual . . .
lords,] temporal and spiritual lords, made up into one house, and
—25 Parlament:] Parlament;   happens] happ'ns   —27 wel-
being] well-being   —28–p. 137, l. 6 What . . . him.] NOT IN 1

PAGE 137

—7 But] And NO PARAGRAPH monarchie] monarchy —8 nations;] nations, receivd] received —9 kings] the kings —11 arm] arme —12 hereafter] heerafter —13 watchd] watch'd —13–14 that . . . treasure,] as that besides the loss of all thir blood, and treasure spent to no purpose, though they would never so fain and at the same rate, —17 them:] them. —17–p. 138, l. 12 nor . . . us:] Besides this,

PAGE 138

—13–14 a new episcopal . . . both] NOT IN 1 —15 privat persons] private persons, assign'd] assing'd —16 recoverd] recovered —16–17 detriment and] NOT IN 1 —17, 18 mens] men's —17 heavie] heavy —18 purses;] purses. —18–22 benifit . . . . . the] Not to speak of —22 offences] offences that will be —24 suites,] suites and —25 inquiries . . . informations,] NOT IN 1 —26 whom] whom, —27 banishment,] banishment; —28 or molestation;] NOT IN 1 if] or if disfavor] disfavour

PAGE 139

—1 royalist] royalist, —2 favors] favours plenteous] plentious —2–p. 141, l. 10 nor . . . repeat,] whatever conditions be contriv'd or trusted on.

PAGE 141

—14 other side] otherside, uncertainties,] uncertainties —16 wherin] wherein —19 kingship] kinship

PAGE 142

—2 I have heretofore] hath been heertofore —2–3 another treatise] other treatises furder] further public] publick —4 confessions] confessions, churches] Churches 5 states] States historie] historie, Reformation.] Reformation. He who cannot be content with this libertie to himself, but seeks violently to impose what he will have to be the only religion, upon other men's consciences, let him know, bears a minde not only unchristian and irrelgious, but inhuman also and barbarous. And in my judgement civil States would do much better, and remove the cause of much hindrance and disturbance in publick affairs, much ambition, much hypocrisie and contention among the people, if they would not meddle at all with Ecclesiastical matters, which are both of a quite different nature from their cognisance, and have thir proper laws fully and compleatly with such coercive power as belongs to them, ordaind by Christ himself and his apostles. If ther were no medling with Church matters in State counsels, ther would not be such faction in chusing members of Parlament, while every one strives to

chuse him whom he takes to be of his religion; and everie faction hath the plea of Gods cause. Ambitious leaders of armies would then have no hypocritical pretences so ready at hand to contest with Parlaments, yea to dissolve them and make way to thir own tyrannical designs: in summ, I verily suppose ther would be then no more pretending to a fifth monarchie of the saints: but much peace and tranquillitie would follow; as the United Netherlands have found by experience: who while they persecuted the *Arminians*, were in much disquiet among themselves, and in danger to have broke asunder into a civil war; since they have left off persecuting, they have livd in much more concord and prosperitie. And I have heard from *Polanders* themselves, that they never enjoid more peace, then when religion was most at libertie among them; that then first began thir troubles, when that king by instigation of the Jesuites began to force the *Cossaks* in matters of religion.   —6 This] NO PARAGRAPH   liberty] libertie   conscience] conscience,   —8 to favor only] only to favour   —12 every ombrage] everie umbrage —17 Queen] Q.   —18 Subjects love] subjects love,   —20 *Camden*] *Cambden*   very] verie   —22 therof;] therof,   &] and   —23 autoritie] authoritie   liberty] libertie   —24 of others,] from others   —24–25 wors principl'd] worse principld —25 *Popish*] Popish   —27–p. 143, l. 13 Especially . . . discipline?]
NOT IN I
PAGE 143
—13 for] For   gospel] Gospel   —14 libertie;] libertie, —15 hate,] hate;   favors] favours   —17–25 But . . . calumniated.] NOT IN I   —27 advancements] advanc'ments   —28 enjoyment] enjoiment
PAGE 144
—1–2 Both which] And both   —3 countie] county   —3–5 kinde . . . they] little commonwealth, and thir chief town a city, if it —7–8 from . . . citie,] NOT IN I   —8, 9, 10 thir] their   —9 laws] lawes   —9–10 or . . . are,] NOT IN I   —10 judicatures] judicatures,   —11 and judges] NOT IN I   —12 So] I So   2 so —13–15 law . . . then] and none   —16 administerd;] administerd.   —16–28 and . . . union.] NOT IN I   —28 imploiments] imployments
PAGE 145
—1 much . . . now,] NOT IN I   themselves,] themselves   —2, 3, 13 thir] their   —6 citie,] citie.   —6–11 or . . . both.] NOT IN I   —14 education] education,   —15 arts] I arts   2 ars —16 religion] religion,   —17 land,] land: —17–19 by . . .

neglected,] this   —21 honorable] honourable   —26 wealthie]
wealthy   —27 well fleec't,] wel-fleec't   shearing and] shearing,
and for   supplie] supply

Page 146

—6 public] publick   —7 travelling] traveling   —9 supreme]
supream   —10 Republic] Republick   —11 happy] happie
mentiond] mentioned   —12–14 as . . . occasions)] NOT IN I
—14 Sovranties] sovranties   united] NOT IN I   —15–16 united
and entrusted] NOT IN I   —16 Sovrantie] sovrantie   —16–p.
147, l. 3 And . . . cause.] NOT IN I

Page 147

—9 citie] cite   —10 mercie] mercie,   felt] left   —11
more] more,   —12 *Germanie,*] *Germanie*   Low-Countries] Low
Countreys,   —14 tradesmen,] tradsmen   —19 &] and   —20
honor] honour   Divine] divine   —23 returne] return   —25
plentie] plenty

Page 148

—1 all] that is to say all   —3–4 government, whatever] government; what ever   —5 duty] dutie,   —6 and] &   forewarne]
forewarn   countrey] country   —7 ther] there   —10 wherof]
whereof   —11 in] into   —13 circumstances;] circumstances,
—16 that . . . amiss] NOT IN I   *the . . . Cause*] the good old cause
—19 said] said,   —20 stones;] stones,   —21 *earth!*] *earth:*
very] verie   self,] self   —21–26 what . . . libertie.] what God
hath determined of *Coniah* and his seed for ever.   —26 trust]
trust,   —27 perhaps] perhaps,   —28 stones] stones,

Page 149

—1 reviving] NOT IN I   —1–11 may . . . multitude.] may
enable and unite in thir noble resolutions to give a stay to these our
ruinous proceedings and to this general detection of the misguided and
abus'd multitude.   —12 *end*] *End*

*Brief Notes Upon a late Sermon, titl'd, The Fear of God
and the King; Preachd, and since Publishd, By Matthew
Griffith, D.D. And Chaplain to the late King. Wherin many
Notorious Wrestings of Scripture, and other Falsities are
observd by J. M.* was published in London in 1660 without
indication of printer or bookseller. The sermon which Mil-

ton took occasion to refute was preached in the Mercers' Chapel on March 25, registered with the Stationers' Company on March 31, and shortly afterwards published (Masson, *Life* V, 667). Milton's reply to Griffith seems to have been made almost immediately. Sir Roger L'Estrange's *No Blinde Guides,* written in reply to Milton, appears in the Thomason Collection with the date "April 20" on the title-page. The text of the present edition has been set up from a photostat of an original copy in the New York Public Library. One or two slight typographical defects have been rectified.

Of True Religion, Haeresie, Schism, Toleration, and what best means may be us'd against the growth of Popery, The Author J. M. was first published in London in 1673 without indication of printer or bookseller. On March 15, 1672, Charles II issued his Declaration of Indulgence suspending the penal statutes against non-conformists. This at once provoked a "no popery" agitation. Parliament, assembling on February 4, 1673, compelled the cancellation of the indulgence (Masson *Life* VI, 687, 690–6). At some time in the discussion of this measure Milton issued the present work, probably in the early months of 1673. The text of the present edition has been set up from a photostat of an original copy in the New York Public Library.

ARTICLES OF PEACE

"ARTICLES of Peace" was published in 1649 in a small octavo of sixty-five pages. Only the commentary of twenty pages is by Milton. Though no name is attached, the authorship is not doubted. The full title-page is: "Articles Of Peace, made and concluded with the *Irish* Rebels, and Papists, by James Earle of Ormond, for and in behalfe of the late King, and by vertue of his Autoritic. Also a Letter sent by *Ormond* to Col. Jones, Governour of *Dublin,* with his Answer thereunto. And A Representation of the *Scotch* Presbytery at *Belfast* in *Ireland*. Upon all which are added Observations. *Publisht by Autority*. London; Printed by *Matthew Simmons* in *Aldergate-streete*. 1649." The date, May 16, is written on the title-page of the copy in the Thomason collection. The present edition is printed from a photostat of the copy in the Thomason collection in the British Museum.

LETTERS PATENTS

"LETTERS Patents" was published in 1674 with no name attached; Toland reprinted it in 1698 in the collected edition of Milton's prose. There seems to be no doubt of Milton's authorship (Masson VI, 725). The full title-page is: "A Declaration or Letters Patents of the Election of this present King of Poland John *the Third* Elected on the 22d of *May* last past, *Anno Dom.* 1674. Containing the Reasons of this Election, the great Vertues and Merits of the said Serene Elect, His eminent Services in War, especially in his last great Victory against the Turks and Tartars, whereof many Particulars are here related, not published before. *Now faithfully translated from the Latin Copy.* London, Printed for *Brabazon Aylmer,* at the Three Pigeons in *Cornhil,* 1674." The present edition is printed from a photostat of the copy in the British Museum.

ACCEDENCE COMMENC'T GRAMMAR

THE text of this edition of "Accedence Commenc't Grammar" is printed from a photostat of a copy of the first edition in the Yale University Library. The full title-page is: "Accedence Commenc't Grammar, Supply'd with sufficient Rules, For the use of such as, Younger or Elder, are desirous, without more trouble then needs, to attain the *Latin Tongue;* the elder sort especially, with little teaching, and thir own industry. J.M. London, Printed by *S. Simmons* next door to the *Golden Lion* in *Aldersgate-street,* 1669."

PAGE 295
　—1 lebes] libes　　—2 phœnix] phænix
PAGE 321
　—19 sarcio sarsi sartum] REPEATED IN THE ORIGINAL TEXT.　　—21 vincio] vinclo　　—22 vinctum] vinctumo　salui] alui

COLUMBIA UNIVERSITY PRESS
COLUMBIA UNIVERSITY
NEW YORK

———

FOREIGN AGENT
OXFORD UNIVERSITY PRESS
HUMPHREY MILFORD
AMEN HOUSE, LONDON, E.C.

p. 76 – Chin. Theo. not so diff. to learn.